More *Matrix*
and Philosophy

Popular Culture and Philosophy™
Series Editor: William Irwin

More *Matrix* and Philosophy

Revolutions and *Reloaded* Decoded

Edited by
WILLIAM IRWIN

OPEN COURT
Chicago and La Salle, Illinois

Volume 11 in the series, Popular Culture and Philosophy™

To order books from Open Court, call toll-free 1-800-815-2280, or visit our website at www.opencourtbooks.com.

Open Court Publishing Company is a division of Carus Publishing Company.

Library of Congress Cataloging-in-Publication Data

More Matrix and philosophy : revolutions and reloaded decoded / edited by William Irwin.
   p. cm. — (Popular culture and philosophy ; v. 11)
   Includes bibliographical references and index.
   ISBN-13: 978-0-8126-9572-4 (trade pbk. : alk. paper)
   ISBN-10: 0-8126-9572-0 (trade pbk. : alk. paper)
   1. Matrix (Motion picture) 2. Matrix revolutions. 3. Matrix reloaded. I. Irwin, William, 1970- II. Series.
   PN1997.M395M67 2005
   791.43'72—dc22
                                   2004028947

For Megan and Daniel

Contents

Acknowledgments

Many thanks to the contributing authors for their hard work, timely production, and oracular insights. Special thanks to the good folks at Open Court, Carolyn Madia-Gray, Kerri Mommer, Cindy Pineo, and especially David Ramsay Steele, aka the Architect, for bountiful support. Abigail Myers served as editorial assistant for the book, read and commented on the entire manuscript, and provided vital corrections and invaluable feedback on the work in progress. Mitu Pandya, the student assistant to the philosophy department at King's College, read much of the manuscript and offered very helpful comments. Last but not least, I thank my friends, colleagues, and students with whom I discussed the *Matrix* trilogy and philosophy, who helped make this book possible. A list such as this is almost inevitably incomplete, but among those to whom I am indebted are: Greg Bassham, Dave Baggett (aka Buck Naked), Kimberly Blessing, Jonathan Decarlo, Bill Drumin, Scott Higgins, Joe Kraus, Megan Lloyd, Henry Nardone, the Socratic Society of King's College, Barry Vacker, and Joe Zeccardi.

Coming Attractions: "Where Have You Gone, Mr. Anderson?"

Upon the release of *Reloaded*, film critics engaged in *Matrix*-bashing with glee. Many did not like the attention, particularly the intellectual and academic attention, the first film received and were eager to sound the death knell for the franchise. I believe the sequels will fare better among fans in the long run than they did among critics in the summer and fall of 2003. In my experience, the sequels get better with each re-viewing, as I distance myself from the initial disappointment. Yes, some of the dialogue was stilted, stiff, and contrived. But part of the problem was that the dialogue is exchanged too rapidly to contemplate properly as the action of the movie progresses. In this book we take the opportunity to linger over the words, finding that what seemed like garbled gibberish on first viewing the films frequently turns out to be quite reasonable, at times even profound.

More Matrix and Philosophy: Revolutions and Reloaded Decoded is a sequel about sequels. That may not sound like a formula for success. But having spent time decoding *Revolutions* and *Reloaded*, it is clear to me that there is much in the sequels to discuss, debate, and clarify. Most people didn't need *The Matrix and Philosophy* to start them thinking philosophically. The first *Matrix* movie clearly and provocatively raised questions that kept college kids up late. The sequels left many confused, frustrated, and annoyed. *More Matrix and Philosophy* is all the more necessary, then, to help to alleviate those conditions and to continue the tradition of staying up late talking about *The Matrix*.

More Matrix and Philosophy deals with all three movies and the *Animatrix*. Some chapters focus more on the sequels. Other chapters deal primarily with the first movie, though they do so in light of the sequels. For example, David Detmer's chapter, "Challenging *Simulacra and Simulation*: Baudrillard in *The Matrix*," largely focuses on the first film in debunking the connections between *The Matrix* and *Simulacra and Simulation*, while showing its author, Jean Baudrillard, to be a charlatan. Readers of *The Matrix and Philosophy* suggested through e-mail that in addition to the Christian and Buddhist connections considered in that book Hindu and Islamic connections could also be made. *More Matrix and Philosophy* follows up on those reader requests with chapters entitled "*The Matrix* and Vedanta: Journeying from the Unreal to the Real" and "The Cosmological Journey of Neo: An Islamic Matrix."

In the years since the 1999 release of *The Matrix*, concern about media violence and gun violence has only increased. The Columbine killings were linked—rightly or wrongly—to *The Matrix*, and John Lee Malvo, one of the D.C. Snipers, offered a "*Matrix* made me do it" defense for part of his trial. In "Pissin' Metal: Columbine, Malvo, and the Matrix of Violence," Henry Nardone and Gregory Bassham reflect on the *Matrix* trilogy and its legacy of violence. Additionally, race continues to be an issue of great concern in contemporary America. In "Race Matters in *The Matrix*: Is Morpheus Black? Is Race Real?" Jorge Gracia and I turn our attention to Zion, where there is racial harmony despite—or maybe because of—the war with the machines. No love-fest, some chapters in *More Matrix* attack the trilogy. Slavoj Žižek continues his criticism of the movies, the fans, and even this book. Martin Danhay calls the *Matrix* sequels "The Prozac of the People."

As road signs in a city should be placed there for the benefit of those who are not familiar with the city, so the philosophy in this book is largely for the benefit of those not already familiar with philosophy. We hope to guide you through the Matrix of philosophy as well placed signs should (but often don't) guide you through the winding roads and one-way streets downtown. The aim of this book is the same as the original and the same as other books in this series: to bring the reader from popular culture to philosophy. The series has been a critical and commercial success so far. *The Matrix and Philosophy: Welcome to the Desert of the Real*, briefly spent time in uncharted territory for philosophy, *The New York Times* bestsellers list. *More Matrix and Philosophy*, like its predecessor, is not a substitute for reading Plato, Descartes, Nietzsche and company. It is meant to generate interest in them. In fact if the e-mail I receive is representative, many readers who would not otherwise have read or been interested in the great philosophers will go on to read them, their interest sparked by connections to *The Matrix*. That's a good thing.

More Matrix and Philosophy does not in every instance attempt or purport to convey the intended meaning of the writers and artists responsible for *The Matrix*. Rather, the book highlights the philosophical significance of the film. Who knows what the Wachowski brothers think? When I read the stories about Larry I'm not sure I want to know what they think. Certainly puts Trinity in a new light, though.

At the close of *Revolutions* Sati asks, "Will we ever see him again?" The Oracle replies, "I suspect so. Someday." I doubt it. It's sad to see him go, but it's time you became the one yourself, the anomaly who reads this book cover to cover.

Scene 1

The Sequels:
Suck-Fest or Success?

1

The Matrix and Plato's Cave: Why the Sequels Failed

LOU MARINOFF

The Matrix and Philosophy

The Matrix and its sequels—*The Matrix Reloaded* and *The Matrix Revolutions*—embody many deep connections to philosophy. Movie-goers immediately began to make some of these connections for themselves. When professional philosophers chimed in, thanks to *The Matrix and Philosophy*, public awareness of these connections deepened, and public interest grew. Movies have potentially great power to entertain us, or to provide a temporary escape from daily routine. But beyond this, some movies also have the power to stimulate thought about important issues in life, or to help us rethink such issues in a new light. This is exactly why *The Matrix* was so successful. Let me give you an example of what I mean.

I teach philosophy at a large American public university (The City University of New York). There is a required core course in Philosophy, which every student must take in order to graduate. All the philosophy professors teach some version of this course, in multiple sections, to hundreds of students every year. Many students take this course without ever realizing the relevance of philosophy to their everyday lives. They sometimes struggle to make sense of the required readings, without really appreciating why the ideas of philosophers like Plato, Descartes, or Nietzsche form an integral part of their undergraduate education, and preparation for adult life. *The Matrix* changed all that, and in a powerful way. In order to

make the first two points of this chapter, I will explain both how
and why *The Matrix* makes a difference to students of philosophy. Since we are all "students of philosophy" in one way or
another, these points have broad applications to you, the general reader, and by extension to society as a whole.

A bit later in this essay, we are going to touch on one of
Plato's key concepts: "mimesis," or imitation. According to Plato,
a work of art imitates or represents something, for better or
worse. Sequels to a movie imitate the original movie, also for
better or worse. In the case of *The Matrix*, we'll see why its
sequels are poor imitations of the original, and we'll also discover why that's a grand philosophical irony.

How *The Matrix* Makes a Difference

How does *The Matrix* make a difference to students' apprecia-
tion of Plato or Descartes? That's easy to illustrate. The Allegory
of the Cave is one of Plato's most famous, and important, teach-
ings. One of its purposes is to make us think about the distinction between appearance and reality. After all, the world is not
exactly WYSIWYG ("What you see is what you get"). On the
contrary, the world is often a place in which you don't necessarily see what you are getting, and don't necessarily get what
you are seeing. Appearances can be very important, but are also
notoriously deceiving at times.

Philosophy students know this perfectly well, or at least as
well as anyone. And yet most of them don't immediately "get"
the relevance of Plato, and certainly don't rush off to read Plato
enthusiastically on their own, before he is assigned. But most of
them have already rushed off to the theater or Blockbuster to
see or rent *The Matrix*, enthusiastically on their own, without
having it "assigned." So to introduce Plato's Allegory of the
Cave, all I have to do is ask "Have any of you seen a movie
recently that addresses the difference between appearance and
reality?" The response is instantaneous. Dozens of hands shoot
up, and voices call out "*The Matrix*!" This sets up Plato beauti-
fully. Students who have seen *The Matrix* are predisposed and
curious to read the Allegory of the Cave. Why? For two reasons.
First, The Matrix speaks to their personal experiences in having
been deceived by appearance, and stimulates their desires to
penetrate veils of deception and glimpse reality. Second, stu-

dents thus impacted by *The Matrix* acquire immediate interest in Plato, as soon as they find out that he had contemplated this very theme millennia before the advent of visual technologies.

This applies just as forcefully, if not more so, when we come to Descartes's *Meditations*. When Descartes speculates that some "evil genius" may be deceiving us entirely about the nature of reality, so that for all we know we are merely "brains in vats" hard-wired to stimuli-generating devices that make us think we have bodies and lives, Descartes has literally antici- pated the holding tanks and program architecture of *The Matrix*. (Or else *The Matrix* has adapted Descartes's speculations to the silver screen.) Either way, the students immediately make this connection, and they demonstrate a vested interest in learning more about Descartes's proposed resolutions of the fundamen- tal problem he and Morpheus raise: "What is real? How do you define real? If you're talking about what you can feel, what you can smell, what you can taste and see, then real is simply elec- trical signals interpreted by your brain" (said Morpheus to Neo).

The Matrix has made Plato's and Descartes's questions directly relevant to contemporary youth, and so has awakened in them the perennial spirit of philosophical inquiry. In this sense *The Matrix* is not only an artifact of the entertainment industry, but also a bridge to philosophical culture. In so far as it motivates students to read Plato and Descartes (among many other philosophers), it serves a worthwhile educational purpose. Very few movies accomplish that much these days.

Why *The Matrix* Makes a Difference

That's an overview of how *The Matrix* makes a difference. Now let's look at *why*. For better or worse, our civilization has shifted from a written tradition to a visual one. Let me explain how sig- nificant this is. Our earliest cultural traditions were oral, not writ- ten. All tribal lore—including history, mythology, music, and so forth—was originally preserved by memorization and dissemi- nated by recitation. A few people had to remember everything, which drastically limited the amount of information that could be stored and transmitted, but which also developed imagina- tion on the part of the myth-makers, memory and verbal skills on the part of the story-tellers, and attentiveness, visualization, and understanding on the part of the audience.

With the advent of writing, human civilization as we know it began to emerge. Writing and reading allow us both to store information externally and also to retrieve it at will, thus freeing up human memory, stimulating our capacity for imagination and invention, and boosting attention span to optimum levels. Given a cumulative written tradition, each generation can build on what previous generations have accomplished.

Thanks to the written tradition, we can still read Plato and Descartes. But the written tradition has also enabled the invention of movies, television, computers, video games, and the Internet. And these products of the written tradition have collectively ushered in the visual tradition. The visual tradition differs from the written one in many key respects. Visual media reduce attention span instead of increasing it, reinforce the processing of images instead of language, evoke primitive emotions instead of refined ideas, diminish memory and enculturation instead of enhancing them. The net effect of this—as a few bright young philosophy students are beginning to realize—is that *The Matrix* has become more of a reality than a fantasy. The deceptions of the visual tradition are becoming more and more difficult to penetrate. By making viewers more aware of the real power of technological deception, *The Matrix* impels many of them to read the philosophers who warned us long ago about such deceptions—before the advent of the visual tradition itself.

Just look at the history of movies, and you will realize that most great movies, along with many not-so-great ones, were once typically adapted from books. The written tradition preceded the visual one, so it was natural for books to be the source of screenplays. (Similarly, the oral tradition preceded the visual one, so it was equally natural for the earliest television programs to be visual renditions of radio broadcasts.) Movie fans of Hollywood's "Golden Age" were also serious readers, and the consensus in those days (and probably today too) was that movies were rarely as good as the books they were adapted from. Whenever someone succeeds in making a movie better than its corresponding book, that movie usually wins Academy Awards. For example, David Lean's movie of *Dr. Zhivago* in many ways improved upon the Boris Pasternak novel from which it is adapted; and Francis Ford Coppola's *The Godfather (Parts I and II)* similarly improved upon the Mario Puzo novel from which they are adapted.

But nowadays this order has become completely reversible: It is increasingly common for popular movies to inspire popular books. *The Matrix* itself gave rise to the book *The Matrix and Philosophy*, and sequels to *The Matrix* have inspired the very book you are now reading. In general, this shows that culture is malleable and multi-directional. A work of art in one medium can always stimulate a corresponding work in another medium, or a continuing work in the same medium. With specific reference to *The Matrix*, we currently see numerous works of art: three movies and several books. Quantitatively, that is pretty impressive output in a fairly short time.

But now I want to raise a qualitative question, both in general and specifically applied to *The Matrix*. The question is: Are sequels to movies generally better, or worse, than the original from which they are derived? We can think of many sequels, because Hollywood loves to produce them: *Jaws*, *Rocky*, *Airplane*, *Scream*, *Austin Powers*, and *The Matrix* are just a few of the many movies that have been "sequelled." In general, most viewers find that the original of any series tends to be the best, with sequels representing worse and worse copies of the original. The same opinion has been widely expressed about *The Matrix*: audiences and critics loved the original, disliked the sequel, and thought the third one was not even worth watching.

Why? Here is a synopsis of the opinions I have heard consistently expressed, by students and other mainstream moviegoers. *The Matrix* was a brilliant and innovative movie. For reasons elaborated in this book and the previous one, *The Matrix* raised vital philosophical questions in a dramatic and engaging context.

The sequel, however, was disappointing. *The Matrix Reloaded* degenerated into comic-book style sequences of gratuitous violence. Its characters were imbued with physical superpowers to make up for the movie's lack of plot and intellectual content. The storyline itself was blurred by a haze of special effects. The one significant piece of mytho-philosophical content was Neo's encounter with the Architect. Neo learned that history repeats itself, that character types reincarnate to play archetypal roles assigned by forces greater than themselves. The deeper message was almost a confession about the movie itself: Governed by market forces greater than creative ones, this sequel is bound to be worse than the original.

The third part, and last act of this downward spiral, was *Matrix Revolutions*. It was reminiscent of the Alamo, as the "good guys" wage a desperate but doomed battle against the forces that threaten to overwhelm them. That Neo returns to fight for love is a great idea, but the tragedy of Trinity's death is dwarfed by the larger tragedy: that the story-tellers cannot find a way to end this movie. It seems as if they need the Oracle mostly for this reason: to tell the audience the point of the whole trilogy before the virus that clones infinite copies of Smith wipes her and everyone else out.

How did this happen? Why did a movie that started so promisingly fall so flat and end so badly? In the case of the *Matrix* trilogy, there is a philosophical explanation that the movie itself hints at but fails to reveal. I will reveal it to you here.

The Matrix and Plato's Cave

Let us return to Plato's Cave, and to its fundamental question posed by Plato and restated by *The Matrix*: How can we reliably distinguish between Appearance and Reality? Plato's answer is that we must exit the world of Appearances, leaving behind its fleeting illusions and fuzzy shadows, and step into the real world of Ideas, in which we begin to understand what Plato called the "Pure Forms" of things.

According to Plato, all artifacts of culture—from chairs to concertos, from makeovers to movies—are copies of their respective Pure Forms. The creators of these artifacts are not bringing something out of nothing. In the best cases, they have each glimpsed the Pure Form (or Ideal) of the object of their respective craft, and have copied it to the best of their abilities. In the worst cases, they are merely copying fuzzy shadows from the Cave wall, and so have no Idea (literally) of what they are doing. Every chair that a craftsman designs is a better or worse copy of the Ideal Chair. Every concerto that a composer writes is a better or worse copy of the Ideal Concerto. Every makeover that a stylist implements is a better or worse copy of the Ideal Makeover. And every movie that an individual or team writes, produces, and directs is a better or worse copy of the Ideal Movie.

Plato was especially concerned about two art-forms of his day: poetry and painting. He thought that poets and painters tended to imitate fuzzy shadows of things, rather than represent their Pure Forms. While such imitations distracted people with emotionally compelling imagery and images alike, these works of art did not help guide people out of the Cave. In fact, they had the opposite effect, serving to reinforce prejudices, inflame passions, and to encourage other kinds of irrational and counter-productive mind-states.

Plato thought that artisans were often better imitators than were artists. For instance, a skilled bed-maker can learn to make increasingly comfortable beds, which improve the quality of sleep. Similarly, a skilled flute-maker can learn to make increasingly sonorous flutes, which improve the quality of music. Plato believed that bed-makers and flute-makers could glimpse the Pure Forms of beds and flutes respectively, and by doing so could make better and better copies of these Forms. In the process, they would come to understand reality outside the Cave. Their souls would be flooded with light, as would the souls of those who slept in their beds, or who played or heard their flutes.

At the same time, Plato worried that poets could pen poetry about flutes or beds, and painters could paint pictures of flutes or beds, without understanding anything about their Forms or essences; that is, about reality outside the Cave. These art-forms, if badly done through poor imitation, could make people desirous to sleep in uncomfortable beds, or to listen to unharmonious music. Their souls would remain in darkness, chained to the Cave wall, mistaking fuzzy appearance for illuminating reality.

So mimesis, imitation, can lead to improvement, or to degeneration. If you start outside the Cave but retreat inside, then you will replace your clear vision of the Pure Forms with the blurred images of shadows dancing on the cave wall. Before long you will be copying those shadows instead of the Forms, and your art will degenerate accordingly. That is why Plato was so opposed to what we would today call "pop" culture: The artist is "an imitator of images and is very far removed from the truth" he said. (*Republic* X, 27). If we apply this concept to movie sequels in general, and to *The Matrix* and its sequels in particular, we can understand how American culture itself has become self-imitating in a degenerative sense, and also far removed from truth.

The Platonic artist is concerned with making better and better copies of the Form in question; the anti-Platonic artist, with making worse and worse ones. American mass culture has become increasingly anti-Platonic, with predictable and observable results. Artists who are successful with an initial creation, be it a book or a movie, are not encouraged to improve upon it in a Platonic way; on the contrary, they are asked to make an inferior copy of it. The inferior copy will be less popular than the original, but will still attract an audience because of the original. Nonetheless, it is a well-known maxim of the entertainment business that sequels rarely do as well as originals. Similarly, sequels to sequels fare even less well, and so forth, until it becomes pointless to continue the process because of diminishing returns on increasingly inferior products.

Why Sequels Fail

Both the movie and the book industry abound with cases of anti-Platonic (that is, increasingly degenerate) copying. In book publishing, an extreme example of this phenomenon is surely the "Chicken Soup" series. The initial volume in this series, namely *Chicken Soup for the Soul*, was a best-selling self-help book. Why? Because, Plato might say, it captured a great Idea: Just as chicken soup can have a healing effect on the ailing body, so wise thoughts can have a healing effect on the ailing soul.

But the success of this book made American anti-Platonism kick in, and saw the industry generate a huge number of increasingly bad copies of this original work: chicken soup for every possible kind of soul—old, young, married, divorced, and so forth. At one point, you could hardly go into a bookstore without tripping over an array of "chicken soup" books. At least one cynic remarked that they should have published a final title in this degenerate series; namely, "Chicken Soup for the Souls of the Sick-and-Tired-of Chicken-Soup-for-the-Soul Books."

Similarly (but not too similarly, I hope!), I'm sitting here writing a chapter for a sequel to a successful book, a chapter which deals with unsuccessful sequels to a successful movie. I don't know whether these books are improving or worsening; that's for you (the reader) to decide. Meanwhile, you see how the process works: It's all about representation and imitation, or what Plato called "mimesis."

The commercial scenario is this: Every copy or the original gets worse and worse, just like photocopies of photocopies, and so every copy is also less and less popular, and therefore also less and less profitable. Eventually, some copy becomes so degenerate and unpopular that the revenues it generates are smaller than the costs of making and marketing it. At this point, the series of sequels is terminated.

While everyone in the book and movie industries knows that a sequel rarely performs as well as the original from which it is copied, and that the sequel to a sequel performs even less well, and so forth, both *ad infinitum* and *ad nauseam*, I'll bet that very few producers or publishers ever consulted a philosopher to find out why.

With *The Matrix* and its sequels, we confront a special irony. On the one hand, this trilogy performed exactly as the allegory of Plato's Cave predicts: The original was both brilliant and popular; the sequel was a degenerate copy and less popular; while the final "episode" was even more degenerate and unpopular. Mercifully, that spelled the end of this mimesis. Ironically, however, the original movie in the sequence was based on the allegory of Plato's Cave itself, the whole point of which is to help us distinguish between appearance and reality, to assist us in emerging from the dim cave of fuzzy images (and their degenerate copies) into the sunlit world of pure forms. While *The Matrix* seemed to lead in that direction, namely out of the Cave, *The Matrix Reloaded* made a rapid U-turn and led its viewers back into the Cave, while *Matrix Revolutions* (rather, "devolutions") re-chained viewers to the Cave wall itself.

2

The Matrix of Control: Why *The Matrix* Still Has Us

WILLIAM IRWIN

I was disappointed in *Reloaded* and *Revolutions*. But should I have been? Lou Marinoff argued in the previous chapter that it's a pretty safe bet a sequel won't be as good as the original. And the more sequels we make the worse they tend to get. Plato predicted this and Xerox confirmed it. When you make a copy you have something less real, less genuine than the original, and making copies of copies takes you down the ladder of reality rather quickly. Just try taking a photograph of your dog and making a photocopy of it and then a copy of the copy. A good movie taps into an original idea or concept; the sequel tends to mimic what worked in the original. And so it goes down the line from there.

Then again, some sequels have been as good as or better than the original. *The Empire Strikes Back* and *Spider-Man 2* come to mind. So it's not an iron-clad law that a sequel will be worse than the original. But I think Marinoff has hit the nail on the head. *Reloaded* and *Revolutions* sought too much to mimic what worked in the first movie. They did not go beyond the first *Matrix* to the ideas and concepts that truly inspired it. They didn't go back to take a better photograph of the dog. They just worked from the photo they already had.

Disappointed as I was in the lack of originality in the sequels, I should not have been surprised—not just because it's the way of sequels but because of the history of Western philosophy. The first *Matrix* film raises the classic philosophical question of appearance and reality: How do you know that the world is actually as it appears? Philosophers long ago had raised this question, most notably Plato with his allegory of the cave and Descartes with his speculations on the possibility of dreams and evil deceivers.[1] Indeed, the twentieth-century philosopher Alfred North Whitehead once remarked that all of European philosophy is a series of footnotes to Plato. (See yet another footnote for the source of Whitehead's observation.[2]) Whitehead had a point, and not just on the top of his head either. Plato raised most, if not all, the big questions with which Western philosophy has grappled ever since. Philosophers mostly agree on the questions—but as for the answers, that's another matter. The first *Matrix* succeeded brilliantly in bringing philosophy and its canonical questions to the big screen. By contrast, the sequels were out in largely uncharted territory, with the burden upon them to deliver what no philosopher has: universally convincing answers to questions of appearance and reality, free will, and causality.

Nonetheless, allow me to suggest that we give the sequels a second chance. There is, I think, one theme they consistently treat well—CONTROL—and it is the key to the enduring popularity of the *Matrix* trilogy. It's not just that Über-cyber-geeks identify with nerdy Neo. "It's the question that drives us." It's *The Matrix* that has us. A message flashes on the screen: "The Matrix has you." Clueless Keanu and the audience have no idea what this could mean. No one can tell you what the Matrix is; you have to see it for yourself. So begins the adventure. With a little help from his friends, Neo escapes from the Matrix. But have we? Does *The Matrix* still have us? And, does *a* Matrix still have us?

Control

The first *Matrix* film appeals to what is universal, the struggle to overcome traps and oppression, illustrating what the philosopher Georg Hegel called the "master-slave dialectic."

---

[1] See my "Computers, Caves, and Oracles: Neo and Socrates," in William Irwin, ed., *The Matrix and Philosophy: Welcome to the Desert of the Real*, pp. 5–15 and Gerald J. Erion and Barry Smith, "Skepticism, Morality and *The Matrix*," pp. 16–27.

[2] Alfred North Whitehead, *Process and Reality*. Corrected Edition (New York: Free Press, 1978), p. 39.

The master becomes so dependent on the slave that eventually the tables are turned. This scenario gets much play at the movies, including the prequels to the original *Planet of the Apes* in which humans use domesticated apes as slaves. Eventually we become so dependent on the apes, who grow stronger and smarter, that we are vulnerable to attack. When the astronauts crash land on earth—now "the planet of the apes"—the truth about humans is known only to a few and is hidden from the rest. "The Second Renaissance I and II" from *The Animatrix* reveals that a similar Hegelian reversal is prelude to the first *Matrix* film. But instead of hiding the truth about the past, the machines create a virtual reality in which humans believe they are living in the past.

In a memorable scene inside the Construct Morpheus asks Neo, "What is the Matrix?" Morpheus answers his own question, "Control." The machines have us under their control, as we sleep peacefully oblivious to the reality that they use us for an energy source. We are being controlled and most of us don't even realize it. Continuing his speech in the Construct, Morpheus remarks that

> The Matrix is a system, Neo. That system is our enemy. But when you're inside, you look around. What do you see? Businessmen, teachers, lawyers, carpenters. The very minds of the people we are trying to save. But until we do, these people are still a part of that system, and that makes them our enemy. You have to understand, most of these people are not ready to be unplugged. And many of them are so inert, so hopelessly dependent on the system that they will fight to protect it.

This control and dependence is strange, but it is not unfamiliar. Fans of the *Matrix* trilogy relate to it. Most or all of us are controlled to one extent or another by forces outside us. Often these forces are subtle and insidious, such that most people are fooled into thinking they are not being controlled. Sometimes we resent these forces, and, like Morpheus and Neo, we may try to save others from them. Other times, deep in denial, we actually act to protect and preserve the control. The control is not so much Orwellian as Huxleyan. It is not a matter of totalitarian interference and brainwashing *à la Nineteen Eighty-Four*; it is giving the people what they want but which subdues them, like the soma of *Brave New World*. Addiction works much the same way. Eventually the addict is so controlled, so dependent upon his poison, that he will do anything to keep smoking, spending, drinking, eating, shooting up, jacking in, jacking off, whatever.

Allow me to suggest a few possible sources of Matrix-like control: the government, the media, the entertainment industry (including films like *The Matrix*), advertising (like the Matrix, it's everywhere), consumer culture, your job, your education, your diet, your gender role, your race or ethnicity, your family, your religion, your drug of choice.[3] The list could go on. In one way or another we're likely each already caught in a Matrix.

Subtle Structural Control

What is the Matrix? Control. Next question: What is control? The answer at first seems obvious. Control is the exercise of power over another person or thing. But the nature of that exercise of power warrants our close attention.

In *Reloaded* an insightful dialogue between Councilor Hamann and Neo refines the issue and points to how subtle the exercise of power can be.

> COUNCILOR HAMANN: Have you ever been to the engineering level? I love to walk there at night, it's quite amazing. Would you like to see it?
>
> NEO: Sure.
>
> COUNCILOR HAMANN: Almost no one comes down here, unless, of course, there's a problem. That's how it is with people—nobody cares how it works as long as it works. I like it down here. I like to be reminded this city survives because of these machines. These machines are keeping us alive, while other machines are coming to kill us. Interesting, isn't it? Power to give life, and the power to end it.
>
> NEO: We have the same power.

---

[3] If it takes buying tickets to see mediocre sequels and buying a book about them to feel the splinter in your mind about consumer culture, then so be it. See Chapter 4 in this volume for the argument that the *Matrix* sequels were a commercial trap.

COUNCILOR HAMANN: I suppose we do, but down here sometimes I think about all those people still plugged into
the Matrix and when I look at these machines, I . . . I
can't help thinking that in a way, we are plugged into
them.

NEO: But we control these machines, they don't control us.

COUNCILOR HAMANN: Of course not, how could they? The
idea's pure nonsense, but . . . it does make one wonder
just . . . what is control?

NEO: If we wanted, we could shut these machines down.

COUNCILOR HAMANN: Of course... that's it. You hit it! That's
control, isn't it? If we wanted, we could smash them to
bits. Although if we did, we'd have to consider what
would happen to our lights, our heat, our air.

NEO: So we need machines and they need us. Is that your
point, Councilor?

COUNCILOR HAMANN: No, no point. Old men like me don't
bother with making points. There's no point.

As this late-night Zion conversation illustrates, control is most
effective when it makes the other dependent on the one with
power. The control does not have to be complete. It doesn't
have to be such that, "If we wanted, we could smash them to
bits." Such heavy-handed control will only be tolerated for so
long before we get a Hegelian master-slave reversal as in *The
Planet of the Apes*. Rather, control is perhaps most effective
when it creates a subtle dependence about which we are hardly
aware—or not aware at all. It can even be a control that is not
purposely exercised by an individual or group. Such is the case
with Zion's dependence on the machines that clean the air and
water, keeping the people alive.

A "system" or structure that forces or causes dependence is
a kind of control, a trap. It may not be purposely designed to
be one, but when unscrupulous people become aware of it (in
whole or in part) and take advantage of it we have a trap.
Structurally, for example, Americans seem forced to vote for
either the Democrat or the Republican for president. Any third
party candidates have so little chance to win that a vote for them
seems wasted. But truly it is not. To depend on the two-party
system, to accept it as inevitable, is to be controlled by it, to fall
victim to the trap.

Traps, particularly large structural traps, do not ordinarily originate through conspiracy. Conspiracies are incredibly tough to pull off, as they require people to be both smart and silent, as Bill Maher remarks. Most traps are not designed to be traps, and they persist as traps because they are effective as such, even when not acknowledged or even recognized as traps. Order ordinarily emerges spontaneously without a designing intellect, "architect," or central planner. Traps spread because they work and so can replicate successfully, like a "virus," as Agent Smith would say. As genes without intellect nonetheless "selfishly seek" to replicate themselves, so similarly do systems of control persist.[4]

The most dangerous and insidious traps are not intentionally or purposely set. Traps purposely set have a guilty conscience behind them. Those not purposely set have no guilty conscience, no sense of responsibility behind them. Such traps are much more difficult to disassemble—no one and nothing looks to be at fault. Still, people benefit from the traps. Sometimes they even realize they are benefiting from a trap they did not devise, a boon for which they feel wickedly grateful but not guilty. Again, the two-party system is a trap no one maliciously set but which is selfishly maintained by those who benefit from it. As the Oracle says of the Merovingian, "What do all men with power want? More power."

The Merovingian is not the Architect, not the designer of the Matrix, just a parasite who knowingly takes advantage of the structural control that is the Matrix. The Merovingian mistakenly believes the world is an inescapable Matrix of cause and effect. He chides Neo and the gang that they are powerless to act, that the laws of cause and effect have already determined the outcome of events, that the best they can hope for is to understand their choices. Demonstrating his ability to exploit the power of cause and effect, the Merovingian points to the causal sequence set in motion by the cake he designed for the fetching young woman at the next table.

MEROVINGIAN: You are here because you were sent here, you were told to come here and you obeyed. [Laughs] It is, of course, the way of all things. You see, there is only one

---

[4] See Richard Dawkins, *The Selfish Gene*, second edition (Oxford: Oxford University Press, 1990).

constant, one universal, it is the only real truth: causality.
Action. Reaction. Cause and effect.

MORPHEUS: Everything begins with choice.

MEROVINGIAN: No. Wrong. Choice is an illusion, created
between those with power, and those without. Look
there, at that woman. My God, just look at her. Affecting
everyone around her, so obvious, so bourgeois, so boring.
But wait . . . Watch—you see, I have sent her dessert, a
very special dessert. I wrote it myself. It starts so simply,
each line of the program creating a new effect, just like
poetry. First, a rush . . . heat . . . her heart flutters. You
can see it, Neo, yes? She does not understand why—is it
the wine? No. What is it then, what is the reason? And
soon it does not matter, soon the why and the reason are
gone, and all that matters is the feeling itself. This is the
nature of the universe. We struggle against it, we fight to
deny it, but it is of course pretence, it is a lie. Beneath our
poised appearance, the truth is we are completely out of
control. Causality. There is no escape from it, we are forever slaves to it. Our only hope, our only peace is to
understand it, to understand the "why." "Why" is what
separates us from them, you from me. "Why" is the only
real social power, without it you are powerless. And this
is how you come to me, without "why," without power.
Another link in the chain. But fear not, since I have seen
how good you are at following orders, I will tell you what
to do next. Run back, and give the fortune teller this message: Her time is almost up. Now I have some real business to do, I will say adieu and goodbye.

The Merovingian "holds the keys" in the form of the
Keymaker to what Neo needs access to, the source, and he has
the power to deny them. Merv's name is apt, as, according to
legend, the Merovingian Kings of France believed themselves to
be descended from Mary Magdalene and in possession of the
Holy Grail. Merovingians are not benevolent keepers but jealous
hoarders, exercising control over something we should all have
access to but the very existence of which is in doubt.

Our freedom too seems in doubt, but structurally we only
need a little wiggle room to have freedom. Structures and traps
never fully control us. They may bump, steer, and influence us,

but we remain free to resist. Consider what the Architect says about the choice people in the Matrix are given.

> ARCHITECT: Please, as I was saying she stumbled upon a solution whereby nearly ninety-nine percent of all test subjects accepted the program as long as they were given a choice, even if they were only aware of the choice at a near unconscious level. While this answered the function, it was obviously fundamentally flawed thus creating the otherwise contradictory systemic anomaly, that if left unchecked might threaten the system itself. Ergo those that refuse the program, while a minority, if unchecked would constitute an escalating probability of disaster.

An anomaly is possible, indeed inevitable, even within the super-control of the Matrix. A free choice remains ours.

Deciding to take the red pill is just the beginning of the adventure, though. Many more choices and obstacles await. It is not just a matter of coming to know that there is a trap. One must understand the trap. As the Oracle says, "We can never see past the choices we don't understand." Denying real, genuine freedom, the Oracle tells Neo, "You've already made the choice, now you have to understand it." But the Merovingian and the Oracle are wrong in believing that all the choices have been made, that all one can do is understand them. Perhaps as she believes she is destined to, the Oracle benevolently misleads Neo and Morpheus, to "unbalance the equation." As she says, "We're all here to do what we're all here to do. I'm interested in one thing, Neo, the future. And believe me, I know—the only way to get there is together."

Assuming we have free will, however—as the *Matrix* trilogy ultimately assumes—there is more to life than the therapy of the Oracle in which we come to understand the reasons for our actions. There is the confrontation with the Freudian-looking Architect, who sees that though Neo and we are pushed about by stormy forces inside and outside us, we can ultimately come to not just understand these forces but to act against them. As with the two-party system, so too with the Architect. To choose an alternative is to take a step to undermine the structure. Just because success remains a long shot does not mean that we are throwing away our vote.

Consider consumer culture and the "affluenza" virus it spreads. Affluenza, in case you're not aware, is "a painful, contagious, socially transmitted condition of overload, debt, anxiety, and waste resulting from the dogged pursuit of more."[5] Advertising is everywhere. The pressure is on to buy designer label clothes, even if they're not any better quality than the no-name stuff. We fall into the trap of "conspicuous consumption," as Thorsten Veblen called it. We keep up with the Joneses for the sake of letting the Joneses know we are keeping up. It's the consumer culture that Jack (Edward Norton) has bought into, becoming the "Ikea boy" of *Fight Club*, leading a perfectly meaningless and empty life. As Tyler Durden tells him, "You are not your job. You are not the money in your bank account. You are not the car you drive. You are not how much money is in your wallet. You are not your fucking khakis." And as Trinity tells Neo, "The Matrix cannot tell you who you are."

Affluenza is another structural trap without an architect. No vast capitalist conspiracy set it up. You are not what you buy. Worse, you buy what you are. Empty inside you buy objects outside to fill the internal void. You live in a consumer society and the pressure is put on you in any number of ways to conform, to be a "good citizen." People judge you in terms of what you own and drive, where you live. To prove your worth you buy to display your ability to buy. You conspicuously consume. As Tyler Durden says, "The things you own end up owning you." Worst of all, you may not even have realized it. You may be one of the nearly ninety-nine percent who accept the program. Contrary to Cypher, ignorance is not bliss; what you don't know sure can hurt you.

After 9/11, there were exhortations to spend, to go to the mall, lest the terrorists should win. Such consumption may seem to benefit the producers we patronize and the larger economy, but such benefits lack real fecundity. They do not encourage producers to make better quality, more affordable products, but rather more expensive, more enticing, less necessary products. In the long run that serves no one well. "It was all another system of control."

---

[5]John de Graff, David Wann, and Thomas Naylor, *Affluenza: The All-Consuming Epidemic* (San Francisco: Berrett-Koehler, 2002), p. 2.

Free Your Mind

In the first film Neo tells Morpheus, "I don't like the idea that I'm not in control of my life." But it's true that Neo cannot control his life, at least not what happens outside his own mind—though even there he has more power than most of us both inside and outside the Matrix. What Neo can control is his own mind, a lesson he begins to learn in the Dojo and which he more fully comes to believe as he sees through the code and opposes the Agents.

Even if it can't bend spoons, how can your mind shape your perception of reality? What connections, if any, are there between your thoughts and your emotions? Can you control your thoughts? Can you control your emotions? According to the Merovingian, "Beneath our poised appearance, the truth is we are completely out of control." That may often be true, but it doesn't have to be.

Stoicism is the philosophy that counsels self-control, detachment, and acceptance of one's fate. The two most important ancient stoics, a slave named Epictetus (A.D. 50–130) and the emperor Marcus Aurelius (A.D. 121–180), shared the insight that thoughts control emotions and thoughts are under our control. In his *Meditations*, Marcus Aurelius advises: "Put from you the belief that 'I have been wronged', and with it will go the feeling. Reject your sense of injury and the injury itself disappears."[6] Epictetus sums up stoicism when he says, "Do not seek to have everything that happens happen as you wish, but wish for everything to happen as it actually does happen and your life will be serene."[7] Bring your mind into conformity with reality and your mind will master reality.

How misguided and misdirected most of us are in our attempts at control. As Marcus Aurelius says, "Our anger and annoyance are more detrimental to us than the things themselves which anger or annoy us" (Book XI, §18). We foolishly break ourselves against the rocks and let potentially strong muscles atrophy. Better to wear down rocks passing over and to the

---

[6] Marcus Aurelius, *Meditations*, translated by Maxwell Staniforth (New York: Penguin, 1964), Book IV §7.

[7] Epictetus, *Encheiridion*, translated by W.A. Oldfather (Cambridge, Massachusetts: Harvard University Press, 1928), §8.

side like gentle stream water. Nothing outside my mind is under my complete control. Things outside my mind, especially people, are, at most, subject to my influence. And exerting my influence comes always at a price, a trade-off. Learning to control the mind is not easy. Still, I can control what I see by closing my eyes or averting my glance, and with effort and practice I can control what I think and hence what I feel. I can learn the wisdom of Marcus Aurelius that "If you are distressed by anything external, the pain is not due to the thing itself but to your own estimate of it" (Book VIII §47). The message is to stop seeking control of what is beyond your control. Instead, get in control of your thoughts. Build your mental muscles through repetition, through practice.

The master is the one who is master of himself. It is not commanding armies, like Lock, or fortunes, like the Merovingian, that makes one a master. Such things are never fully commanded or controlled; they cannot be. And if one's inner weather changes as they change, one is not the master but a slave. The master, like Neo, is not cold, insensitive, indifferent. He is compassionate, though he controls his emotional temperature.

So what can I control concerning the Matrix of consumer culture and the virus of affluenza? East and West agree, you can and should control and resist the creation of desire and the illusion of need. The second Noble Truth of Buddhism tells us that suffering is ultimately caused by desire (*trsna*). Marcus Aurelius cautions, "Do not indulge in dreams of having what you have not" (Book VII, §27). You truly need very little if you are unconcerned with impressing others with what you have. In the *Tao te Ching,* Lao Tzu offers the wisdom that "He who knows he has enough is rich."[8]

Become conscious of living in a consumer society. Realize the vested interest that companies have in getting you to buy their products. Companies do this by getting you to desire and, in some cases, believe you need their product. Resisting on your own is difficult when those around you are still plugged in to the Matrix. They do not resist, often not realizing there is anything to resist. They become walking advertisements and agents

---

[8] Lao Tzu, *Tao te Ching*, translated by Gia-Fu Feng and Jane (New York: Vintage, 1972), §33.

of coercion, more difficult to resist than the ads. But the habits and pressures of others are no excuse. Why not take some satisfaction in refusing to conform, in refusing to be like those you don't even like? As Marcus Aurelius says, "To refrain from imitation is the best revenge" (Book VI, §6).

"Free your mind." It's yours to control.

Cast off the Fruit of Action

Stoicism does not tell us to just give up, to do nothing. Rather it tells us to realize that our attempts at influencing the world through our actions always come at a price and the results are far from guaranteed. Neo does not cease action. In *Revolutions* he comes to know what he must do, go to the machine city and attempt to save Zion. Neo is a reluctant warrior. Much as he does not relish the task, it is his duty as the One. Worse, there is no certainty in the outcome. He must simply do it because it is his duty, the right thing to do.

Here Stoicism finds an Eastern cousin in the *Bhagavad-Gita*, the story of another reluctant warrior, Arjuna. The god Krishna tells Arjuna that he must perform his sacred duty as a warrior, that "The wise who have obtained devotion cast off the fruit of action."[9] The *Bhagavad-Gita's* message is subtle and steers the course between obstacles, like Niobe through the support line. Yes, identify the right action and visualize doing it well, as that will likely bring good results. But the results, "the fruit of action," are ultimately not under your control and in some way not even your business. What impact you have on the world outside your own mind is not for you to determine. Neo in this way acts on his duty. The results are good—Zion is saved—but not ideal—many millions will remain connected to the Matrix. Consider too Hamann, who with stoical serenity allows Morpheus to take the *Nebuchadnezzar* despite Lock's insistence that he needs every ship available. Hamann didn't know Neo would ultimately succeed, but he made a decision and let the outcome unfold. Finally, consider what the Oracle reveals at the end of *Revolutions*. Seraph asks, "Did you always

---

[9] *The Bhagavadgita*, translated by Kasinath Trimback Telang, in *The Sacred Books of the East*, edited by F. Max Müller, Volume VIII, second edition (Oxford: Clarendon, 1908), p. 50.

know?" She responds, "Oh no. No, I didn't. But I believed. I believed."

What does this tell us concerning action in response to consumer culture? Be a one-percenter. You don't have to "accept the program." Downshift your consumption and voluntarily simplify your life.[10] If your credit cards are a problem, cut them up. Steal this book or borrow it from the library. Resist the car, clothes, and jewelry. Live below your means and be frugal. Caught in the trap of conspicuous consumption, too many people drive—and otherwise wastefully display—their wealth. If you're fortunate enough to have money, drive a car of less value and prestige than what the consumer culture might expect a person in your line of work and making your money to drive. Same too with your house. Live in a nice, clean, safe neighborhood among people who generally make less money than you do. Do not spend great amounts on clothes, shoes, and jewelry. Buy nice items, but not impressive ones.

A need to impress belies an inner bankruptcy. If you don't have much money, don't buy the lie that you need it to be rich. To know you have enough *is* to be rich. Get right with yourself on the inside; it's a lot cheaper than covering up on the outside. Neo will not bail you out of debt; you have to "save yourself." In the Gnostic Gospel of Thomas (Mr. Anderson's namesake evangelist), Jesus says,

> Rather the Kingdom is inside you and outside you. When you know yourselves, then you will be known, and you will understand that you are children of the living father. But if you do not know yourselves, then you live in poverty, and you are poverty. (v. 4)[11]

So resist the products that tell your friends and neighbors that you have money to burn when you don't. Such behavior only encourages them to burn money they don't have. Far better for both individuals and the larger economy would be to save the money and invest part of it in companies that meet genuine needs with quality products, thereby benefiting the

---

[10] See *Affluenza*, pp. 177–182.
[11] See Elaine Pagels, *Beyond Belief: The Secret Gospel of Thomas* (New York: Vintage, 2004), p. 227.

individual investor, the company, and the larger economy. Does this guarantee that you will become wealthy, the next "millionaire next door"?[12] No, the results of your actions are not under your control.

But maybe the Matrix of consumer culture is a trap you've already overcome or one that doesn't interest you. Maybe you're not even convinced that it is a trap. So what can *you* do about the kind of control that *The Matrix* draws to our attention? It's unlikely that you'll be able to free yourself from all Matrix-control, but pay attention to that splinter in your mind driving you mad. At first, it's more likely to be something you feel in the pit of your stomach than something you see with your eye. If there is something about the world that you sense is not right, look closely. Don't worry about what other people do or think. Find out what your job, your government, your religion, your whatever, is doing to control you. And then do something about it. Make your life meaningful. Take the red pill. Make the choice to bring about change, to subvert the dominant paradigm—to face what is difficult and do what is worthwhile. Be the anomaly, the One to resist. Show them "a world without rules and controls."[13]

---

[12] Thomas J. Stanley and William D. Danko, *The Millionaire Next Door: The Surprising Secrets of America's Wealthy* (Athens, Georgia: Longstreet, 1996).

[13] Thanks to all those who provided helpful feedback and criticism including Greg Bassham, Dave Baggett, Kim Blessing, Jorge Gracia, Rebecca Housel, Joe Kraus, Jim Lawler, Megan Lloyd, Abby Myers, Joe Zeccardi, and an audience at Wesleyan University.

3

Only Love Is Real: Heidegger, Plato, and *The Matrix* Trilogy

JAMES LAWLER

The ordinary inhabitants of the Matrix have no idea that their world is an artificial one. They are like the occupants of Plato's cave, who live out their entire lives in the false belief that the shadows they projected on the wall in front of them are reality.[1] With some few but notable exceptions, they do not ask Descartes's question: What if the world we experience is like a dream, created by a malign intelligence to deceive us? Like most of us before being awakened from our dogmatic slumbers, they believe that the objects of their experience exist independently of them. They therefore fail to recognize the implications of Kant's Copernican revolution in philosophy—that the world of our experience is in large part a projection of our own minds.[2]

Reloaded pursues these themes of *The Matrix* with even greater deliberateness. Philosophical themes that had earlier been only suggested or intimated—and so often ignored for the compelling visuals—now themselves compel the attention of the audience. The lengthy and spectacular sixty-million-dollar car chase to end all car chases is a welcome interlude allowing us time to ponder the questions previously raised concerning the nature of cause and effect, freedom and destiny, love and death.

---

[1] See William Irwin, "Computers, Caves, and Oracles," in William Irwin, ed., *The Matrix and Philosophy* (Chicago: Open Court, 2002), pp. 5–15.

[2] See James Lawler, "We Are (the) One! Kant Explains How to Manipulate the Matrix," in William Irwin ed., *The Matrix and Philosophy* (Chicago: Open Court, 2002), pp. 138–152.

If the themes of freedom, determinism, and destiny are prominently thematized in *Reloaded*, we also see more clearly the background texture woven from the conflicting strands of love and fear. That the *Matrix* trilogy is above all a love story is suggested from the very beginning. As the film title in *The Matrix* is displayed in a rain of computer digits, we hear the intrusive voice of the navigator Cypher saying to Trinity—"You like him, don't you?" If we look carefully, we note that the opening sequence in which Trinity battles policemen and Agents takes place in a hotel named "Heart o' the City." The capital letters H, E, A, R, and T, vertically descend the height of the shabby inner city building. In a world dominated by Artificial Intelligence, there is still a place for the heart.

Two Tests for Finding the One

Trinity is watching out for the computer programmer, Thomas A. Anderson, a denizen of the Matrix who moonlights as a computer hacker, known to his grateful clients as Neo. The company of the *Nebuchadnezzar* is intent on extracting Neo from the Matrix because the captain of the *Nebuchadnezzar*, Morpheus, believes that Neo is "the One," the individual prophesied by the Oracle to be the liberator of enslaved humanity from the Matrix. Secretly, however, Trinity's interest in Neo is more personal. Near the end of *The Matrix*, we learn that the Oracle once told her that the person she would love would indeed be "the One." While others on the *Nebuchadnezzar* see the test of Neo's special destiny in his unusual ability to assimilate downloaded programs of martial arts and other weapons of battle, for Trinity there is a quite different test—the test of her heart. She doesn't love him because she believes he is the One. She finally believes he is the One because she knows that she loves him.

When Neo awakens out of the dream-like illusion of the Matrix, Morpheus greets him: "Welcome to the real world." We soon learn, however, that the distinction between reality and illusion is not as sharp as common sense would suggest. After an early training sequence in the virtual reality space called the Construct, Neo, on returning his consciousness to his body, discovers that he is bleeding. "I thought it wasn't real," he says. "Your mind makes it real," Morpheus replies. Neo: "If you're killed in the Matrix, you die here?" Morpheus: "The body cannot live without the mind." Hence Morpheus keeps insisting that Neo free his mind from all restrictive beliefs—beliefs that continue to affect and shape reality outside of the Matrix. One of the main restrictive beliefs, apparently confirmed over and over by experience within the Matrix, is enunciated to Neo by the slimy Cypher: "You see an Agent, you do what we do. Run. Run your ass off." Thus fear of the Agents, fear of death, persists within the parameters of the Matrix even for those who understand its artificiality. So when Neo finally turns to fight Agent Smith, Morpheus, observing the events in their digital computer form, says, "He is beginning to believe." He is beginning to believe that he is indeed the One—that he has the power to destroy the Matrix and liberate its slaves. Beginning to believe in his power and destiny, he ceases to be afraid.

However, all Neo's stupendous feats of strength, speed and agility finally fail to defeat the Agents. Racing to find a telephone hookup that would take his consciousness back to his body on the ship, Neo finds himself at the business end of a gun. As he is killed in the pseudo-reality of the Matrix, the computer monitor connected to his brain in the real world flatlines. The tests of strength and speed, the test of doing battle in the Matrix, seem to prove that Neo, after all, is not in fact the One. But Trinity has not been applying this test. Blaise Pascal (1623–1662) wrote that "The heart has its reasons, which reason does not know."[3] Trinity is following the test of her heart, which has reasons of which ordinary scientific-technological reason knows nothing. The Oracle prophesied that the one she loves would be the One. Trinity loves Neo. Therefore Neo must be the One. Thanks to her love, Trinity is no longer afraid of death. When it looks as if all is over for both Neo and the *Nebuchadnezzar*, Trinity says to Neo's dead body: "Neo, I'm not afraid anymore. The Oracle told me that I would fall in love, and that man, the man who I loved, would be the One. And so you see, you can't be dead. You can't be. Because I love you. You hear me, I love you." She kisses Neo, and he comes back to life. The place in which Neo dies and is then resurrected is that same dreary building with the word HEART prominently displayed on its marquee.

---

[3] *Pascal's Pensées* (New York: Dutton, 1958), p. 78; #277.

The names of the main characters in *The Matrix* each have some significance. "Neo," which indicates that something new will happen despite the controls of the Matrix, is also an anagram of One. "Morpheus" is appropriately named after the god of the dream world. "Cypher," who betrays his crew and strives to return to comfortable oblivion back in the Matrix, wants to be the non-entity his name indicates. So then what does "Trinity" mean? I suppose that most people watching the film, and recognizing that these other names have been chosen for their obvious meanings, are reluctant to do the same for the name "Trinity." But who is it that is capable of creating life, as Trinity does when her love restores life to Neo? In the Christian tradition, only the triune God has such power. And in God's secular ordinance the power of creating life is given to a woman in love. In Trinity, the God that is Love takes flesh and creates life.

The Oblivion of Being

Beyond the excitement of its simulated battles and the allure of its technological theses of virtual reality, is there a meaning to the trilogy that the audience can apply to their "real" lives? According to the philosopher Martin Heidegger (1889–1976), the history of the Western world is the history of the forgetfulness of Being. In the course of this history, technocratic intellect has become a quasi-demonic force, creating a world of objects and a dominant mentality based on the artificial ideas of the intellect. This frame of mind blinds us to the truth of experiences that are found only outside this technological framework—such as the power and beauty of the natural world as expressed in ancient religions and early Greek philosophy, in the nature philosophy of Chinese Daoism, or in the works of certain modern poets such as Hölderlin. Our modern world is therefore dominated by a Technocratic Matrix which we take to be reality, but which hides from us a deeper truth about our human being.

Heidegger argues that the oblivion of Being through the mesmerizing spell of technological rationality has its origins in the rationalism of Plato—in Plato's disjunction between the Idea, with its transcendent realm of true being, and the mere appearance of reality accessible to the senses. In this interpretation,

Plato's allegory of the cave, which instructs us to look for ultimate reality outside of the sensory material world of immediate
experience, contributes to the oblivion of Being. It conceals our
spontaneous awareness that there is another, more fundamental
truth than that which scientific intellect attains and applies
through its technology. Christianity later adopts the perspective
of a transcendent realm of heaven, which implies a degradation
of the sensory world of earth, and so Heidegger concludes that
"Nietzsche was right in saying that Christianity is Platonism for
the people."[4] It is a paradox that Christianity, with its other-
worldly perspective, contributes to technological domination of
this world. But the scientific-technological mentality depends
precisely on the notion that the natural world is not something
inherently sacred, and so can be exploited and manipulated for
egotistical goals.

Heidegger therefore gives us a philosophical perspective for
recognizing truth in the *Matrix* trilogy: our own world is in fact
dominated by the technocratic mentality, shutting off from
awareness the deeper reality of the human being. Philosophical
reflection of this type reinforces the power of an aesthetically
gripping work of popular commercial art. But the relation
between art and philosophy works in both directions. The
Matrix trilogy suggests possibilities for understanding what
Heidegger could possibly mean. How can technocratic intellect
take on an independent power over human minds without
being embodied in entities of the type described by film?
Heidegger once argued that the United States and the Soviet
Union had incarnated this spirit of sheer, soulless technology.
He had hoped that his native Germany, with its super-hero
Leader, had retained that connection to Being, to what is ultimately real, that could liberate mankind from its mind-induced
shackles.[5] But this conception of salvation through the high-tech
armies of Hitler's racist nationalism proved to be another illusion, perhaps an even more insidious dimension of the unfold-
ing demonic Matrix of technocratic control.

In *Reloaded* the possibility that the promised salvation is

---

[4] Heidegger, *An Introduction to Metaphysics*, pp. 89–90.
[5] On Heidegger's assertion of the "inner truth and greatness" of Hitler's
National Socialism, see Martin Heidegger, *An Introduction to Metaphysics*
(Garden City: Doubleday Anchor), p. 166.

really just another illusion is clearly raised. The One is not the liberator of humanity from the control of the Matrix, but a function of the program whose purpose is the preservation of the Matrix itself. When, at the end of this second film, Neo uses the power of his mind outside of the Matrix to stop the advance of the threatening sentinels, our simplistic distinction between the illusion of the Matrix and the "real world" of the *Nebuchadnezzar* and Zion is seriously challenged. Is there no independent truth outside the projections and so the power of the technocratic mind? Is everything therefore illusion?

While this pessimistic perspective is prominently suggested, other strands in the film indicate a different possibility. Two paths of liberation have been proposed from the beginning. The first is to confront the technological power of the machines with the superior techniques of power, speed, and agility of the One. But in such a war of technologies, isn't it technology itself that inevitably wins? In a somber scene in *Reloaded*, the wise old councilor of the free city of Zion takes Neo on a tour of the underground machinery that supports the life of the city. We too are dependent on machines, he says. Where is there really a difference between this and the Matrix?

There is however another approach which sidesteps this confrontation of machines, of technologies and their mind-based powers. This is the way of the heart, Trinity's way of love. In the open sequences of *Reloaded* Neo has fully reciprocated Trinity's love. The hearts and bodies of the two lovers are entwined in passionate yet solemn embrace, as the whole city of Zion celebrates its freedom to the sensual drumbeats of love. The people have been released from their fear of the weapons of terror by the impassioned declaration of Morpheus: "This is Zion! And we are not afraid!" As the enemy advances, rather than prepare for battle, the people of Zion dance in the fires of love.

Who Was the Teacher of Socrates?

If Heidegger was himself under the mesmerizing spell of technocratic rationality in his belief that mankind's salvation lay in the countervailing technological might of National Socialism, how can we trust his interpretation of Plato? In the history of interpretations of Plato, there are two approaches, comparable to the two paths of liberation outlined in the *Matrix* trilogy: Plato as the exponent of the all-controlling Forms or Ideas detected by technically agile reason, and Plato as the philosopher of love.

In the allegory of the cave, Plato compares the life of the majority of human beings to that of lifelong prisoners, preoccupied solely with the shadows of reality. The philosopher is The One—the One who has been liberated from this shadow world and returns to free his fellow humans from illusion. How is the liberation of the philosopher achieved in the first place? Is it by conquering false reasons with the technical superiority of true reasons on the battlefield of rationality—and thereby forgetting, as Heidegger would argue, that Being is not something that yields to force? Or is there another approach: the path of love, the way of the heart?

There is indeed a strange kind of forgetfulness in the history of Western philosophy which also persists in the historical recollections of Heidegger. In the canonical genealogy of Western philosophy, Socrates was the teacher of Plato, Plato was the teacher of Aristotle, and Aristotle the philosopher who inspired the European Middle Ages. But who taught Socrates in the first place? Did his philosophy step forth fully formed from the mind of Zeus? Socrates himself tells us, in *The Symposium*, that his teacher was a woman, Diotima of Mantineia. Diotima taught the philosophy of the heart with its own reasons, not the philosophy of a heartless, self-aggrandizing rationality.

Philos means love and *sophos* means wisdom. The philosopher, etymologically, is a lover of wisdom. The stress is generally placed not on love but on wisdom, which then is interpreted as the transcendent Idea that Heidegger says is responsible for the oblivion of Being. But Diotima proposes the following curriculum for her Philosophy 101: "For he who would proceed aright in this matter should begin in youth to visit beautiful forms; and first, if he be guided by his instructor aright, to love one such form only—out of that he should create fair thoughts . . ."[6] The first step in Diotima's philosophy is not a matter of the mind but an affair of the heart. It is to fall

---

[6] Plato, *Symposium* in *Great Books of the Western World*, Volume 7 (Chicago: Encyclopaedia Britannica, 1952), pp. 167, 210.

deeply in love with someone. It is physical, erotic love that breaks the mental shackles that bind the individual to the darkness of the cave. In recounting his allegory, Socrates says that the One, the potential philosopher, is first dragged from his position in the cave. He does not say who does the dragging. But the ascent out of the cave exactly parallels the ladder of love taught by Diotima. And she teaches that it is the person whom I love who first introduces the light of beauty into the darkness of mind-based illusion. Enflamed by the fire of love, ordinary, self-centered reason is lost, and a new life with its fair thoughts opens up to the student of love. For the person in love the world glows with a new intensity; it becomes transparent to ultimate reality.

The next, crucial step is to keep on loving—to follow the path of love wherever it leads. When reason is linked to love, it keeps telling us not to stop at this or that person, but to recognize the beauty that potentially shines forth in every person. It reminds us that institutions too have their own beauty—if only their leaders would recognize it. It resists the temptation to close off the ultimate nature of reality with limiting beliefs. It teaches us to free our minds to see the light of beauty everywhere, and the power of darkness only in the attempt to direct our love *exclusively* to one person, one institution, one set of beliefs. In *Revolutions*, Neo, whose eyes are blinded, sees with heart-opened vision the light in the enemy machines themselves: "It's unbelievable, Trin. Lights everywhere. Like the whole thing was built with light."

As we universalize our love, discovering beauty in everyone and everything in the harmony of their multiple colors and textures, we do not have to abandon our first love. If she too is a whole-hearted lover, she accompanies us on our journey—one's true Soul Mate who, says Aristophanes in the same *Symposium*, comes in the soul's earthly journey to those authentically devoted to the gods. True "Platonic love" is that same first love of one beautiful person that has been expanded to the entire universe through the heart-felt vision of the universal presence of Beauty Itself. Through the philosophical eyes of love, the world of matter shines with the splendor of spirit. The power of darkness, the illusory world of fear and death, is only dispelled by the fiery light of love.

Neo Chooses the Path of Love

In *The Matrix,* Neo has to choose between the red pill and the
blue pill. Morpheus explains: "You take the blue pill, the story
ends, you wake up in your bed and believe whatever you
want to believe. You take the red pill, you stay in Wonderland,
and I show you how deep the rabbit hole goes." But why is
the path down the rabbit hole symbolized by the *red* pill? The
reference to Lewis Carroll's *Alice in Wonderland* suggests
another book by Lewis Carroll, *Silvie and Bruno*, in which
Silvie is given the choice between a blue locket and a red one.
On the blue locket are the words: "All will love Silvie." On the
red locket are the words "Silvie will love all." Silvie chooses
the red locket: "It's *very* nice to be loved, but it's nicer to love
other people!"[7]

The choice between self-love and loving other people is
given to Neo in *Reloaded* as the choice between two paths,
opened up by two facing doors. As the Architect puts this
choice: "The door to your right leads to the Source, and the salvation of Zion. The door to your left leads back to the Matrix,
to her [Trinity] and to the end of your species." It is really a
choice between mere survival, rooted in self-love, and Neo's
love of Trinity—the love of one person that is the starting point
of Diotima's ladder of universal love. Neo chooses the latter,
and this turns out indeed to be the path that leads beyond mere
survival to authentic freedom.

Revolutions therefore distinguishes between two opposing
approaches to revolution. Previous Neos, in their efforts to bring
about the revolutionary overthrow of the Matrix, chose to sacrifice the one to save the many. Many revolutionaries in human
history, believing that the end justifies the means, were willing
to sacrifice some for others. They promoted the sacrifice of one's
loved ones for the higher cause. But such a mentality is perpetuated in the outcome—a world in which some continue to be
sacrificed for others. Our beliefs are inevitably manifested in the
world that we create.

The truly revolutionary approach is that of Diotima, who, like

---

[7] Lewis Carroll, *Silvie and Bruno*, Chapter V, "The Magic Locket." Internet
source: http://www.hoboes.com/html/FireBlade/Carroll/Sylvie/ Thanks to
Theodore Gracyk for this reference. Ted says he got it from his son,
Thelonious.

Silvie, teaches that *all* must be loved, because there is beauty in everyone and everything. The path to the free world cannot begin by abandoning your partner, your Soul Mate. Such hard-hearted revolutionaries, like the previous Neos, only perpetuated the cycles of war.

Neo follows the path of love, the path of Trinity, to the very end. In *Revolutions*, Trinity must guide Neo, "the blind Messiah" as Smith calls him, to the threshold of the Machine City, where she dies. But the spirit of her love, the nature of the path she has chosen from the very beginning, lives on in him when he faces Mr. Smith and his clone army.

The Matrix has been criticized as "a naïve fantasy of overcoming human flesh. The hero moves from being 'penetrated' and connected to others to being self-controlling and intact—even immune to bullets. . . . This fantasy suits geeky young males who yearn for autonomy and mental powers."[8] This appraisal may have been justifiable on the basis of the first film, before the love theme of the trilogy moves definitively to the foreground. The feminist criticism recognizes the seductive primacy, for some, of the path of technocratic intellect and the resulting wars of technologies. For the geeky males who were captivated by this illusory surface appearance, the emerging real theme of the trilogy, subverting the dominant paradigm of technocratic intellect with its climax of self-effacement, must have been quite disappointing.

At the beginning of their final struggle, Smith taunts Neo for his effeminate weakness:

> Why keep fighting? . . . Is it freedom or truth, perhaps peace—could it be for love? Illusions, Mr. Anderson, vagaries of perception. Temporary constructs of a feeble human intellect trying desperately to justify an existence that is without meaning or purpose. And all of them as artificial as the Matrix itself. Although, only a human mind could invent something as insipid as love.

But which is the real illusion? The endless spiral of the technologies of war—represented by the infinitely expanding clone

---

[8] Cynthia Freeland, "Penetrating Keanu: New Holes, but the Same Old Shit," in William Irwin ed., *The Matrix and Philosophy* (Chicago: Open Court, 2002), p. 205.

army of Mr. Smith—that is characteristic of the male-dominant societies of the past five thousand years of "civilization," or the truly revolutionary path of love on which Trinity guides Neo?

Heidegger argues that Plato separated soul from body, the ideal world from the world of sensory experience, and thereby legitimated the rule of the technocratic intellect over what must become, as a result, a blighted earth. However, it was not Plato, but the Stoics, during the time of imperialist Roman rule, who radically separated soul and body, believing that the external physical world is beyond the control of the individual, and so subject to an unknowable higher will. The German Philosopher Georg Hegel (1770–1831) therefore called the Roman religion, in which individuals are sacrificed to the will of the gods and the Emperor, "The Religion of Expediency."[9] Here indeed we see the technological relationship of power over the earth that is criticized by Heidegger. This is the true forgetfulness of Being. But this is not the earth-loving teaching of Diotima that is passed on to us through the works of Plato, if we know how to read them. Hegel therefore calls the Greek religion of the time of Plato "the Religion of Beauty."[10]

Neo puts an end to the spiral of destruction due to the dominance of the technocratic intellect when he finally stops fighting and adopts the feminine position, allowing himself to be "penetrated" by Smith. In his realization that the war between technocratic intellects is unwinnable, Neo also follows the lead of the Mother of the Matrix, the Oracle, who previously refused to fight Smith on his own terms.

Revolutions concludes with the grandmotherly Oracle complimenting the little girl Sati, a computer program, for her breath-taking sunrise—Sati's gift of gratitude to Neo. When Sati first meets Neo on the underground train platform, she asks him: "Are you from the Matrix?" Neo says that he was from the Matrix, but had to leave. Sati replies: "I had to leave my home too." For Sati there is no hierarchy, no discrimination between a real world and an artificial, illusory one. It is all reality. It is all someone's home. She is the embodiment of acceptance. She can create beauty because she sees it everywhere. In place of the

---

[9] Georg Wilhelm Friedrich Hegel, *Lectures on the Philosophy of Religion*. Volume 2 (Berkeley: University of California Press, 1987), p. 498.
[10] Hegel, *Lectures on the Philosophy of Religion*, p. 455.

pessimistic possibility that all is illusion, *Revolutions* concludes with Sati's belief that all is real, because beauty can be found, and created, everywhere. The final outcome of *The Matrix* trilogy is not the victory of the real world over the illusory one, of the humans over the machines, or vice versa, but compromise, acceptance of the differences, and so peace between all the worlds and the beginning of a reign of love. Let us not forget, Diotima teaches Socrates, that there is beauty, and so love, everywhere.

4

The Matrix Is the Prozac of the People

MARTIN DANAHAY

"Religion is the opium of the people." The words have shock value, apparently relegating all religions to the status of a drug designed to numb the intellect and to help the believer escape from reality. This most frequently cited quotation from the works of Karl Marx is, however, widely misunderstood and is actually saying something much more interesting than at first appears. In fact, Marx was not advocating abolishing religion because it was a drug, but was simply using an analogy to describe its social function.

Marx was not critical of religion itself, but was very critical of the combination of the profit motive and religion under capitalism, which he termed "hucksterism." Marx would view the *Matrix* sequels as yet another example of hucksterism. The *Matrix* trilogy abounds with religious references, but the movie itself has very little in common with any recognizable organized religion. The religious messages function more as a comforting veneer. The movie's main goal is to sell a lot of tickets and create a profit for the industry. *Reloaded* was marketed alongside other products like the drink PowerAde, and this easy cross-marketing shows how much a movie is a product just like any other. Like the movie itself, the ad for PowerAde was actually exhorting us to buy more products as Agent Smith urged us to "keep up our energy levels." The spiritual pretensions of the movie become untenable if it is analyzed in Marx's terms as an example of religious hucksterism that is indistinguishable from the marketing of any other commodity.

When Marx compared religion to opium he was not saying that it was a "drug" in the sense of an addictive substance, but more like a medicine. Opium for most of the nineteenth century was used for medicinal purposes and was not a controlled substance. It was freely available over the counter in pharmacies and was found in a wide range of medicines. A much better synonym for opium in the contemporary context would be Prozac, a widely prescribed antidepressant. Everyone can understand why Prozac is prescribed, as people would have understood the use of opium in the nineteenth century. Marx while not condemning the drug would ask why it was necessary in the first place, just as he would ask why people needed religion. Marx's comments on religion as medicine can help us understand the therapeutic function of religion on which movies like *Reloaded* and *Revolutions* draw.

Religion for Sale

Neo is consistently identified with Jesus as "the One" in the *Matrix* trilogy, and even undergoes a kind of crucifixion in the climactic scene, but he has serious deficiencies as a spiritual or religious leader. The problems with Neo as a Jesus-like figure become increasingly difficult to ignore as the trilogy progresses. In Marx's terms the first movie in the trilogy seemed to offer the possibility of "real human emancipation," but what Neo ends up offering in *Revolutions* is a much more restricted compromise between humans and machines. The Matrix will continue to exist in some form, and so presumably human batteries will still be necessary to provide power for the machines. Jesus offers in this case not salvation but a standoff. While Zion will still exist complete liberation is not a possibility for all human beings.

Religion in the trilogy is amorphous and undemanding. In *Reloaded*, after an "opening prayer" by Councilor Hamann, which we do not see, Morpheus gives a very short "sermon." Church, the state, and the military do not seem to be distinguished from one another in this system. After Morpheus's "sermon" everyone gets to dance and have sex because church services are really no more than raves in the Zion version of religion. This is almost a parody of attempts by religions to update their services to appeal to a younger congregation. It has become commonplace in the United States to incorporate rock bands into services, but the movie takes things a step further and makes a church into a dance club. Religion in Zion is a form of entertainment and is so pervasive that it is impossible to tell where it begins and ends. This mixing of religion and entertainment makes *Reloaded* a particularly American movie.

There is a long-standing connection between capitalism, the media, and religion in the United States. I live in Texas where this connection is glaringly obvious because religion and commercialism are pervasive throughout the media in my local environment. Churches in Texas are very successful commercial enterprises, and many are expanding their buildings to include their own movie theaters and bowling alleys. Like the church in Zion, they meld religion and entertainment. There are also several huge churches that have created their own TV networks. Through my cable provider I have access to four TV channels devoted exclusively to religious programming; in addition, there are several radio stations in the area devoted to religion twenty-four hours a day, seven days a week. The churches and the radio stations are local versions of the more famous national broadcast operations run by such "televangelists" as Pat Robertson. Indeed, the movie theater where I watched *Reloaded* doubles as a church on Sunday mornings. The Connect Church, whose web site is at http://www.connectchurch.com, meets every Sunday for worship in one of the theater's screening rooms.

The Connect Church is a material sign of the mixing of religion and movies in the United States. The photos of services at the Connect Church show members of the congregation sitting in movie-theater seats looking at a religious message on the screen. They are watching a rock band play, but not dancing like the actors in the "service" in *Reloaded*. Their website studiously avoids naming itself as any particular denomination and seems to want to convey a vague Christian spirituality without defining itself as Methodist, Baptist, Catholic, or any other denomination. The website tries to present a broad spirituality that, like that of the *Matrix* trilogy, will appeal to the greatest number of customers. This accords with the statistics cited by Gregory Bassham in *The Matrix and Philosophy* that sixty-two percent of American adults professed a pluralistic outlook, although as Bassham points out it's easier to be pluralistic in theory than practice (p. 116). Bassham refers to this as "cafeteria pluralism," perspicuously pointing out the contradictions in such an approach (pp. 118–19).

It is striking that the Connect Church does not feel the need to explain overtly that the services will be conducted in a movie theater. The setting of a movie theater, I suppose, can be seamlessly integrated into religious services, and a religious message can be adopted by a Hollywood movie because both function as "the Prozac of the people." People can leave the Sunday morning services feeling uplifted, or leave an evening showing of *Revolutions* confident that a power greater than themselves is going to solve humanity's problems. The common denominator between the church services and the movies is capitalism, which will readily adapt to any ideology so long as it is profitable. Indeed, the conjunction of religion and capitalism is extremely profitable in the United States. Witness the proliferation of Christian churches and media outlets.

Neo Wrestles with an Angel

The most obvious example of the mixing of religion and commerce in *Reloaded* occurs in the scene in which Neo encounters Seraph. The scene opens with a shot of a table with a number of religious and other products. On the table rest not just a Barbie doll, a small plastic soccer ball, and other toys, but also an image of Jesus and a Buddha. The very last items are a votive candle and a toy computer. This compilation of products could be signaling a criticism by the Wachowski brothers of cheap commercialism, but I will read this image as a visual embodiment of what Bassham referred to as "cafeteria pluralism" and what Marx would call "hucksterism." The table symbolizes the way in which in the contemporary United States religious icons are like any other commercial product. The commercialization of religion is neatly summed up by the chance to buy a plastic Buddha or a cheap image of Jesus.

The table makes all commercial goods, whether sacred or profane, equal as commodities. The images of Jesus or the statue of Buddha are as much a product as the soccer ball. The table unintentionally symbolizes the approach to religion in *Reloaded*, which is to mix together references to several different religions and use them to sell a product, in this case a movie. The religious traditions of any particular group are not as important as the drive to make a profit. The trilogy espouses a very bland, non-specific spirituality that is designed not to offend any particular religion while giving the movie a veneer of transcendence that makes its more venal aspirations less evident. It is "feel good" spirituality with an emphasis on hedonism that marks the *Matrix* trilogy as a part of a commodity culture.

The mixing of religious references is most obvious in the character of Seraph. The word "seraph" invokes a Christian image of angels, although our first view of Seraph through Neo's eyes turns him into a Buddha-like figure composed of golden code. Instead of the traditional halo, the golden code conveys the idea that Seraph is a spiritual figure unconstrained by any one religious doctrine. Seraph also proves to be a master of martial arts, immediately starting a fight with Neo to see if he is the One.

This scene invokes the Biblical account of Jacob wrestling with an angel (Genesis 32), although in this case Neo does not have his hip knocked out of joint and does not have to fight all night. After a bit of sparring, which looks more like a dance than a fight, Seraph is satisfied that Neo is the One. But Seraph's assertion that "You do not truly know someone until you fight them" trivializes both the violence and the religious references. The violence is so aestheticized in this scene, as it is throughout the *Matrix* movies, that it becomes a matter of admiring the choreography of two bodies in motion and not of fearing damage to real, physical bodies. A similar aesheticizing of religion takes place so that the equation of God with computers is an intellectual exercise rather than a blasphemy, which is how it might appear to devout followers of one of the religions sampled in the trilogy.

It is difficult to become upset at the cavalier mixing of religions in the *Matrix* trilogy because it is meant to comfort, and not to challenge or unsettle the beliefs of its audience. In Marxist terms the trilogy is a form of "opium of the people" meant to allay peoples' fears and make their lives more bearable. To understand what Marx meant by "opium of the people," we must understand the status of opium in the early and mid nineteenth century.

The Opium of the People

When Marx referred to opium he was not necessarily thinking solely in terms of opium dens and hopeless addicts. Throughout the nineteenth century opium was widely prescribed as a medicine and was used in preparations such as laudanum, which was often taken for coughs. Opium was viewed in much the same way as aspirin is today. Before the invention of aspirin at the end of the nineteenth century by the Bayer Corporation (along with heroin, ironically enough), opium was one of the few reliable substances in the doctor's medicine chest to soothe the pain and quiet the nerves of patients. In fact, the metaphor of disease would more accurately capture Marx's attitude to religion than contemporary images of drug addiction; Marx felt that religion, like opium, was useful in soothing pain. He was, like a doctor, quite prepared to condone medication that brought relief to suffering, but he was also anxious to diagnose the underlying illness that created the need for medication in the first place. This comes across very strongly if one restores the "opium of the people" quotation to its original context in "A Contribution to the Critique of Hegel's Philosophy of Law" (1844):

> Religious distress is at the same time the expression of real distress and the protest against real distress. Religion is the sigh of the oppressed creature, the heart of a heartless world, just as it is the spirit of a spiritless situation. It is the opium of the people (175).[1]

Marx clearly sees religion as a response to stress and anxiety, and recognizes that it provides "heart" or human caring and emotion in a "heartless" capitalist system that cares only about profits. Like opium, religion provides an antidote to pain, but to a spiritual rather than a physical distress. Religion makes up for the deficit of spirit in a capitalist system. To turn to religion is in some unconscious way to protest against the capitalist system which is itself indifferent to the spiritual and emotional state of workers, who are viewed solely in terms of productivity. Like

---

[1] All quotations in this article are from the *Collected Works of Karl Marx and Frederick Engels*, Volume 3 (1843–44) (New York: International, 1975). Page numbers are cited parenthetically in the text.

opium, religion provides relief from distress by numbing the pain of having to live under such an oppressive system.

Marx felt that religion was an understandable reaction to the stress and anxiety of being a worker in a capitalist system. He was not interested in "curing" people of their use of opium or religion; he wanted to change the system that caused such pain, and to reshape society into a healthier alignment. Once you had changed the system, Marx believed, the need for the medicine of religion would disappear. Marx expressed this idea in the following terms:

> To abolish religion as the illusory happiness of the people is to demand their real happiness. The demand to give up the illusion about its condition is the demand to give up a condition which needs illusions. (176)

The key term here is "illusion." People need illusions in a capitalist system simply to survive in such a harsh environment. If you can persuade people to give up their illusory relationship to reality then they will no longer need palliatives such as opium or religion in order to survive. He believed that through critique you could perceive the real economic and social conditions under which people lived, rather than through the distorting ideological lens that he compared at one point to a "camera obscura," a device that turned reality into its mirror image. In his "Critique of Hegel's Philosophy of Law" Marx said that "state and this society produce religion, which is an inverted consciousness of the world" so that a religious consciousness was for him the product of a distorted political and social condition that made an "upside down" view of reality inevitable (p. 175). Marx was not interested, therefore, in abolishing religion but in changing the conditions that gave rise to the need for religion in the first place. He was not hostile to religion but rather indifferent to it, believing that religious belief would become obsolete once the social conditions that created the need were restructured.

Marx on Religion in the United States

Marx makes several perceptive comments about religion and the state in the United States that help explain why the Wachowski brothers, as American citizens, would have produced movies like *Reloaded* and *Revolutions* in which they turn Neo into a Jesus figure and exploit a vaguely defined spirituality. The United States was and still is a very contradictory country when it comes to religion; it possesses one of the most churchgoing populations of any industrialized nation, yet follows an ideal of the separation of church and state. As Marx notes, even in the nineteenth century the United States was "pre-eminently the country of religiosity," having already earned a reputation for being exceptionally devout (p. 151).

Marx discusses the status of religion in the United States in reference to the Constitution of New Hampshire which declares the "right of conscience" for its citizens. Marx says of this declaration:

> Incompatibility between religion and the rights of man is to such a degree absent from the concept of the rights of man that, on the contrary, a man's *right to be religious*, is expressly included among the rights of man. The privilege of faith is a universal right of man. (p. 162)

Marx's point is that New Hampshire is not so much a secular state as one that turns religion into a question of individual belief, just as the state is not hostile to the concept of property but views it as a question of being indifferent to the uses of "private" property if they do not infringe on others. This is not real freedom, says Marx.

If freedom in the United States had really been perfected then religion would not still be needed according to Marx. As it is, the United States only achieved partial emancipation. Religion was turned into an entirely individual, private matter and thus separated from the state and from civic life. The fragmentation of religion in the United States discourages full and direct participation in the communal human life that Marx valued so highly. The United States approach to religion and the state is therefore seen as defective by Marx because it encourages individualism and selfishness instead of communal values.

The root of the problem for Marx is mediation. He has a dream of a direct, unmediated relationship between the emancipated citizen and reality. Both religion and the state as they exist in the United States are symptoms of a defective social organization.

Marx argues that the secular state simply takes the categories of religion, such as heaven and Jesus, and translates them into citizenship and idealized images of political leaders. Marx opposes both religion and the capitalist state as mediators and wants a direct expression of human emancipation that does not require using an intermediary. Do away with this mediation and both the state and religion become obsolete. If Neo is a Christ figure, then Marx would say that his existence shows that people in the United States have not yet achieved real freedom.

Marx, *The Matrix*, and Liberation

It might seem that in apparently aiming at human liberation Marx and the *Matrix* movies would have the same goal, but in fact the *Matrix* movies reaffirm the need for mediation. Neo apparently offers emancipation for human beings that would restore them to an unmediated relationship to reality, but in fact Neo becomes the intermediary between humans and machines. Neo does not liberate humans but through his sacrifice helps bring about a truce. He creates a "separate but equal" scenario in which both humans and machines can continue to operate and does not provide the freedom from domination that the trilogy seemed to promise. Under the very messy compromise with which *Revolutions* ends, it seems that large numbers of human batteries will still be necessary to supply power to the machine-based dream of the Matrix.

Neo becomes a combination of political and religious leader during the course of *Reloaded* which codifies the casual Biblical references in the first movie. Neo suddenly takes to wearing what looks like a cassock, and people start making offerings to him. Morpheus consolidates his John the Baptist role by showing a sudden talent for short but stirring sermons in the cave-like church, and Zion turns out to be a theocracy in which the Church and state happily coexist. While many may dismiss *Reloaded* as filler just designed to get you to pay some more money before seeing *Revolutions*, from Marx's perspective the movie would be crucial in understanding Neo's role as a representative of religion and the State.

Religion and Hucksterism

Marx predicted the close connection between religion and commercialism in "The Jewish Question," but he did so solely in terms of Judaism, which makes his statements sound anti-Semitic today.[2] If we replace the term "Judaism" with "commercialism" in the places where Marx refers to Jews then he is describing the situation that prevails in the commercial market for *Reloaded* and *Revolutions*. Marx calls this situation "hucksterism," which connotes the activities of somebody who makes excessive profit from selling shoddy goods. Marx criticizes the commercialism of the United States, where trade and religion have, from his perspective, become indistinguishable. Spirituality has been reduced to a commodity in the United States, he argues. While he unfairly blames this on Judaism, Marx's words do ring true for religion and commerce generally in the U.S. Religion and commercialism are deeply intertwined in the American context to a much greater extent than in many other industrialized countries. This is especially true in the visual media. Televangelism and business deals are an acceptable combination of activities for most Americans who see no contradiction between becoming rich from preaching a religious message and the otherworldly ideals of Christianity.

Working within this context, the Wachowski brothers also did not see a contradiction between making a movie with religious overtones and overt commercialism. The *Matrix* movies had product affiliations with many companies, including the PowerAde commercial mentioned above, and the Samsung "Matrix phone." While *The Matrix* seemed to promise liberation, the sequels proved indistinguishable from any other Hollywood product on the market. The Samsung "Matrix phone" promised to unlock "the prison of your mind," but this "liberation" has nothing to do with freedom, only with buying air time for a phone. From Marx's perspective the *Matrix* movies are therefore just another example of the "hucksterism" of religion in the United States, which continues to be more developed in the American context than in any other industrialized nation.

Movies like the *Matrix* trilogy function much like religion in the contemporary U.S. commercial context. The ultimate result of the *Matrix* movies is to reassure us that, while real freedom is not possible, a compromise kind of existence where we learn

---

[2] Marx's essay on "The Jewish Question" is a review of a book by Bruno Bauer, which argued that German Jews could only be emancipated if they repressed their religious identity, an argument with which Marx disagreed sharply.

to live with the situation is possible if we surrender our fates to a figure like Neo. The *Matrix* movies are celluloid Prozac that functions the same way as religion in Marx's formulation, offering an antidepressant that helps cure the symptoms of anxiety and depression, but does not address the structural issues that led to this situation in the first place. This suggests that we should reevaluate the scene in which Morpheus offers Neo the choice between red and blue pills. In keeping with his name, Morpheus may just be offering a sleeping aid in the blue pill, and the much vaunted red pill is perhaps just an antidepressant. In both hands he is offering short-term pharmaceutical solutions.

The Matrix itself is a very good metaphor for how the entertainment industry functions as a whole in American society as a form of antidepressant much like Prozac. When people are immobilized in front of the movie or TV screen they are functioning like the human "batteries" that power the very illusion that enslaves them. It really doesn't matter what images move across the screen so long as people continue to pay to be temporarily distracted and anesthetized by the product. Far from liberating people from production, the *Matrix* movies aim to keep them in the cycle of production and consumption that dominates most peoples' lives. This is why some people are still functioning as batteries by the end of the movie.

Marx would view Hollywood movies as part of the problem of capitalism in the U.S., not as the source of a possible solution. Like religion, the *Matrix* movies provide an illusory solution to real problems. The original *Matrix* movie raised serious issues about how we can perceive reality and control our own lives in an environment dominated by media and technology. However, the Matrix is itself part of the media system that is in the business of marketing illusions. It is therefore unreasonable to ask *Reloaded* and *Revolutions* to provide an antidote for the very commercial system of which they are a part.

In keeping with the spirit of Marx's inquiry we should ask then "what are the conditions that make movies like *Reloaded* and *Revolutions* necessary?" Rather than dismiss the *Matrix* movies by calling them "the Prozac of the People" I am, like Marx, suggesting that the movies are serving a medicinal function, but that we need to move beyond Prozac and examine the problems that give rise to peoples' suffering within the system in the first place. Only by changing peoples' living conditions will movies like *Reloaded and Revolutions* and drugs like Prozac become unnecessary. Change peoples' real living conditions and they can stop being batteries and stop watching movies like *Reloaded* and *Revolutions*.

5

"The Purpose of Life Is to End": Schopenhauerian Pessimism, Nihilism, and Nietzschean Will to Power

MARK A. WRATHALL

The German philosopher Friedrich Nietzsche (1844–1900) predicted that our age would be a nihilistic age. Nihilism, Nietzsche explained, means *"that the highest values devaluate themselves. The aim is lacking; 'why?' finds no answer."*[1] In a nihilistic age, all that seems valuable or important, everything that gives life purpose, now comes to appear as empty or meaningless.

The world of the *Matrix* is a nihilistic world. The characters of the *Matrix* trilogy, like Nietzsche himself, are struggling to come to grips with the consequences of nihilism. The problem for everyone in the world of the *Matrix* (and, if Nietzsche is right, for everyone in our age) is: how can we do anything meaningful or worthwhile in a world where nothing shows up as having inherent value?

In this chapter, we'll see that the characters of the *Matrix* exemplify different strategies for answering this question. In fact, they reflect Nietzsche's own view of the possible responses to nihilism. But before exploring the responses to nihilism, we need a more thorough description of Nietzsche's account of nihilism, and of his proposal for a new value that could survive the nihilism of our age.

---

[1] Friedrich Nietzsche, *The Will to Power*, translated by Walter Kaufmann and R.J. Hollingdale (New York: Vintage, 1967), §2.

The Nietzschean World of the Matrix

According to Nietzsche, the loss of meaning and purpose in our age is attributable to an event that he called "the death of God."[2] As long as one believes in God, it is possible to accept that there is a right or true way to understand things and to live one's life. The net effect of the death of God is, ultimately, to deprive us of the ability to distinguish between the true nature of things, and the mere appearance of things—in Nietzsche's jargon, between the "true" world and the "apparent" world (see *Will to Power*, §583). If there is no ultimate source to which we can appeal in deciding what the true meaning or nature of things is (that is, if there is no God), then different appearances of the world are equally "true" or legitimate.

Nietzsche thought of the death of God as a process, and predicted that for centuries to come, God's shadow would continue to have a hold on us (see *Gay Science*, §108), meaning that we would continue to long for and believe in some absolute truth about the universe or some ultimate purpose to life. But Nietzsche also thought that his philosophy was a destiny (see "Why I am a Destiny"[3]), meaning that everyone will eventually come to see things in just the way that he does. There will come a day, in other words, when it is simply not possible to believe in good conscience that there is a "right way" to live our lives, inherent goodness or justice or truth in the world, or that there is something ultimate to which we can appeal in justifying what we do or think.

Let's consider more closely the ways in which the world of *The Matrix* reflects the Nietzschean interpretation of the world. How does the death of God—an inability to believe in an ultimate arbiter of what is good, true, or just—manifest itself? Perhaps the most immediate consequence is the moral one— once God is dead, then, Nietzsche argued, "the whole of our European morality" which is ultimately grounded on God's justice and goodness will break down (*Gay Science*, §343). What we lose, with the death of God, is precisely the notion that we

---

[2] Friedrich Nietzsche, *The Gay Science*, translated by Walter Kaufmann (New York: Vintage, 1974), §125.

[3] In *Ecce Homo*, Friedrich Nietzsche, *On the Genealogy of Morals / Ecce Homo*, edited by Walter Kaufmann (New York: Vintage, 1989), p. 326.

have an obligation to do or refrain from doing anything. Instead, the "goodness" of the act can henceforth only be judged in terms of its consequences for me, given my desires. Interestingly enough, in the entire *Matrix* trilogy, there is only one appeal ever made to anything like an obligation to do what is moral, what is ethical, what is just, or what is right. This appeal is made by Agent Smith to Thomas Anderson in the interrogation room: "My colleagues believe," Smith tells Anderson, "that I am wasting my time with you, but I believe you wish to *do the right thing.* . . . all we're asking in return is your cooperation in bringing a known terrorist to *justice*" (emphasis supplied). The irony should be as obvious as the implications—no one in the world of *The Matrix* is genuinely moved by considerations of justice or what is right.

Beyond the moral effects, Nietzsche argues that, with the death of God, a distinction collapses that, for centuries, has structured our understanding of ourselves and the world. This is the distinction between a true and an apparent world. In both the Platonic and the Judeo-Christian tradition, the world we inhabit has been viewed as a mere appearance, or a fallen and imperfect approximation of the true reality, which is the world of the forms (the ideal versions of everything), or the world as God envisions it, and into which he will someday introduce the blessed. But if we cannot believe in God any longer, then we also have to give up the idea that there is some final arbiter of what is real or true. And that means that we are no longer in a position to treat any world as a "mere" appearance, because, as Nietzsche notes, "we possess no categories by which we can distinguish a true from an apparent world" (*Will to Power*, §583(A)). Thus, every appearance will be equally legitimate.

If the world of the *Matrix* trilogy is free of the shadows of God with respect to morals, the story is more complicated with respect to the idea of a true world. Morpheus is the main character who most maintains a sense for God. Zion has religious rituals, but only Morpheus, with his discussion of "providence," ever implies that God can actually be counted on to help out. Not surprisingly, then, Morpheus is also the only one who consistently insists that the world of the Matrix is a mere appearance and that the world outside the Matrix is the true world. The Merovingian has a different but interesting view. The worlds of the Matrix and the outside world are equally worlds of appearance; the true world is operating at a level below the ordinary appearances of things. Those, by contrast, who have accommodated themselves to the death of God have no trouble in treating the worlds simply as different worlds, without need for qualifiers like "real" or "true." Smith/Bane, for example, says to Neo: "I see you're as predictable in this world as you are in the other." Neo (after the first movie) and the Oracle also refer to the two worlds consistently as "this world and the machine world."

Finally, Nietzsche also argued that the idea that life has a purpose was also built upon the idea of God as final arbiter of what is true and good. In a world in which God is dead, nothing is capable of giving life deep meaning or purpose. The discovery that existence is "without meaning or purpose" wouldn't create a problem if we were mere machines or mere animals. It's only because we, unlike automatons, *need* a purpose that it creates a problem. This need, Nietzsche believed, was nothing essential, but something of an historical accident resulting from centuries of religious and moral teachers—the "teachers of the purpose of existence." As a result of these teachers, he wrote, "human nature has been changed . . . : It now has one additional need–the need for the ever new appearance of such teachers and teaching of a 'purpose'. Gradually, man has become a fantastic animal that has to fulfill one more condition of existence than any other animal: man *has to* believe, to know, from time to time *why* he exists; his race cannot flourish without a periodic trust in life—without faith in *reason in life*" (*Gay Science*, §1).

If the Agents Smith are any indication, this is a need that humans passed along to programs in the Matrix:

> There's no escaping reason, no denying purpose—because as we both know, without purpose, we would not exist. It is purpose that created us, purpose that connects us, purpose that pulls us, that guides us, that drives us, it is purpose that defines, purpose that binds us. We're here because of you, Mister Anderson, we're here to take from you what you tried to take from us. Purpose.

Rama-Kandra later informs Neo that "every program that is created must have a purpose; if it does not, it is deleted."

Unfortunately, the ability to have a purpose or believe in a purpose can't survive the death of God. If there is no "true" world, no right way to live one's life, no fate, then no purpose can really have a hold on us. "The problem is," as Neo succinctly puts it, "choice." A genuine freedom to choose entails that no reason or purpose can compel us to act, and this means that no choice can show up as the indubitably correct one. But that, in turn, implies that all one's purposes appear as arbitrary and, well, purposeless. Such a recognition will produce a genuine crisis and force one to confront what Camus called the only truly serious philosophical problem: "judging whether life is or is not worth living amounts to answering the fundamental question of philosophy."[4]

Life—A Nietzschean Revaluation of the World

In summary, then, the world of the *Matrix* is very much a Nietzschean world. No one is really moved by moral categories any more. But the breakdown of the old metaphysical understanding of the world is not yet complete, because there are still some attempts to hold on to the idea that there is a true world, or that there is a purpose to life, whether or not there is freedom. From Nietzsche's perspective, such efforts at justifying life by appealing to an ultimate truth or a transcendent purpose represent a kind of weakness, an inability to own up to the possibilities opened up by the collapse of God. But what allows him to make this judgment? If we can't appeal to morality, to truth, or to freedom in deciding what makes a life worthwhile, what can we appeal to? Nietzsche's answer is: life itself. The central focus of the revaluation of values is life.

According to Nietzsche, the essence of life—what characterizes all living things—is a striving for more power. "Power," for Nietzsche, is the ability to overcome resistances and constraints. So the essence of life is constant overcoming—a constant increase in its ability to "become master over that which stands in its way" (*Will to Power*, §696). What makes life worthwhile, then, is simply an ascending life, a life which is more and more capable of overcoming. It's thus a sign of decadence and weakness, for Nietzsche, when someone, like Commander Lock, set-

---

[4] Albert Camus, *The Myth of Sisyphus*, translated by Justin O'Brien (New York: Vintage, 1991), p. 3.

tles for mere survival, or distracts himself from the problem of life through either conformity or pursuit of pleasure, like Cypher.

Using this understanding of life, Nietzsche works out a taxonomy of, and a basis for evaluating different approaches to life after the death of God. This taxonomy can also be taken as a key to understanding the characters in the *Matrix* trilogy.

The guiding presupposition of Nietzsche's taxonomy is that "every philosophy may be viewed as a remedy and an aid in the service of growing and struggling life; they always presuppose suffering and sufferers" (*Gay Science,* §370). That is, he sees suffering as an essential component of life, and he thinks that all philosophies—approaches to life—can be best interpreted in terms of how they help us deal with that suffering. But it's crucial to recognize that there are "two different kinds of sufferers": "first, those who suffer from the *over-fullness of life* . . . and then those who suffer from the *impoverishment of life*" (*Gay Science,* §370). Suffering from an impoverishment of life is the suffering one experiences at being unable to impose one's will on things, or to satisfy one's desires. Given that what makes life worthwhile for Nietzsche is precisely ascending life—getting better and better at overcoming restraints—those who suffer from an impoverishment of life will not be living worthwhile lives. As we will see, from Nietzsche's perspective the Merovingian, Morpheus, and Smith all fall into this category.

Suffering from an over-fullness of life is more complicated. Nietzsche's name for those who possess an over-fullness of life is *Übermensch*, "superman." Neo is a good example of what Nietzsche means with this term (no surprise, then, that the "Shooting Script" of the first movie tells us that he "flies faster than a speeding bullet,"[5] and Link in *Reloaded* explicitly says that "he's doing his superman thing"). A Nietzschean superman is one who is maximally alive—that means, maximally able to overcome himself (that is, go beyond the limitations that his way of living impose on him) and overcome resistances he encounters in the world. Such a person, Nietzsche writes, "would take leave of all faith and every wish for certainty, being practiced in

---

[5] Larry and Andy Wachowski, *The Matrix: The Shooting Script* (New York: Newmarket Press, 2001), p. 122.

maintaining himself on insubstantial ropes and possibilities and dancing even near abysses" (*Gay Science*, §347). But such a figure will "often appear *inhuman*," because she will not be bound by "all that was hitherto called holy, good, untouchable, divine" (*Gay Science*, §382).

But in what sense does such a person suffer from an "over-fullness" of life? Nietzsche describes this suffering as the suffering of someone who is "most full of oppositions and contradictions."[6] The "oppositions and contradictions" of the superman are the contradictions of always having to go beyond any set way of existing—the suffering of, one might say, never being at home in the world. This is, in fact, the metaphor that the *Matrix* films use to distinguish those like Morpheus and Link, who are at home in Zion, from Neo (the Keymaker sends Morpheus in one direction—"that door will take you home"—but there is no such direction for Neo, only the observation that "you'll know which door"). Or consider this exchange between Sati and Neo:

SATI: Are you from the Matrix?
NEO: Yes. No. I mean, I was.
SATI: Why did you leave?
NEO: I had to.
SATI: I had to leave my home too.

Neo, in other words, is clearly identified as no longer being at home—indeed, he's not even sure what answer to give about where he is from.

Returning, now, to Nietzsche's taxonomy of forms of life, in addition to distinguishing kinds of suffering, Nietzsche distinguishes what sort of desire drives the overall approach to life: is it "the desire for *being*," or for "*becoming*" (*Gay Science*, §370). The desire for being is the desire "to fix, to immortalize" some way of life or some configuration of the world. The desire for becoming is "the desire for *destruction*, change."

Using these two axes, we can develop the following chart to discover the relationship between different forms of life:

---

[6] "An Attempt at Self-Criticism," §5, in Friedrich Nietzsche, *The Birth of Tragedy and Other Writings*, edited by Raymond Geuss and Ronald Speirs (Cambridge: Cambridge University Press, 1999).

	Over-fullness of life	**Impoverishment of life**
desire for Being		
desire for Becoming/Destruction		

For Nietzsche, the important distinction is that between super-abundant and impoverished life, and Nietzsche advocates as worthwhile only the forms of life in the left-hand boxes. Let's now look at how to plug *Matrix*-characters into this taxonomy. We'll start in the upper-right corner, and move clockwise.

Sympathy for the Devil: Morpheus Meets the Merovingian

We're looking now at possible ways to deal with the loss of purpose and meaning in a nihilistic world. One way to respond is pessimistically—that is, to rest one's hopes on some other "true" world and, in the process, devalue this one. But to the degree that one does this, one manifests an impoverishment of life, an inability to impose one's will on *this* world. The characters who best represent this form of response to a Nietzschean-Matrix world are Morpheus and the Merovingian, who meet for the first time, interestingly enough, in the restaurant *Le Vrai*, French for "The True." There, Morpheus and the Merovingian argue over the truth—over what the "true" world is. The argument is succinctly stated in the following dialogue:

> MEROVINGIAN: You see, there is only one constant, one universal, it is the only real truth: Causality. Action. Reaction. Cause and effect.
> MORPHEUS: Everything begins with choice.
> MEROVINGIAN: No. Wrong. Choice is an illusion. . . .

To understand the significance of this exchange, we need to look more closely at the characters of Morpheus and the Merovingian. The secret to Morpheus's character is his name—Morpheus, in mythology, was a shaper or guardian of dreams. In the *Matrix* movies, the character Morpheus has a twofold relationship to dreams. In the first place, he awakens Neo (and others) from the "computer generated dream world" of the Matrix and educates them concerning the supposed "unreality" of the Matrix world. In this respect, of course, Morpheus betrays a prejudice that he should have lost in the Nietzschean world of the Matrix—namely, a prejudice that any world is more or less true or real than any other: "The Matrix is the world," he tells Neo, "that has been pulled over your eyes, to blind you from the truth."

But Morpheus is also a guardian of dreams in a second sense. For him, the "real" world is truer than the Matrix world, but not as true as the ideal world of which he dreams, and for the realization of which he struggles—a world without the Matrix. After rallying the people of Zion to fight against the encroaching machine armies, he turns from them, saying: "Good night, Zion. Sweet dreams." This dream of a new world is one that Morpheus believes he is being directed toward by Providence itself.

The truest reality, in other words, is one that Morpheus believes in as a dream to be realized, arrived at through our choices and actions. But Morpheus also sees our choices and actions as set into motion by a kind of divine providence: "There are no accidents," he tells the assembled group preparing to pave the way for Neo to reach the Architect. "We have not come here by chance. . . . I do not see coincidence, I see Providence, I see purpose. I believe it is our fate to be here. It is our destiny. I believe this night holds for each and every one of us the very meaning of our lives." With such declarations, Morpheus betrays himself as someone who still views the universe as if there were a God guiding everything. But, as we've already suggested, living for a dream world is sign of an impoverished life—one that is still lived under the shadows of the dead God, because it still believes that there is such a thing as the "true" world.

In the dispute between Morpheus and the Merovingian over the role of choice in producing the world, Nietzsche's sympathies would be with the Merovingian. But Nietzsche would be just as critical of the Merovingian's claim that causality is the "real truth" of the world. To see why, we need to say a word about how the Merovingian looks through Nietzsche's eyes.

Decoding the Merovingian with Schopenhauer

The *Matrix* films have a lot of fun with casting the Merovingian as a satanic figure (he dresses in red and black, he reigns in Club Hel surrounded by ghosts and other monsters, his wife is Persephone, a goddess in Greek mythology married to Hades, and so on . . .). But the true key to understanding the Merovingian, at least from a Nietzschean perspective, is to be found in his reading preferences. The most important book in the library in his Chateau—the one Persephone uses to open the trap door and lead Neo and the others to the Keymaker—is a copy of Schopenhauer's *Die Welt als Wille und Vorstellung, The World as Will and Representation*.[7] The Merovingian is a Schopenhauerian (or, more precisely, he has a Schopenhauerian view of the world).

In *The World as Will and Representation*, as the title indicates, Schopenhauer argued that the world can be regarded in two ways. The world as it appears to us is a mere representation, a mere appearance. In this world of appearance, everything shows up as completely and inescapably governed by the laws of causality. The causal chains of the world of appearances, Schopenhauer taught, are what we inevitably discover when we seek to understand the world, and ask about its "why" (WWR I, p. 80). This is, of course, precisely the point that the Merovingian was making in his debate with Morpheus: "there is only one constant, one universal, it is the only real truth: causality. Action. Reaction. Cause and effect."

But at some point—namely, when we confront the ultimate reality of things and not just their appearances—the answers to the "why" give out: "the *Why* is subordinated to the *What*" (WWR I, p. 82). The most profound kind of knowledge of the world doesn't explain the causal relations between appearances, but the nature, the "what" of the world as it really is in itself. The world as it really is, as it is in itself, is a world of will, where by "will" Schopenhauer means a blind, irrational, driving, and striving force with no purpose to give it meaning:

---

[7] Arthur Schopenhauer, *The World as Will and Representation*, translated by. E.F.J. Payne (New York: Dover, 1966). Volume I will be cited as WWR I; Volume II as WWR II.

"the will dispenses entirely with an ultimate aim and object" (WWR I, p. 308). All individuals and worldly objects are mere appearances. The truth of the world is that "the will alone is; it is the thing-in-itself, the source of all those phenomena" (WWR I, 184). We are at the mercy of this source, of which we ourselves are manifestations. So while our best knowledge of the world of appearances is to understand causality and the "why," as Schopenhauer and the Merovingian both believe, the apparent causes and reasons for things can't touch the deeper truth of the world. In the words of the Merovingian (describing the woman overcome by passion as a result of the dessert program he wrote),

> She does not understand why—is it the wine? No. What is it then, what is the reason? And soon it does not matter, soon the why and the reason are gone, and all that matters is the feeling itself. This is the nature of the universe. We struggle against it, we fight to deny it, but it is of course pretence, it is a lie. Beneath our poised appearance, the truth is we are completely out of control.

So when the Merovingian says that everything is causality, he means what Schopenhauer refers to as the "causal nature of the cause at the point where this causal nature is etiologically [that is, causally] no longer explicable at all" (WWR I, p. 112). In other words, he wants to understand the way that the will drives or produces appearances.

The Schopenhauerian/Merovingian view of the relation between appearance and reality is also pessimistic. It entails that there can be no true happiness or end of suffering in this world. Because the "kernel and in-itself of everything" is striving or will, which only exists insofar as it lacks satisfaction, it follows that there is constant suffering. Such satisfaction as there is can only be temporary; "it is always merely the starting-point of a fresh striving."[8] On top of it all, our striving brings us into conflict with other entities which are also striving for satisfaction. The end result is that we find "everywhere struggling and fight-

---

[8] This, by the way, explains Persephone's and the Merovingian's mutual disenchantment. As Schopenhauer said it himself, "everyone who is in love will experience an extraordinary disillusionment after the pleasure he finally attains" (WWR 2, p. 540).

ing, and hence always suffering. Thus that there is no ultimate aim of striving means that there is no measure or end of suffering" (WWR I, p. 309). Or, elsewhere, "the truth is that we ought to be wretched, and are so. The chief source of the most serious evils affecting man is man himself. . . . He who keeps this last fact clearly in view beholds the world as a hell, surpassing that of Dante by the fact that one man must be the devil of another" (WWR II, p. 578).

Thus, Schopenhauer concludes, "so long as our consciousness is filled by our will, so long as we are given up to the throng of desires . . . we will never obtain lasting happiness or peace." But if knowledge is "freed from the thralldom of the will," so that we can comprehend and understand the true nature of things, then, Schopenhauer argued, "all at once the peace, always sought but always escaping us on that first path of willing, comes to us" (WWR I, p. 196). Or, in the Merovingian words, "Causality. There is no escape from it, we are forever slaves to it. Our only hope, our only peace is to understand it, to understand the 'why,'" where understanding the "why" means seeing that the whys and the causes are mere appearances of a deeper source of striving in the world. Of course, the Merovingian has not yet learned the full lesson of Schopenhauerian denial of the will, a fact demonstrated by the way that he still suffers because he is driven by his passions and desires (his first words, upon meeting Trinity are "si belle qu'elle me fait souffrir", "she's so beautiful that she makes me suffer").

From a Nietzschean perspective, Morpheus and the Merovingian are flip sides of the same error. Although they no longer believe in God in a traditional sense, they both approach life "from the same ideal that created Christian theism." Namely, they "still seek . . . true 'reality', the 'thing-in-itself' compared to which everything else is merely apparent. It is their dogma that our apparent world, being so plainly *not* the expression of this ideal, cannot be 'true'" (*Will to Power*, §17). In doing this, they betray a fundamental inability to accept the world in which they find themselves, and a need to find behind this world a true world. That they are meant to represent two opposed reactions to the same problem is signaled by the near paraphrases they offer of one another. Morpheus: "I do not believe in chance . . . . I do not see coincidence, I see providence, I see purpose." The

Merovingian: "Where some see coincidence, I see consequence. Where others see chance, I see cost."

For Nietzsche, their refusal to accept what they see in this world and to posit instead some "true" other world are signs of their desire for being, permanence, and immortality. But, more importantly, they are also signs of an impoverished life. This comes out in the *Matrix* in the way both Morpheus and the Merovingian end up frustrated, unable to overcome the constraints they face. Every scene involving the Merovingian ends in his palpable frustration. Morpheus ends up literally in the passenger seat, watching helplessly as others drive the action.

But, if Morpheus and the Merovingian were the only options, it is clear where Nietzsche's sympathies would lie. Like Schopenhauer, Nietzsche believed that the world needs to be understood at its most fundamental level as wills striving with each other. "I bring a new interpretation, an 'immoral' one," he wrote: "Expressed in a vulgar fashion: God is refuted, but the devil is not."[19] And the Merovingian, unlike Morpheus, attained "the high point of the spirit imagined by Schopenhauer," namely, "the recognition that there is no meaning in anything." The task is to find a way to make this recognition compatible with an expansive notion of life.

"Trying Desperately to Justify an Existence that Is Without Meaning or Purpose": Neo versus Smith

We've now filled in the upper right-hand box of the chart: Morpheus and the Merovingian, each in their own ways, desire a fixed, immortalized, true world, and they do this, from Nietzsche's perspective, because they suffer from the inability to satisfy their desires. Smith, on the other hand, belongs in the lower right-hand box. His inability to satisfy his need for a purpose drives him to desire the destruction of everything. In Nietzsche's words, Smith embodies "the hatred of the ill-constituted, disinherited, and underprivileged, who destroy, *must* destroy, because what exists, indeed all existence, all being,

---

[9] Friedrich Nietzsche, *Kritische Gesamtausgabe Werke*, volume VIII-3, edited by Giorgio Colli and Mazzino Montinari (Berlin: De Gruyter, 1972), p. 355.

outrages and provokes them" (*Gay Science*, §370). It is in these terms that we should understand the Oracle's claim that Smith can't stop until he has destroyed all life: "very soon he's going to have the power to destroy this world, but I believe he won't stop there; he can't. He won't stop until there's nothing left at all."

Neo, like Smith, wants destruction as well (Smith tells him twice: "I want what you want"). But his desire for destruction grows, not out of the suffering of an impoverished life, but out of the suffering of an over-fullness of life. He needs to destroy current conditions in order to move beyond them, and over-come them. But to understand this, it is worth tracing Neo's growth into the superabundant life. Here, Neo's evolution into a destroyer mirrors Smith's in interesting ways.

The first stage is for each to lose their sense of purpose. We've already looked at Smith's discussion of his lost sense of purpose. Once Neo took his purpose from him, Smith notes, "I understood what I was supposed to do but I didn't." It takes Neo somewhat longer to come to terms with his lack of pur-pose. In *Reloaded*, he confesses to Trinity: "I just wish . . . I wish I knew what I'm supposed to do. That's all. I just wish I knew." Two possibilities hold themselves out—one is to be the savior of Zion, as Trinity points out in response to Neo's worries: "It's all right. They need you." The other possibility is to give his life meaning and purpose as the lover of Trinity—hence, Neo's reply: "I need you."

In Nietzschean terms, the love of Trinity becomes Neo's "condition of preservation"—it stabilizes his life and allows him to act meaningfully in a world that's otherwise lacking in purpose. As we realize in his meeting with the architect, this condition allows him to outgrow the purpose with which everyone else would like to saddle him, namely, being savior of Zion. "The relevant issue," the Architect quite rightly points out, "is whether or not you are ready to accept the responsi-bility of the death of every human being in this world." From Neo's choice, it is clear that he is willing to accept this respon-sibility. But he is only able to do this once he realizes that no-one, not even the Architect, can answer his question: "Why am I here?"

From that point on, he can choose to define himself as the lover of Trinity. His desire then becomes to destroy in order to overcome obstacles to this. But he also realizes that at some point he will need to also be able to overcome the constraints that even this condition sets on his life. Until, at the end of the movie, he can affirm the truth he has realized: that he does what he does, not for any purpose, but simply because he chooses to do so.

The final, climactic fight in *Revolutions* between Neo and Smith, in other words, depicts the Nietzschean struggle between active nihilism and the affirmation of the will to power. Smith takes the side of active nihilism in an effort to bring to an end the meaninglessness of human existence. All the things we live for ("freedom or truth, perhaps peace—could it be for love?") are dismissed by Smith as "illusions . . ., vagaries of perception. Temporary constructs of a feeble human intellect trying desperately to justify an existence that is without meaning or purpose." Despairing that anything could justify existence, Smith concludes that there is only one purpose left—that of actively pursuing an end to the world: "the purpose of life is to end," he declares.

Neo, like Nietzsche himself, doesn't deny the arguments of the active nihilist. Neo and Nietzsche are very much aware of the inevitability of death and the ultimate meaninglessness of life. But both see also that a worthwhile life is possible in the face of such facts, provided that one can become so well-disposed to life that one smiles at the notion of eternal recurrence. One embraces life, and one would even willingly live the same life over and over again, despite its ultimate meaninglessness. Neo, by the end, is not deceived that there is anything which could make his life ultimately meaningful. Smith asks him incredulously why he keeps on struggling, given the inescapable fact of his demise: "You must be able to see it, Mr. Anderson, you must know it by now! You can't win, it's pointless to keep fighting! Why, Mr. Anderson, why, why do you persist?" Neo replies simply: "because I choose to." There is, in other words, nothing which could ultimately give him a reason for acting, and Neo recognizes this. But he nevertheless wills himself to keep going. In so willing, he embodies the ideal of a life that strives for constant overcoming.

With Neo filling in our lower left-hand square, the chart now looks like this:

	Over-fullness of life	Impoverishment of life
desire for Being		**Morpheus/ Merovingian**
desire for Becoming/Destruction	**Neo**	**Smith**

Sati and the Eternal Recurrence

Of course, there's one box left to be filled. This would be a life driven by a desire to immortalize some approach to the world, not because it is the "right" or "true" one, but merely out of "gratitude and love" (*Gay Science*, §370). It would be a life that is "bright and gracious like Goethe, spreading a Homeric light and glory over all things" (*Gay Science*, §370). None of the major characters in the *Matrix* live such a life, but we're told enough about a minor character to suspect that she is a candidate for this box. To qualify, she must have an overfullness of life, and only one other character is explicitly identified as not being at home anywhere—Sati. Sati is explicitly acknowledged by Rama-Kandra as being without purpose. And she, appropriately enough, closes the trilogy by spreading light and glory over the world, prompted by gratitude.

Sati and Neo are linked, then, by the fact that each is well-disposed to life. For Nietzsche, the test of the super-abundant life is the response one has to the thought experiment known as "Eternal Recurrence." "What if," Nietzsche wrote,

> some day or night a demon were to steal after you into your loneli-est loneliness and say to you: "This life as you now live it and have lived it, you will have to live once more and innumerable times more; and there will be nothing new in it, but every pain and every joy and every thought and sigh and everything unutterably small or great in your life will have to return to you, all in the same suc-cession and sequence—even this spider in this moonlight between the trees, and even this moment and I myself. The eternal hour-glass of existence is turned upside down again and again, and you with it, speck of dust!" Would you not throw yourself down and gnash your teeth and curse the demon who spoke thus? Or have

you once experienced a tremendous moment when you would have answered him: "You are a god and never have I heard anything more divine." . . . how well disposed would you have to become to yourself and to life *to crave nothing more fervently* than this ultimate eternal confirmation and seal?"

Sati anticipates this eternal cycle of recurrence in asking hopefully: "will we ever see him [Neo] again?" The Oracle responds: "I suspect so. Someday."[10]

---

[10] I am indebted to Hubert Dreyfus and Iain Thomson for their thought-provoking responses to this paper, as well as for many enjoyable discussions of *The Matrix*.

Scene 2

A Splinter in Your Mind: Freedom and Reality

6

Choice, Purpose, and Understanding: Neo, the Merovingian, and the Oracle

THEODORE SCHICK, Jr.

"The problem is choice," Neo realizes during his conversation with the Architect. But "Choice is an illusion," proclaims the Merovingian. "Beneath our poised appearance," he contends, "the truth is, we are completely out of control." If the Merovingian is correct, Neo is mistaken; choice is not a problem because no one—not even Neo—can make free choices. In that case, the experience of choice in the real world is just as illusory as the experience of objects in the Matrix.

Ironically, the Oracle seems to take choice more seriously than the Merovingian. When Neo asks her whether he has to choose whether Trinity lives or dies, she says, "No, you've already made the choice; now you have to understand it." Notice: the Oracle doesn't say that Neo has no choice, which would be the case if choice were an illusion. She says instead that Neo has already chosen. The implication here seems to be that even though Neo's choice is determined, it is nevertheless a real choice. Is that possible? Can there be real choices in a world where the future is fixed? Or is the Merovingian right in claiming that there are no real choices? To answer these questions, we'll have to flesh out the Merovingian's and the Oracle's views.

Hard Determinism

The Merovingian is what William James, the great American philosopher and psychologist, calls a "hard determinist" because he does not "shrink from such words as fatality, bondage of the will, necessitation, and the like."[1] On the contrary, he embraces them. In his view, "we are all victims of causality. There is no escape from it; we are forever slaves to it." Strong words. But many have defended causal determinism in equally strong language.

In the eighteenth century, Baron Paul Henri d'Holbach (1723–1789) eloquently described the human condition this way:

> [Man] is connected to universal nature, and submitted to the necessary and immutable laws she imposes on all the beings she contains . . . Man's life is a line that nature commands him to describe upon the surface of the earth without his ever being able to swerve from it, even for an instant. He is born without his own consent; his organization does in no way depend upon himself, his ideas come to him involuntarily; his habits are in the power of those who cause him to contract them; he is unceasingly modified by causes whether visible or concealed, over which he has no control, which necessarily regulate his mode of existence, give the hue to his way of thinking, and determine his way of acting.[2]

We are natural objects, made out of atoms and molecules just like everything else in the world. And like every other natural object, we are governed by natural laws which, unlike political laws, are unbreakable. We can no more violate a law of nature than a leopard can change its spots or a billiard ball can change its direction of travel. Just as a billiard ball must follow the path determined by the forces acting on it, so we must follow the path determined by the forces acting on us. According to the hard determinists, the future is fixed. There is only one possible future, and we are powerless to change it.

The Merovingian illustrates the power of causality with the example of the wine: "I drink too much wine, I must take a piss. Cause and effect." Hard determinists claim that this sort of reasoning can be applied to all of our actions. The principle that

---

[1] William James, "The Dilemma of Determinism," in *The Will to Believe and Other Essays in Popular Philosophy* (Cambridge: Harvard University Press, 1979), pp. 117–18.

[2] Baron Paul Henri d'Holbach, "Of the System of Man's Free Agency," *The System of Nature* (1770), Chapter XI.

underlies their claim is known as *the principle of universal causation*, which says that every event has a cause that makes it happen. Since human actions are events, all of our actions are caused. As a result, we can't act freely. In their view, the principle of universal causation is incompatible with the existence of free will; if every event is caused, no actions are free.

The Oracle, however, seems to suggest that principle of universal causation does not rule out free will. On the one hand, she often speaks as if everything is determined. "We're all here to do what we're all here to do," she informs Neo, implying that we can do nothing but what we're destined to do. She also tells him that he can see the world without time, implying that, like God, he can see the world under the aspect of eternity (*sub species aeternitatis*) with past, present, and future spread out before him. On the other hand, the Oracle seems to believe that we can make real choices. In her first meeting with Neo, she tells him that he will have to make a choice between Morpheus's life and his own. In their second meeting, she reveals that programs can make a choice between exile and deletion. And in their final meeting, she claims that she has choices to make just like Neo does. So, unlike the Merovingian, the Oracle seems to believe that the principle of universal causation is compatible with free will.

Soft Determinism

William James calls those, like the Oracle, who see no conflict between determinism and free will "soft determinists" because, for them, "freedom is only necessity understood, and bondage to the highest is identical to free will."[3] What distinguishes a free action from an unfree one, they claim, is not that it is uncaused, but that it is uncoerced.

According to the soft determinists, to act freely is to do what you want to do. Only when you are forced to do something against your will are you not acting freely. Consider a bank teller who has a gun pointed at his head. If he's a loyal employee, he doesn't want to give the robber the money. If he does give up the money, we don't blame him because he was forced to do it against his will. Soft determinists readily admit that what you

---

[3] William James, p. 118.

want to do is entirely determined by your genetic makeup and your upbringing (nature and nurture). Nevertheless, they claim that as long as your actions are caused by your own beliefs and desires—as long as their cause is internal rather than external—your actions are free.

The Oracle, however, seems to suggest that there's more to acting freely than simply doing what you want to do. During her conversation with Neo in the park, she tells him that although he's already made the choice to save Trinity, he must now understand it. Why? Perhaps because understanding it will enable him to see its consequences. When we understand the cause of an action, we are better able to predict its effects. If we don't know why an event occurred, then, as the Oracle tells us, we can't see past it; we can't know what's coming next.

But perhaps the Oracle wants Neo to understand his choice because understanding it will give him the power to successfully act on it. The Marxist writer Georgi Plekhanov (1856–1918) explains:

> Let us examine more closely the case in which a man's own actions—past, present or future—seem to him entirely colored by necessity. We already know that such a man, regarding himself as a messenger of God, like Mohammed, as one chosen by ineluctable destiny, like Napoleon, or as the expression of the irresistible force of historical progress, like some of the public men in the nineteenth century, displays almost elemental strength of will, and sweeps from his path like a house of cards all the obstacles set up by the small-town Hamlets and Hamletkins. . . . When the consciousness of my lack of free will presents itself to me only in the form of the complete subjective and objective impossibility of acting differently from the way I am acting, and when, at the same time, my actions are to me the most desirable of all other possible actions, then in my mind necessity becomes identified with freedom and freedom with necessity. . . . I am unfree only in the sense that I cannot disturb this identity between freedom and necessity, I cannot oppose one to the other, I cannot feel the restraint of necessity. But such a lack of freedom is at the same time its fullest manifestation.[4]

---

[4] Georgi Plekhanov, "The Role of the Individual in History," *The Fundamental Problems of Marxism* (New York: Beekman, 1962), p. 140.

Far from enervating our actions, Plekhanov claims, knowledge of their necessity may actually strengthen them. Believing that one is destined for great things may help one achieve greatness. Being a perceptive student of human nature, the Oracle may have realized that getting Neo to understand his destiny might help him realize it. If so, the Oracle's suggestion that Neo understand his choice should be seen for what it is: another kind of control.

After the failure of the prophecy (that the war would end once the One reached the Source), Neo realized that the Oracle had been manipulating him. As he tells Morpheus, Trinity, and Link after his conversation with the Architect, "The prophecy was a lie. The One was never meant to end anything. It was all another system of control." The Oracle manipulated Neo by lying to him; both in the sense of saying something that's false (lying by commission) and in the sense of not giving him certain information (lying by omission). Lying in any form is considered wrong because it attempts to get someone to do something against their will. By giving someone information that's false, or by not giving them full information, you may get them to do something that they wouldn't have done if they had all the relevant information. So it could be argued that the choices Neo made while under the influence of the Oracle were not free because they were caused, at least in part, by someone else.

Once Neo is no longer controlled by the Oracle, can his actions be considered free even though they are determined? According to soft determinism, they can. But soft determinism seems to be inconsistent with other things that the Architect tells Neo about the Matrix. Here's the Architect's encapsulated history of the Matrix:

ARCHITECT: The first Matrix I designed was quite naturally perfect; it was a work of art, flawless, sublime. A triumph equaled only by its monumental failure. The inevitability of its doom is apparent to me now as a consequence of the imperfection inherent in every human being. Thus I redesigned it, based on your history to more accurately reflect the varying grotesqueries of your nature. However, I was again frustrated by failure. I have since come to understand that the answer eluded me because it required a lesser mind, or perhaps a mind less bound by the parameters of perfection. Thus the answer was stumbled upon by another, an intuitive program, initially created to investigate certain aspects of the human psyche, If I am the father of the Matrix, she would undoubtedly be its mother.

NEO: The Oracle.

ARCHITECT: Please. As I was saying she stumbled upon a solution whereby nearly ninety-nine percent of all test subjects accepted the program as long as they were given a choice, even if they were only aware of the choice at a near-unconscious level. While this answered the function, it was obviously fundamentally flawed, thus creating the otherwise contradictory systemic anomaly, that if left unchecked might threaten the system itself. Ergo those that refuse the program, while a minority, if left unchecked would constitute an escalating probability of failure.

To make the Matrix work, the Architect had to give humans real choice, even if most humans were unaware of the fact that they possessed it. But the existence of real choice is what creates the systemic anomaly and the need to reboot the system. If all events, including human actions, were causally determined, there would be no anomaly. If everything in the Matrix were governed by deterministic laws, it would, in principle, be possible to predict and control everything that happens in it. But an anomaly is something that violates a law. So it seems that choice introduces an element of indeterminism into the system. If the occurrence of some events is indeterminate, however, the principle of universal causation must be false; not every event has a cause that makes it happen.

Quantum mechanics, the branch of physics that accounts for the behavior of the most basic constituents of matter such as atoms and sub-atomic particles, has found that the occurrence of some events is indeed indeterminate. One of the most well-established principles of quantum mechanics, known as the Heisenberg Uncertainty Principle, claims that certain properties of sub-atomic particles, like their position and momentum, can't be known with certainty. Some, like Einstein, thought that this uncertainty was due to the crudeness of our measuring apparatus. We just couldn't make fine enough measurements without disturbing the system. We now know that Einstein was wrong; the uncertainty in the quantum realm is due to the fact that sub-atomic particles engage in truly random behavior. As physicist Paul Davies explains,

> Quantum fluctuations are not the result of human limitations or hidden degrees of freedom; they are inherent in the workings of nature on an atomic scale. For example, the exact moment of decay of a particular radioactive nucleus is intrinsically uncertain. An element of genuine unpredictability is thus injected into nature."[5]

A random event is an uncaused event. According to modern physics, even if we knew everything about the state of a radioactive atom to an infinite degree of precision, we could not predict when it would decay. The best answer a physicist can give to the question "Why did that radioactive atom decay at that time rather than some other?" is "No reason; it just happened."

This indeterminacy at the heart of our universe means that the universe is open. The future is not fixed; there is more than one possible future. The television screens on the wall of the Architect's room illustrate this openness. While he's talking to Neo, the screens are illustrating some of the possible responses that Neo may have to the information he's receiving. The Architect may be able to calculate the probability of various responses, but he can't know for sure what response Neo will give. (If he could, there would be no anomaly.) So it appears that, contrary to what the Merovingian would have us believe, even those in the Matrix are not slaves to causality; they, too, have some degree of control over their own destiny.

The need to introduce choice into the Matrix along with its attendant indeterminism goes some way toward explaining the structure of the Matrix. The Architect tells us that the first two Matrixes failed. We know from Agent Smith's interrogation of Morpheus in the first movie that the first Matrix gave humans the experience of living in a utopia: "Did you know that the first Matrix was designed to be a perfect human world? Where none

---

[5] Paul Davies, "Chaos Frees the Universe," *New Scientist* 6 (October, 1990).

suffered. Where everyone would be happy." But those plugged into the Matrix realized that it was too good to be true and refused to accept the program. The second Matrix more closely approximated real life by mixing unpleasant experiences in with the pleasant ones. But the people in this Matrix also rejected it because there was no real choice. We can imagine that in the first two Matrixes, the humans were simply passively receiving signals sent from the computer mainframe. There was no real interaction between them and the machines and thus no real choice. We may suppose that upon recommendation from the Oracle, the Architect wired the third Matrix in such a way that the humans could interact with one another. Signals from one brain could be sent to another, thus modifying it. This interaction introduced an element of indeterminism—of chaos—into the system and it began to grow exponentially, threatening to shut down the whole system and thus creating the need for the One to reboot it.

Introducing choice into the Matrix apparently required giving the people in it some ability to control the images they see. This would explain why Morpheus compares being in the Matrix to being in a dream and why Neo is able to manipulate the Matrix in the way he does. The images we see in dreams are produced by our subconscious. Ordinarily, we are not aware of the fact that we are producing these images, just as ninety-nine percent of those in the Matrix are unaware that they have any control over their experiences. It is possible, however to realize while we're dreaming that we're dreaming; to wake up inside a dream, so to speak. Such dreams are called *lucid dreams*, and when we have them, we acquire a power over the dream world similar to that which Neo has over the Matrix: we can fly, defeat monsters, and even stop bullets.

Those in the Matrix, however, are not in an ordinary dream state. Unlike ordinary dreams, their experiences are not purely the product of their own subconscious. Others, as well as the machines, play a role in producing their experiences. In addition, the experiences in the Matrix are much more orderly than dream experiences, presumably because the machines are monitoring them. People in the Matrix respond more like those who are awake than those who are asleep to the bizarre antics of the rebels and agents. Nevertheless, as in dreams, their experiences are not grounded in reality, and the truth is hidden from them.

Libertarianism

We are now in a position to see what was wrong with the soft determinists' analysis of freedom. Real freedom requires real choice, and real choice requires real options. There can be no freedom in a world where the future is fixed. If no alternative courses of action are open to anyone—if no one can do otherwise than they are destined to do—then no one can act freely.

But acting freely requires more than having real alternatives. It also requires the power to choose among those alternatives. The soft determinists, remember, claim that to act freely is simply to do what you want to do. But if you have no control over what you want—if you are unable to determine what you value—you are merely a slave to your passions and can't act freely. The Scottish philosopher Thomas Reid (1710–1796) realized this long ago:

> By the liberty [freedom] of a moral agent, I understand a power over the determination of his own will. If, in any action, he had power to will what he did, or not to will it, in that action he is free. But if, in every voluntary action, the determination of his will be the necessary consequence of something involuntary in the state of his mind, or of something in his external circumstances, he is not free; he has not what I call the liberty of a moral agent, but is subject to necessity.[6]

According to Reid, to act freely we must not only be able to do what we want, we must be able to want what we want. Only if our wants are up to us, can our actions be free.

To see this, consider those who have been brainwashed, like those portrayed in *The Manchurian Candidate*. Those doing the brainwashing don't force their subjects to do anything against their wills; they change their wills. They give their subjects a new set of desires. Since brainwashed people do what they want to do, even when they're doing the bidding of their captors, soft determinists are committed to the view that they're acting freely. But that can't be right. Brainwashed people are merely doing what they've been programmed to do. In that

---

[6] Thomas Reid, *Essays on the Active Powers of Man*, IV, Chapter 1, in *The Works of Thomas Reid*, edited by Sir William Hamilton (Hildesheim: Olms, 1983), p. 599.

sense, they are little better than robots. True freedom, Reid claims, requires the ability to program yourself. This view of free will is known as "libertarianism."

We value freedom because it makes moral judgments possible. People can be praised or blamed for what they have done only if they acted freely. If they were forced to do something against their will, or if they had no control over their will, we don't hold them responsible. There can be no right or wrong actions in a world where people can't act freely. In such a world, as Casy the preacher in Steinbeck's *Grapes of Wrath* realized: "There ain't no sin and there ain't no virtue. There's just stuff people do."

In addition to a free will, acting morally requires having a conscience. Deciding upon the right course of action in a given situation often involves empathizing with others; putting yourself in their shoes, so to speak, and considering how your actions will affect them. Only those who can empathize with others can be connected to them by bonds of affection, friendship, and love. And only those who can be connected to others in these ways can act morally toward them. Those who are capable of acting morally are known as "moral agents."

Not all intelligent human beings are moral agents, however. Some, as a result of neglect, abuse, or genetics, have no compassion, no capacity for remorse, and no conscience. Such people are known as psychopaths. Lacking any fellow feeling and concerned only with themselves, they have committed some of the most horrendous crimes in history. Ted Bundy, the serial killer; Jeffrey Dahmer, the cannibal; and Eric Harris, the Columbine shooter; were all psychopaths.

Although Smith is an agent, he is not a moral agent, for like Bundy, Dahmer, and Harris, he has no conscience. He is incapable of empathizing with others because he has no moral sentiments. Love, in particular, is foreign to him. Thus not only is he incapable of acting morally, his is also incapable of finding purpose in his existence.

Neuroscientists have recently discovered that the ability to feel emotions is essential for leading a purposeful life. Those unable to feel emotions are unable to formulate or follow any life plans. Neurophysiologist Antonio Damasio provides the following description of one of his patients, Elliot, who lost the ability to feel emotions as a result of a brain operation.

He needed prompting to get started in the morning and prepare to go to work. Once at work he was unable to manage his time properly; he could not be trusted with a schedule. When the job called for interrupting an activity and turning to another, he might persist nonetheless, seemingly losing sight of his main goal. Or he might interrupt the activity he had engaged, to turn to something he found more captivating at that particular moment.[7]

Although Elliot had a high degree of intelligence and could be quite charming in conversation, nothing mattered to him. When he was shown gruesome pictures of people in burning buildings or bloody accidents, he showed no reaction whatsoever. His lack of emotions made it impossible for him to value the sorts of things that give life purpose. As a result, he is adrift in the world, unable to find any course of action that has meaning for him.

Smith is in a similar situation. He hates Neo because he took away the only purpose Smith ever had by disconnecting him from the mainframe. Without positive emotions to guide him, he is incapable of formulating his own purpose. Consequently, he finds Neo's behavior incomprehensible:

SMITH: Why, Mr. Anderson, why? Why, why do you do it? Why, why get up? Why keep fighting? Do you believe you're fighting for something, for more than your survival? Can you tell me what it is, do you even know? Is it freedom or truth, perhaps peace—could it be for love? Illusions, Mr. Anderson, vagaries of perception. Temporary constructs of a feeble human intellect trying desperately to justify an existence that is without meaning or purpose. And all of them as artificial as the Matrix itself. Although, only a human mind could invent something as insipid as love. You must be able to see it, Mr. Anderson, you must know it by now! You can't win, it's pointless to keep fighting!. Why Mr. Anderson, why, why do you persist?

NEO: Because I choose to.

---

[7] Anthony R. Damasio, *Descartes' Error: Emotion, Reason, and the Human Brain* (New York: Putnam's, 1994), p. 36.

Smith's psychopathology is here clearly revealed. Concepts like peace and freedom and positive emotions like love have no meaning for him. He can't value such things because he doesn't understand them. Without such an understanding, he cannot create his own purpose or meaning.

Truly free people, as we have seen, are self-programming. They can decide for themselves what sort of things they want and what sort of people they will become. Smith can't program himself because he has no understanding of the sorts of things that give life meaning, point, purpose, and value. All he can do is what he was originally programmed to do: destroy Neo.

Neo is capable of acting both morally and autonomously. Since he values the lives of his fellow human beings, he is willing to give his life to save them. His sacrifice brought peace to the machines and the humans, and it also seems to have signaled a new stage in the evolution of machine consciousness. For Sati and her parents seem to have arrived at a rudimentary understanding of love. If the machines can come to a better understanding of such moral sentiments, then perhaps the peace that Neo bartered can be a lasting one.

7

Why Make a Matrix? And Why You Might Be in One

NICK BOSTROM

The Purpose of the Matrix

Why the Matrix? Why did the machines do it? (Human brains may be many things, but efficient batteries they are not.) How could they justify a world whose inhabitants are systematically deceived about their fundamental reality, ignorant about the reason why they exist, and subject to all the cruelty and suffering that we witness in the world around us? Children dying of AIDS; lovers separated by war and poverty; cancer patients tormented by unbearable pain; stroke victims deprived of their use of language and reason . . . One would think nobody but a sadist could have the imagination to think up these horrors, much less possess the desire to create a world that contains them in such abundance. But the machines did it; at least that's how the story goes.

Although the world of the Matrix they created is far from perfect, it is—arguably—better than no world at all, the elimination of all human beings. Still, the machines could have created a world containing much more goodness, happiness, wisdom, personal growth, love and beauty, a world that was free of most of the natural and manmade evil that pervades our world. Indeed, as the story goes, they tried that, but supposedly it didn't work.

> AGENT SMITH: Did you know that the first Matrix was designed to be a perfect human world. Where none suffered.

81

Where everyone would be happy. It was a disaster. No
one would accept the program. Entire crops were lost.
Some believed that we lacked the programming language
to describe your perfect world. But I believe that as a
species, human beings define their reality through misery
and suffering. The perfect world was a dream that your
primitive cerebrum kept trying to wake up from. Which is
why the Matrix was redesigned to this, the peak of your
civilization

The existence of unnecessary evil is one of the most powerful arguments against the belief that the world was created by
an all-powerful, all-knowing, and perfectly good God.
Theologians have spent centuries trying to answer it, and with
very questionable success. But the problem of evil is only a
problem if one assumes that the world was created by an
omnipotent and perfectly good being. If one assumes instead
that the creator was not perfectly good, and perhaps not even
omnipotent, then it would be much easier to reconcile the view
that our world was created with its seemingly obvious ethical
shortcomings.

What about you? You're not all-powerful, all-knowing, or
perfectly good. But what if you had the ability to create this kind
of Matrix, would you do it? Even if *you* would not have chosen
to create a world like this, there are many other people who do
not share your scruples. If these people had the ability to create
Matrices, some of their works might well look like the world in
which we find ourselves.

Why might they choose to build a Matrix like our reality? One
can think of many possible reasons—setting aside the daft idea
of using human brains as batteries. But perhaps future historians
would create a Matrix that mimicked the history of their own
species. They might do this to find out more about their past, or
to explore counterfactual historical scenarios. In the world of the
Architect(s), Napoleon may have succeeded in conquering
Europe, and our world might be a Matrix created to research
what would have happened if Napoleon had been defeated. Or
perhaps there will be future artists who create Matrices as an art
form much like we create movies and operas. Or perhaps the
tourist industry will create simulations of interesting historical
epochs so that their contemporaries can go on themed holidays

to some bygone age by entering into the simulation and inter-acting with its inhabitants. The possible motives are myriad, and if future people are anything like present people, and if they have the technological might and the legal right to create Matrices, we would expect that many Matrices would be created, including ones that would look like the world that we are experiencing.

The Simulation Argument

If each advanced civilization created many Matrices of their own history, then most people like us, who live in a technologically more primitive age, would live inside Matrices rather than outside them. If this were the case, where would you most likely be?

The so-called Simulation argument, which I introduced a few years ago, makes this line of reasoning more precise and takes it to its logical conclusion. The conclusion is that there are three basic possibilities at least one of which is true. The first possibility is that the human species will almost certainly go extinct before becoming technologically mature. The second possibility is that almost no technologically mature civilization is interested in building Matrices. The third possibility is that we are almost certainly living in a Matrix. Why? Because if the first two possibilities are not the case, then there are more "people" living in Matrices than in "real worlds." As a "person" then the chances are that you are living in a Matrix rather than in a "real world."

The Simulation argument does not tell us which of these three possibilities obtain, only that at least one of them does. The argument employs some math and probability theory, but the basic idea can be understood without recourse to technical apparatus.[1]

Building a Matrix

Creating comprehensive Matrices that are indistinguishable from non-simulated reality is, of course, far beyond our current

---

[1] For the full story, see "Are You Living in a Computer Simulation?" *Philosophical Quarterly*, Vol. 53, No. 211 (2003), pp. 243–255. This and other related papers are available at www.simulation-argument.com.

technological capability. Even so, we can estimate the computational requirements for creating such virtual realities.

Rather than confining the construction project to creating a virtual reality simulation, we can consider a more ambitious project that also involves the creation of the inhabitants of the Matrix. Instead of having pink gooey pods with biological humans floating in them being fed sensory input from a simulated reality, it would be more efficient to replace the brains with simulations of brains. Many philosophers and cognitive scientists believe that such brain-simulations would be conscious, provided the simulation was sufficiently detailed and accurate.

Estimates of the human brain's computational power have been given and estimates of the computational power that would be available to a technologically mature civilization can also been made. While these estimates are very approximate, it turns out that even when allowing for a large margin of error, the computational resources of a mature civilization would suffice to create very many Matrices. Even a single planetary-sized computer, constructed with advanced molecular nanotechnology, could simulate the entire mental history of humankind by using less than one millionth of its computing power for one second; and this presupposes only already known computational mechanisms and engineering principles. A single civilization may eventually build millions of such computers. We can conclude that a technologically mature civilization would have enough computing power such that even if it devoted but a tiny fraction of it to creating Matrices, there would soon be many more simulated people than there were people living in the original history of that civilization.

These simulations would not have to be perfect. They would only have to be good enough to fool its inhabitants. It would not be necessary to simulate every object down to the subatomic level (something that would definitely be infeasible). If the book you are holding in your hands is a simulated book, the simulation would only need to include its visual appearance, its weight and texture, and a few other macroscopic properties, because you have no way of knowing what its individual atoms are doing at this moment. If you were to study the book more carefully, for example by examining it under a powerful microscope, additional details of the simulation could be filled in as needed. Objects that nobody is perceiving could have an even more compressed representation. Such simplifications would dramatically reduce the computational requirements.

Three Possibilities

Given that the Architects of a technologically mature civilization could create a vast number of Matrices even by devoting just a small fraction of their resources to that end, an interesting implication follows. Consider the set of civilizations that are at similar level of technological development as our own current civilization. Suppose that some non-trivial fraction of these eventually go on to become technologically mature. Suppose, furthermore, that some non-trivial fraction of these devote a non-negligible proportion of their resources to building Matrices. Then most people like us live in Matrices rather than outside them. There are thus three basic possibilities: *either* almost every civilization like ours goes extinct before reaching technological maturity; *or* almost every mature civilization lacks any interest in building Matrices; *or* almost all people with our kind of experiences live in Matrices.

Let us think a little about these three possibilities. If almost every civilization at our current stage goes extinct before becoming technologically mature, then our future looks relatively bleak. For if such a premature ending were the fate awaiting most civilizations, we would have to suspect that the same will hold for our civilization in particular. This is because we seem to lack any reason for thinking that our civilization will be luckier than most other civilizations at our stage.

The second possibility is less depressing. It might turn out that almost all technologically mature civilizations lose interest in building Matrices. Maybe the potential Architects of the future will not share any of the possible motives for building Matrices that we discussed above. Presumably, Architects would have used their advanced technology to improve their own capacities, so they may be superintelligent and have complete control over their own mental states. Rather than resorting to Matrix-building for recreation, they may obtain pleasure more efficiently by direct stimulation of their brains' pleasure centers. Their science may be so advanced that they have little to learn from running simulations of their historical past. Furthermore, they might develop ethical norms that prohibit the creation of

Matrices. So we cannot infer from the fact that many *current* people would be tempted to construct Matrices that the same would hold for the super-advanced folks that would actually have the ability to act on this motive.

The third possibility is the most intriguing. If the vast majority of all people with other kind of experiences live in Matrices then *we* probably live in a Matrix. Unless we had some specific evidence to the contrary, we would therefore have to conclude that the world we see around us exists only by virtue of being simulated on a powerful computer built by some technologically highly advanced Architect.

Not the Old Brain-in-a-Vat Argument

For hundreds of years, philosophers have pondered the question how we can know that the external world exists. René Descartes (1596–1650) posed this question in his *Meditationes*, and considered the scenario where a hypothetical evil demon caused us to have erroneous beliefs about external objects. In more recent years, Descartes's skeptical scenario has been given a more modern finish, and instead of a demon one is now asked to imagine a mad scientist who has extracted one's brain and who keeps it in a vat where the scientist is stimulating it with electrical signals replicating the sensory input that the brain would have had if it had interacted with a very different environment from that which is present in the real world. This is, of course, is the predicament explored in the *Matrix* movies. How can one possibly know that one is not such a brain in a vat, the philosophical skeptic challenges, given that all the appearances we experience could be the experiences of an envatted brain?

The argument outlined above provides a much stronger reason for taking seriously the possibility that we are living in a Matrix. The traditional skeptical argument offers no positive ground for thinking that we are living in a Matrix. At best, it shows that we cannot completely rule out that possibility, but we remain free to assign it a very small or negligible probability. If there are no mad scientists who experiment on conscious envatted human brains, then we are not envatted. Even if there were a few such brains-in-vats, they might be extremely rare compared to the brains-in-crania that interact with the external world in the normal way; and if so, then it may be highly unlikely that we would be among the envatted ones.

The Simulation argument, by contrast, adopts as its starting point that things are the way they seem to be and that science gives us reliable information about the world. Part of this information concerns the technological capabilities that an advanced civilization would be able to develop. Among these would be the capability to create Matrices. Crucially, it seems that they could easily create Matrices in astronomical numbers. From this we can then conclude that *either* technologically mature civilizations that are interested in creating Matrices are extremely rare compared to civilizations at our own current stage of development *or* almost all people like us live in Matrices. And from this, the division into the three basic possibilities mentioned above follows.

The Simulation argument itself doesn't tell us which one of these three possibilities obtain. In fact, we do not currently have any strong evidence either for or against either of these three possibilities. We should therefore assign them all a significant probability. In particular, we should take seriously the possibility that we are living in a Matrix. We might still think that the probability is less than fifty percent. A degree of belief of something like twenty percent would seem quite reasonable given our current information.

How Could You Tell if You Were in a Matrix?

Consider the predicament of Neo and his fellow rebels in the trilogy. They *know* there are many Matrices. They lead parts of their lives inside a Matrix. They know that most of their compatriots spend their whole lives in a Matrix. Given this, they should be extremely reluctant to think that they have escaped their Matrix. What appears to be an escape could easily just be simulated escape, so that they exit one level of the Matrix only to re-emerge at another. The Wachowski brothers can of course stipulate that this is not the case and that the heroes really do get to experience "real" reality. But if Neo were rational, he would never be able to be at all confident that this is what happens.

If the Wachowski brothers had created a *real* Matrix (rather than just a movie *about* a Matrix), then, if they were rational, they would have to conclude that *they* themselves are almost certainly in a Matrix. For if we develop the capability to create

our own Matrices, and if we decide to make use of this capability, we would obtain very strong evidence against the first
two possibilities: that it is *not* the case that almost all civilizations
at our current stage go extinct before reaching technologically
maturity and that it is *not* the case that almost all mature civilizations lose interest in creating Matrices. This would leave us
with only the third possibility—that we almost certainly inhabit
a Matrix.

But what about the situation we actually find ourselves in?
The Simulation argument aside, would it be possible to detect
any direct signs of being in a Matrix? Is there a kind of "splinter
in the mind" that would indicate that all is not right with reality?
Certainly, if the Architects of a Matrix wished to reveal themselves, it would be easy enough for them to do so. For example, they could make a window pop up in our visual field with
the text "YOU ARE LIVING IN A MATRIX. CLICK HERE FOR
MORE INFORMATION."

In the movie, the Oracle tells us that UFOs, Ghosts, and other
strange sights are the manifestations of malfunctions in the
Matrix that are being covered up.

> THE ORACLE: Look, see those birds? At some point a program
> was written to govern them. A program was written to
> watch over the trees, and the wind, the sunrise, and sun-
> set. There are programs running all over the place. The
> ones doing their job, doing what they were meant to do,
> are invisible. You'd never even know they were here. But
> the other ones, well, we hear about them all the time.
> NEO: I've never heard of them.
> THE ORACLE: Of course you have. Every time you've heard
> someone say they saw a ghost, or an angel. Every story
> you've ever heard about vampires, werewolves, or aliens
> is the system assimilating some program that's doing
> something they're not supposed to be doing.

Déjà vu is a sign of a glitch in the Matrix, which is re-running
a sequence to cover something that has changed. Some people
have written to me that they have found signs that we are in a
Matrix. One person, for instance, told me that he could see flickering pixels when he looked in his bathroom mirror. Another
person wrote that he could hear voices in his head. But even if

we are in a Matrix, it is far more likely that such phenomena are the result of imperfections in the reporters rather than in the Matrix itself. There are many perfectly ordinary explanations for why some people should report having these kinds of experiences, including mental illness, over-excited imagination, gullibility, and so forth. Dysfunctional brains could be simulated just as easily as properly functioning ones, and including them in the simulation may indeed add to its verisimilitude.

Building any kind of Matrix at all that contains conscious simulated brains would be tremendously difficult. Any being capable of such a feat would almost certainly also be able to prevent any glitches in their Matrix from being noticed by its inhabitants. Even if some people did notice an anomaly, the Architect could backtrack the simulation a few seconds and rerun it in a way that avoided the anomaly entirely or else could simply edit out the memory of the anomaly from whoever had noticed something suspect.

How to Live in a Matrix

If we knew the Architects' motives for designing Matrices then the hypothesis that we live in one might have major practical consequences. But in fact we know almost nothing about what these motives might be. Because of this ignorance, our best method for getting around in our Matrix (if that is where we are) is to study the patterns we find in the world we experience. We would run experiments, discover regularities, build models, and extrapolate from past events. In other words, we would apply the scientific method and common sense in the same way as if we knew that we were not in a Matrix. To a first approximation, therefore, the answer to how you should live if you are in a Matrix is that you should live the same way as if you are not in a Matrix.

The Simulation argument does, however, have some more subtle practical ramifications, even if we set aside the other two possibilities to which it points (which do not entail that we are in a Matrix). Some scenarios that would otherwise seem to have been foreclosed by our current scientific understanding again become real possibilities if we inhabit a Matrix. For instance, while the physical world cannot suddenly pop out of existence, a simulated reality could do so at any time if the Architect decides to pull the plug. An afterlife would also be a real possibility. When a person dies in a simulation, he or she could be resurrected in another simulation, or the Architect could uplift the deceased into his own level of reality.

It is also conceivable that only some people are simulated in enough detail to be conscious while others may be simulated at a cruder level allowing them to appear and behave much like the real people but without having any subjective experience. The so-called "problem of other minds"—how we can know that other people are really conscious and are not just behaving as if they were—is another old chestnut of philosophy. There is, however, no consensus that such "zombie" people are possible even in principle. Some people have argued that it is necessarily true that anybody who acts sufficiently like a normal human being must also have conscious experience. (Whether this view would entail that your least favorite politicians cannot be zombies is a question on which more research is required.)

Another possibility it that the Architect might decide to reward or punish his simulated creatures, perhaps on the basis of moral criteria. If you might be in a Matrix, this consideration may give you a novel self-interested reason for behaving morally. The situation would be analogous to the case where God is watching and judging you except that the role of the final judge would not be a supernatural being but the physical person or persons who built the Matrix.

It would be misleading to say that if we are in a Matrix then we and the world around us do not really exist. It would be more accurate to say that the reality of these things is of a somewhat different nature than we thought before. Your nose would still be real; only, its reality would consist in being simulated on a powerful computer. The computer and the electrical activity of its circuitry would be physical phenomena in the more basic level of reality inhabited by the Architect of the Matrix.

Matrices Repeated and Stacked

When Neo stopped the Sentinels with his mind outside the Matrix at the end of *Reloaded* the speculation began. Was there a Matrix on top of the Matrix? As *Revolutions* revealed, there was not. But there could have been. A mature civilization would have enough computing power to run astronomically many

Matrices. If we are in a Matrix, therefore, there are probably vast numbers of other Matrices, which differ from ours in some detail or in their overall design. These other Matrices may be run sequentially, as in the movie, or simultaneously by time-sharing the same processor or by using multiple computers. From the viewpoint of the simulated inhabitants, it makes little difference how the Matrices are implemented.

A Matrix may contain a civilization that matures and proceeds to build its own Matrices in the simulation. Reality could thus contain many levels, with computers being simulated inside computers which are themselves simulated, and so forth. How many layers of simulation there could be depends on the computing power available to the bottom-level Architect (who is not simulated). Since all the higher levels of simulation would ultimately be implemented on this Architect's computer, he would have to shoulder the cost of all the simulations and all the simulated people. If his computing power is limited, there may be only a small number of levels.

As we noted above, all Architects would have strong reason to think that they themselves might be in a Matrix. (If the Architects at the basement level believed this they would be mistaken, but only because of bad epistemic luck, not because of any fault in their reasoning.) If we combine this insight with the speculation that moral considerations may play a part in determining the treatment some simulated people receive at the hands of their Architects, we are led to the peculiar thought that everybody—not just the simulated people—may have a self-interested reason for behaving morally. If behaving morally towards somebody includes judging and treating them according to moral criteria, this could further strengthen the reason that everybody has for behaving morally. The stronger that reason is, the more we would expect that people would be motivated by it. And the more people are likely to be motivated to treating their simulated creatures morally, the stronger this reason would become. This reasoning can be iterated indefinitely in a truly "virtuous circle," albeit a rather tenuous one as it relies not only on the possibility that we are in a simulation but also on tenuous speculations about the motives of the Architects.

At a minimum, the Simulation argument provides many exciting avenues for philosophical thinking. But if it is sound—and so far it has not been refuted—it could also provide various suggestions, however tentative and ambiguous, for how we should go about our lives and for what we should expect in the future. When we follow through the logical implications of what we think we know, we discover just how much we don't yet know.

8

Challenging *Simulacra and Simulation*: Baudrillard in *The Matrix*

DAVID DETMER

One scene in *The Matrix* grabs the attention of all those who are familiar with recent French thought: Neo opens a hollowed-out book. The camera lingers on the book's cover long enough for us to read the title: *Simulacra and Simulation*, which just happens to be the title of a book by Jean Baudrillard, a famous contemporary French theorist. Moreover, when the book opens we are able to read a chapter title: "On Nihilism."

But mightn't all of this be insignificant? After all, the filmmakers (the Wachowski brothers) might have chosen any book (and any chapter within it) for this scene, simply at random. So how can we know that their selection really tells us something meaningful about their intentions in the film? Well, for one thing, we have the testimony of Baudrillard that the Wachowskis asked him to serve as a consultant for their movies (he declined their invitation)[1] and of Reeves that they asked him to read Baudrillard's book as part of his preparation for the film ("Oh it's fun! It's fun!" is his reported review).[2] More importantly, we have a direct quote from Baudrillard in the film (when

---

[1] Jean Baudrillard, in an interview with *Nouvel Observateur* ("The Matrix Baudrillard-lerized,") accessed online at http://www.blogalization.info/reorganization/?q=node/view/13 on June 1, 2004.

[2] Keanu Reeves, quoted in "The Quiet Man: The Riddle of Keanu Reeves," *Rolling Stone* (31st August, 2000), accessed online at http://pub207.ezboard.com/fzionresistanceonlinefrm13.showMessage?topicID=21.topic on June 23, 2004.

Morpheus welcomes Neo to "the desert of the real," a phrase that Baudrillard uses on the very first page of *Simulacra and Simulation*[3] and an explicit reference to Baudrillard in a line from the screenplay draft that did not make the final cut for the film (Morpheus tells Neo, "You have been living inside Baudrillard's vision").[4] It seems likely, then, that a look at Baudrillard's ideas might help us to achieve a better understanding of the intellectual content of the *Matrix* films.

Baudrillard's Ideas (Or at Least a Nihilistic Simulation of Them)

Let's begin with the titles of the book and chapter that are shown in *The Matrix*, for they provide us with a good window into Baudrillard's worldview. Simulacra are images or representations of things. A simulation is an imitation. Baudrillard's claim is that we now live—and he says that this is something new, part of the current historical period known as "postmodernity"— in an imitation world, a highly artificial world of images, signs, copies, and models. In this high-tech, computerized world of virtual reality and media saturation, the idea of a "real" world underlying the dizzying parade of images and simulations has dropped out of sight. As Baudrillard himself puts it,

> The real is produced from miniaturized cells, matrices, and memory banks, models of control—and it can be reproduced an indefinite number of times from these. . . . It is no longer really the real. . . . It is a hyperreal, produced from a radiating synthesis of combinatory models in a hyperspace without atmosphere. (p. 2)

The attentive reader will notice not only that Baudrillard's description sounds a lot like the Matrix, but also that he even uses that very term, albeit in the plural form. No wonder the Wachowski Brothers turned to him for inspiration! And the res-

---

[3] Baudrillard, "The Precession of Simulacra," in his *Simulacra and Simulation* (Ann Arbor: University of Michigan Press, 1994), p. 1. Unless otherwise indicated, all further references to Baudrillard are to this book. Page numbers will be found in parentheses in the text.

[4] Larry and Andy Wachowski, *The Matrix* (dated April 8th, 1996), accessed online at http://www.scifiscripts.com/scripts/matrix_96_draft.txt on June 28, 2004. I have corrected their spelling of Baudrillard's name.

onances with the Matrix only intensify as Baudrillard goes on to tell us that we have crossed "into a space whose curvature is no longer that of the real," and have entered

> the era of simulation. . . . It is a question of substituting the signs of the real for the real, that is to say of an operation of deterring every real process via its operational double, a programmatic, metastable, perfectly descriptive machine that offers all the signs of the real. . . . (p. 2)

You will recall that "On Nihilism" is the chapter to which the Wachowskis direct us in *The Matrix*, and the pains the filmmakers have taken in having the camera reveal it are evident and noteworthy. To render this title page visible when the hollowed-out book is opened they have had to move it from the end of the book (it is in fact the final chapter) to the middle, and from the right hand page to the left. Thus, I think it is safe to say that "On Nihilism" doesn't appear in the film by accident.

But what is nihilism? If you've seen the film *The Big Lebowski* you may recall that the hero, known as "The Dude," is repeatedly terrorized by individuals who call themselves "nihilists," explaining that they "believe in nothing." And indeed, *nihil*, the root of the word, means "nothing" in Latin. The term is used, usually without much precision, to refer to any of a number of loosely related doctrines. Someone who denies that anything exists, or, more modestly, that anything can be known, might be called a nihilist. More commonly nihilism refers to the view that traditional values and beliefs are unfounded, or to the idea that existence is meaningless and absurd. Yet another meaning has to do with the denial of objective truth, either generally or in the specific area of values and morality. Finally, nihilism can refer to the belief that social conditions are so bad as to make their destruction by violence desirable.

Baudrillard's thought is distinctive both in that it contains strong elements of nihilism in all of these senses and in that it sees nihilism as a recent arrival to the world stage, a symptom of our postmodern condition. While he doesn't say that nothing exists, he does insist that "reality" has ceased to exist, having vanished in a haze of images and simulations. And Baudrillard further insists that the postmodern world is devoid of meaning. Because it is a world of simulacra and simulations, it has no

depth. Everything is on the surface, and nothing is stable or permanent. The images, signs, simulations, and models that com-
prise contemporary "hyperreality" are constantly moving and
mutating, and are doing so at a perpetually increasing speed.
But meaning depends upon depth, stability, permanence, and
reality. Theories that can't latch on to anything real are ultimately meaningless. Thus, life in our postmodern world is constantly becoming more and more meaningless. As he puts it (in
the chapter referenced in *The Matrix*), "I am a nihilist" [because]
"I observe, I accept, I assume, I analyze the . . . revolution . . .
of the twentieth century, that of postmodernity, which is the
immense process of the destruction of meaning" (pp. 160–61).
And the penultimate paragraph of the essay (and the book)
begins with the simple declaration that "[t]here is no more hope
for meaning" (p. 164).

What about truth? Baudrillard explains:

> The belief in truth . . . is a weakness of understanding, of common-
> sense… [N]obody really believes in the real . . . [O]ur belief in real-
> ity and evidence is . . . obscene. Truth is what should be laughed
> at. One may dream of a culture where everyone bursts into laugh-
> ter when someone says: this is true, this is real . . . [S]imulacra have
> become reality! . . . The simulacrum now hides, not the truth, but
> the fact that there is none, that is to say, the continuation of
> Nothingness.[5]

If Baudrillard is to touch all the bases of nihilism, only one
thing remains for him to do—he must advocate the violent
destruction of the current social order. He's a good sport, and
eager to oblige: "I am a terrorist and nihilist in theory as the others are with their weapons. Theoretical violence, not truth, is the
only resource left us" (p. 163). Here Baudrillard's position once
again makes strong contact with the world of the *Matrix* films,
in which Neo, Morpheus, Trinity, and their comrades engage in
violence and terrorism in their campaign to overturn the reign
of the Matrix. But on second thought, Baudrillard, unlike the
anti-Matrix warriors, advocates only "theoretical" terrorism and

---

[5] Baudrillard, "Radical Thought," translated by François Debrix, accessed online
at http://www.uta.edu/english/apt/collab/texts/radical.html on February 11,
2004.

violence, whatever that might mean. (He doesn't explain, but then again, since he holds that "there is no more hope for meaning" in our postmodern age, perhaps he's just being consistent). But on third thought, maybe the comparison is pretty strong after all, since, in a sense, most killings in the *Matrix* films aren't real. They are "virtual" killings, possibly analogous to Baudrillard's "theoretical" terrorism. Matters are further complicated, moreover, by the fact that Baudrillard retracts his endorsement of theoretical terrorism immediately after issuing it, on the grounds that "such a sentiment is utopian." He explains that, while "it would be nice to be a terrorist," it is no longer possible to be one, since "death, including that of the terrorist," no longer has any meaning (p. 163).

On the Possibility that Baudrillard Might Not Be Absolutely One Hundred Percent Right about Everything

If some of this is starting to sound a bit dubious to you, let me assure you that you're far from alone. I, for one, find Baudrillard to be a consistently sloppy thinker, readily given to hyperbole and exaggeration, *non sequiturs* and logical inconsistencies, the routine misappropriation of scientific concepts and theories, the ignoring of counterarguments and counterevidence, the issuing of sweeping generalizations that obliterate needed qualifications and nuances, and to hiding the weak spots in his project behind pretentious and incomprehensibly jargon-riddled verbiage, among other transgressions.

Other than that I think he's just terrific! But all kidding aside, I will not deny that there is a substantial nucleus of insight and truth in Baudrillard's pronouncements, oracular and exaggerated as they may be. In a little while I'll try to identify this nucleus, and discuss its relevance to our understanding, not only of the *Matrix* films, but also of our lives and times. But first, let me show you just a little of what is wrong with our friend, Monsieur Baudrillard.

Let's begin with his writing. If you thought the sequels, *Reloaded* and *Revolutions*, were confusing, at times perhaps even bordering on gobbledygook or nonsense, try reading Baudrillard. Up to now I've been taking it easy on you, quoting only relatively accessible passages. Here's a more typical specimen:

Our complex, metastatic, viral systems, condemned to the exponential dimensional alone (be it that of exponential stability or
instability), to eccentricity and indefinite fractal scissiparity, can
no longer come to an end. Condemned to an intense metabolism,
to an intense internal metastasis, they become exhausted within
themselves and no longer have any destination, any end, any oth-
erness, any fatality. They are condemned, precisely, to the epidemic, to the endless excrescences of the fractal and not to the
reversibility and perfect resolution of the fateful. We know only
the signs of catastrophe now; we no longer know the signs of
destiny.[6]

Wow! Doesn't it embarrass you that you didn't think of that first?
I mean, it's so obvious, now that he points it out! (Well, okay,
I'm still not sure why fractal scissiparity would be indefinite—
but that's probably just me).

Then there's the issue of his scholarship. *Simulacra and
Simulation*, the book featured in *The Matrix*, begins with the
following epigraph:

The simulacrum is never what hides the truth—it is truth that hides
the fact that there is none.
    The simulacrum is true.

—Ecclesiastes

Now my point, at least at present, is not just that it's hard to
know what this means. I want instead to focus on the attribu-
tion. Notice that Baudrillard claims to have taken this quotation
from Ecclesiastes.

Do you see the problem? Now, while I'm the first to admit
that I'm not much of a Biblical scholar, I am somewhat familiar
with Ecclesiastes. (You see, back in the 1960s Pete Seeger put
music to a portion of it and turned it into an extremely catchy
folk song; the Byrds then gave it a compelling electric arrangement complete with a jangly twelve-string guitar part by Roger
McGuinn . . . but I digress.) And now, having been prodded into
action by Baudrillard's "quotation," I have taken my Bible off the
shelf, dusted it off, and read Ecclesiastes straight through. What
did I find? Well, let's put it this way. If you were disappointed

---

[6] Baudrillard, *The Illusion of the End* (Cambridge: Polity, 1994), p. 114.

with the bogus way *Revolutions* answered the question of how Neo stopped the sentinels outside the Matrix in *Reloaded*, then you know how I felt when I read Ecclesiastes in search of Buadrillard's epigraph. So I wish hereby to make public my offer to pay the sum of five (5) dollars to the first person who can direct me to the passage in Ecclesiastes that Baudrillard claims to find there. And lest you think this an isolated case, I would cite the testimony of Mark Poster, editor of a collection of Baudrillard's writings, who reports that his attempts to complete Baudrillard's rather minimal citations were frustrated on those occasions in which "Baudrillard's quotations have not been located anywhere in the text he cites."[7] So it seems that Baudrillard's scholarship is every bit as careful and meticulous as his prose is lucid!

Tip-toeing into the Matrix with Baudrillard

Baudrillard may indeed be a needlessly opaque writer, and at times a careless (or dishonest? or joking? I'm really not sure) scholar, but that doesn't mean he's wrong about everything. Nor does it prove that he has no stimulating and potentially useful ideas to offer us. So let's look next at some ideas of Baudrillard's that are both defensible (provided that we scale back Baudrillard's hyperbole somewhat, and introduce some needed exceptions, qualifications, and nuances into his thinking) and highly relevant to the *Matrix* films.

Some of the forces that have been moving us away from reality and into something more like the Matrix have been long in coming. Baudrillard's contribution has been to show how these forces have begun mutually to reinforce one another and to intensify in recent years, with the result, according to Baudrillard, that we have now completely abandoned the "real," natural, world, and have instead taken up residence in a fully artificial world of images and simulations—the world of postmodernity, a world much like the Matrix.

One of the many meanings of "real" is simply "not artificial." And indeed, one of the ways in which existence in the Matrix is

---

[7] Mark Poster, "Notes on the Translation," in *Jean Baudrillard: Selected Writings*, edited by Mark Poster (Stanford: Stanford University Press, 1988), p. viii.

unreal is that it, too, is artificial. The experiences of a person living in the Matrix are artificially produced by a computer program; they do not arise naturally from encounters with real human beings or animals, or with natural objects.

Similarly, many of us, perhaps most, spend almost all of our time in highly artificial environments, far removed from nature. We move about, from one building to another, in cars, trains, and airplanes. When we arrive at our destination we stare at computer monitors and television screens. Ours is a world of steel, brick, cement, and glass, not that of mountain, meadow, tree, and stream.

Another way to live an unreal life is to live in a world of illusions, just as those plugged into the Matrix do. Moreover, those who stand to gain from the false beliefs of others sometimes deliberately try to instill them—in short, they practice the art of deception.

Once again, the connection with the Matrix is clear. For the Matrix is a world in which people are shown appearances and invited to confuse them with reality. And this issue has become especially pressing in our own time, with its ubiquitous advertising and public relations campaigns, and its ever more sophisticated techniques of propaganda.

We live in an age of rapidly accelerating media saturation. Many people are plugged into electronic media constantly, and rarely experience unmediated life. If you like music, you can listen to CDs or the radio just about anywhere, including in your car, or while walking or jogging. If you like television, now there are cable and satellite dish options offering not just the seven or eight channels one had to choose from a few decades ago, but rather hundreds of options. And if nothing good is being broadcast, there's always the VCR or DVD player, in addition to the local cinema, which now has sixteen screens, rather than just one. With the advent of cell phones, it's now possible to talk on the phone anytime and almost anywhere. And pretty much everything can be found on the world wide web, which never closes. Finally, there's no escaping advertising. It's everywhere. Even if you avoid newspapers, magazines, radio, television, and movies, you'll still find it on billboards and T-shirts out on the street. The great majority of people, who do not avoid these media, are subjected to hundreds of advertisements daily.

It's easy to lose sight of real life in the midst of that howling blizzard of media. As Baudrillard puts it, "[w]e live in a world where there is more and more information, and less and less meaning" (p. 79).

Moreover, as we have already noted, such meaning as we do find in the electronic mass media has its ominous side, since such media provide the perfect means for the dissemination of propaganda and deception. But such deception need not take the form of explicit claims. Rather, as Noam Chomsky points out,

> A principle familiar to propagandists is that the doctrines to be instilled in the target audience should not be articulated: that would only expose them to reflection, inquiry, and, very likely, ridicule. The proper procedure is to drill them home by constantly presupposing them, so that they become the very condition for discourse.[8]

For example, the media do not say things like: "The U.S. always supports democracy, never aggresses against other nations, and always opposes terrorists." Nor do advertisers explicitly say that the key to happiness and the good life is the unceasing and ever-expanding consumption of purchasable products. But the message still comes through, loud and clear.

Finally, according to Baudrillard, contemporary society is dominated by computers and by other sophisticated technological systems and their signs. Moreover, he suggests that such emerging technologies of cloning, cybernetics, robotics, and holography, are further blurring, or obliterating, the distinction between reality and simulation, creating a hyperreality, not unlike the Matrix, in which we all live.[9] All of this, he further suggests, is by now far beyond anyone's control.

That's Gratitude for You! Baudrillard's Rejection of *The Matrix*

Perhaps this is sufficient to explain why the Wachowskis would turn to Baudrillard for inspiration in creating the *Matrix* trilogy.

---

[8] Noam Chomsky, "Third World, First Threat," in his *Letters from Lexington* (Monroe, Maine: Common Courage Press, 1993), p. 29.

[9] See, for example, Baudrillard's "Clone Story" and "Holograms," in *Simulacra and Simulation*.

And, given their explicit acknowledgment of his influence, you might think that Baudrillard would be glad they did. After all, while Baudrillard's ideas are famous in certain, principally academic, circles, he is largely unknown to the general public. Consequently, one might have expected Baudrillard to feel grateful to the Wachowskis for calling his work to the attention of their huge audience. Instead, he has rather grumpily criticized them for getting his ideas wrong. "What's really embarrassing about *The Matrix*," he remarks, "is that the new problem posed by simulation gets confused with the classical problem of illusion, which one finds already in Plato. That's a serious misunderstanding."[10]

Baudrillard is right to claim that his idea of simulation goes beyond the problem of illusion. The latter problem, which, as he rightly notes, goes back at least to Plato, is that it might be difficult or impossible for us to know that what we perceive is real. Perhaps it is a mere illusion (or shadow, or dream, or hallucination). Thus, the problem is that we might, for all we know, be confusing a mere image of reality with reality itself.

Now, as we have seen, Baudrillard develops and intensifies this problem by noting the unprecedented dominance in the present age of public relations and advertising, of disinformation and propaganda, and, most importantly, of increasingly sophisticated, high-tech tools for artificial reality creation (computers, the mass media, and so forth). The *Matrix* films seem to follow him in this, at least metaphorically and symbolically. But Baudrillard goes further and claims that the forces of artificial reality-creation have become so powerful as to have abolished reality and truth all together—all that is left is the "hyperreality" of simulations and simulacra.

The *Matrix* films firmly reject this further claim. They affirm, as is made abundantly clear in *Reloaded and Revolutions*, that there is a way things really are. The sequels don't follow Baudrillard and say that there is nothing but the Matrix, or one Matrix layered on top of another indefinitely. Instead, they insist that there is a sharp distinction to be drawn between the real truth (that people are the victims of deception and exploitation on a massive scale) and the artificial reality that is used to control and enslave them. Indeed, the central characters in the tril-

---

[10] Baudrillard, "The Matrix Baudrillard-lerized."

ogy are those who recognize the truth and fight to overturn the prevailing system of illusion. The films thus metaphorically assert that there is a reality and truth that the contemporary forces of disinformation and propaganda are attempting, with considerable success, to obscure, much to their enrichment and our detriment.

The Battle of the Titans: Baudrillard versus The Matrix Trilogy

Baudrillard thus appears to be correct in his statement that the *Matrix* films, at least in one crucial respect, misrepresent his ideas. For while the thesis of the *Matrix* trilogy is that images *mask* reality, Baudrillard's claim is that images have *replaced* reality. Well then, this leaves us with the critical task of evaluating these two competing claims. Which of them seems better, or more rational, or more likely to be true, all things considered?

In my judgment it is no contest. The *Matrix* thesis is vastly superior in that it, in radical contrast to Baudrillard's vision, (a) can be expressed clearly and understood readily, (b) is plausible in light of the available evidence and has considerable explanatory power, (c) can be stated in an appropriately qualified and nuanced form (that is, it recognizes exceptional cases, and also acknowledges other cases that hold to a greater or lesser degree than do other cases), and, most importantly (d) is coherent and self-consistent.

One problem is that Baudrillard exerts very little effort in attempting to render his thesis plausible. To the contrary, he makes it extremely hard on all readers who might be concerned to think seriously about whether or not they agree with his pronouncements. The reason, as you may have noticed in the passages I've already quoted, is that he rarely offers arguments or evidence of any kind in support of his pronouncements. Rather, he delivers them in an oracular, declarative manner, and makes minimal attempt at rational persuasion.

Consider, in this connection, his claim that "[o]nly signs without referents, empty, senseless, absurd and elliptical signs, absorb us."[11] Now, since this isn't obviously true, and isn't

---

[11] Baudrillard, *Seduction* (New York: St. Martin's, 1990), p. 74.

widely believed, it would be enormously helpful if Baudrillard would offer a clear, careful statement of his reasons for asserting it. But he declines to give us this help.

Insofar as Baudrillard does offer an argument, it is simply a *non sequitur*. From the true premise that the present age is dominated by image, public relations campaigns, advertising, disinformation, and propaganda, Baudrillard immediately draws the conclusion that therefore there is no such thing as truth or reality. But this does not follow. An alternative possibility, the one presented in the *Matrix* films, is that there is a reality and a truth that these contemporary forces are employed to obscure. To put the point another way, Baudrillard's mistake lies in his fallacious attempt to draw an ontological conclusion (that is, a conclusion about the nature of being or reality—in this case that there is no such thing as reality, because everything is mere image or sign or simulation) from an epistemological premise (that is, a premise about the nature of knowledge—in this case that it is increasingly difficult to determine the nature of reality, since we tend to get lost in the maze of images and signs).[12]

Even more importantly, whereas the *Matrix* thesis (that there really is a way things are but that most of us are deceived into not knowing about it) is perfectly clear and self-consistent, Baudrillard's alternative (that there is no such thing as reality and truth) is utterly incoherent. For Baudrillard must be understood as saying such self-contradictory absurdities as that there *really* is no *reality* and that it is *true* that there is no *truth*! If this is not what he means, then it is difficult to see what the point of his utterances could possibly be.

For example, Baudrillard tells us that

> Disneyland is presented as imaginary in order to make us believe that the rest is real, whereas all of Los Angeles and the America that surrounds it are no longer real, but belong to the hyperreal order and to the order of simulation. It is no longer a question of a false representation of reality (ideology) but of concealing the fact that the real is no longer real . . ." (pp. 12–13)

---

[12] Christopher Norris presents this criticism in "Lost in the Funhouse: Baudrillard and the Politics of Postmodernism," in his *What's Wrong with Postmodernism* (Baltimore: The Johns Hopkins University Press, 1990), p. 182; and in *Uncritical Theory* (Amherst: University of Massachusetts Press, 1992), p. 122.

The problem of incoherence emerges as soon as one asks what the status of these "facts" could possibly be. For what can it mean to say that "the real is no longer real"? Is this claim itself *really* true?

This problem is equally apparent in the work of sympathetic expositors of Baudrillard's brand of postmodernism. Consider in this regard Dino Felluga's contribution:

> Postmodernism . . . tends to understand language and ideology as the basis for our very perception of reality. There is no way to be free of ideology, according to this view, at least no way that can be articulated in language. Because we are so reliant on language to structure our perceptions, any representation of reality is always already ideological. From this perspective, mankind cannot help but view the world through an ideological lens. The idea of truth or objective reality is therefore meaningless. In the view of some postmodernists, this has always been true; in the view of other postmodern theorists, the period that approximately follows the Second World War represents a radical break during which various factors have contributed ever more to increase our distance from "reality" . . .[13]

Let me see if I've got this straight. According to some postmodernists it has always been true that the idea of truth is meaningless? But what on Earth can that mean? If the idea of truth is meaningless, then what does it mean to say, of that very statement, that it is true (let alone that it always has been so, or, as some other postmodernists would have it, merely that it has been becoming increasingly more so since the end of the Second World War)? Felluga shows no sign of noticing this problem, and offers us no help with it. Neither does Baudrillard.

Running Out of the Matrix (And Leaving Poor Baudrillard Behind)

One virtue of the *Matrix* trilogy is that it communicates a good deal of what is valuable in Baudrillard's ideas while jettisoning or at least minimizing their objectionable components. The trilogy

---

[13] Dino Felluga, "*The Matrix*: Paradigm of Postmodernism or Intellectual Poseur?," in Glenn Yeffeth, ed., *Taking the Red Pill: Science, Philosophy, and Religion in The Matrix* (Dallas: Benbella, 2003), pp. 73–74.

can be seen as an allegorical representation of Baudrillard's idea that we are increasingly removed from the real and the true, that we are victims of deception and exploitation on a gigantic scale, and that the tools of this deception and exploitation come largely from the worlds of the mass media and of computers and other advanced technologies. But at the same time, Neo, Morpheus, Trinity, and their group, unlike Baudrillard, clearly believe in reality—in a real world, to be defended against the artificial world of the Matrix. They hold that the real is good, that the fake is bad, and that authenticity is a value worth fighting for—the illusion must be fought and overcome. In that sense the *Matrix* trilogy is profoundly anti-postmodern.

But the trilogy is meaningful to us as an allegory only to the extent that we, too, are in the Matrix, and thus in need of escaping from its clutches and returning to reality, authenticity, and truth. So let me challenge you, dear reader, to consider to what degree you are in the Matrix. I would respectfully suggest to you that you may be in the Matrix if (and to the extent that) you (a) spend almost all of your time in artificial environments, cut off from the natural world; (b) believe that your favorite soft drink or lite beer tastes significantly better than its major competitors; (c) believe that the good life is the life of acquisition and consumption; (d) think that your country, while it may make some mistakes, is always on the side of good, and never, for example, embraces terrorism;[14] (e) spend most of your waking hours immersed in media; or (f) greatly prefer the Internet, video games, and virtual reality to face-to-face encounters with other people.

OK, then, how do we get out of the Matrix? On this issue Baudrillard offers us very little help. During the 1970s he pro-

---

[14] Consider, for example, the little-publicized fact that the two great enemies of the U.S. in recent times, Osama bin Laden and Saddam Hussein, were once allies of the U.S. and recipients of U.S. economic, military, and diplomatic aid. Such aid continued to flow for many years after Hussein had used chemical weapons (against Iranians and Iraqi Kurds) and bin Laden had engaged in many acts of terrorism (mainly directed against Russians and secular Arabs). During the period in which these figures were favored by the U.S. government, the U.S. corporate media (that is, the mainstream or mass media) did not publicize their crimes. And these are far from isolated examples. See, on this issue, my "What is Objectivity? Sartre vs. the Journalists," in my *Challenging Postmodernism: Philosophy and the Politics of Truth* (Amherst: Humanity Books, 2003).

posed that one could overthrow a system, or transform it into something new, different, and possibly better, simply by pushing the logic of that system to its extremes. For example, he declared that "a system is abolished only by pushing it into hyperlogic, by forcing it into an excessive practice which is equivalent to a brutal amortization. 'You want us to consume— OK, let's consume always more, and anything whatsoever; for any useless and absurd purpose'"[15] Yeah, Jean, that's a great suggestion. We'll buy more and more of their stuff, making them even more obscenely rich—that'll show 'em! Little wonder, then, that in recent years Baudrillard has pretty much given up on making suggestions for change, declaring instead that "[n]ever again will the real have a chance to produce itself" (p. 2).

What's worse, Baudrillard's relentless attacks on reality and truth stand as obstacles to any effort to overthrow the Matrix. Indeed, notice how well Baudrillard's position helps liars of all kinds. His is a disabling skepticism, invalidating in advance any critique that would expose the deception, both because he denies the distinction between the image promulgated by the deceivers and the reality about which they are attempting to deceive us, and because he would withhold from us the critical skills (logic, reason, and a concern for facts) needed to accomplish this task.

Unfortunately, the *Matrix* films also disappoint on this score. To be sure, they constitute a distinct improvement on Baudrillard, since they acknowledge that there is a reality and a truth lurking behind the illusion, suggest that the illusion is to be resisted, and do not recommend that we abandon all logic, reason, or concern for facts and truth in going about the project of overthrowing the illusion. But the films ultimately encourage quietism, in that they seem to assert that we must wait for a messiah (Neo, possibly representing Jesus) to come and save us. Moreover, the films' many lengthy and graphic gunfight and martial arts scenes strongly imply that the revolution, if it is going to come at all, will have to come by violence. And the trilogy seems to suggest that not even violent struggle will be sufficient to liberate humanity from the Matrix, as *Revolutions* ends

---

[15] Baudrillard, *In the Shadow of the Silent Majorities*, translated by Paul Foss, Paul Patton, and John Johnston (New York: Semiotext(e), 1983), p. 46.

with a kind of uneasy détente between the humans and machines, with many humans still prisoners to the Matrix.

Well, that may be right, but I hold out the hope that your chances of achieving a Matrix-free resistance may be better than *Revolutions* implies. In any case, here are a few suggestions as to how to resist the Matrix:

(1) Spend a lot of time in the natural world. Hike in mountains. Go camping. Take long walks on nature trails. Don't spend all of your time in office buildings and on city streets.

(2) Devote a little bit of time each day to creative activity— painting, playing music, writing poetry, whatever you like.

(3) Become politically active. I don't recommend going the route of electoral politics, because then you have to hope that the people you work for actually pan out—it's a bit like waiting for Neo. Instead, pick an issue that interests you and work on that.

(4) Spend more time with your friends and less time watching other people's friends on TV or the movies.

For that matter,

(5) radically reduce the amount of time you spend passively enjoying the various electronic media. After all, you're going to have to find some time somewhere so that you'll be able to hike in those mountains, write those poems, and engage in that political activism. This is where you'll find it.

(6) Stop relying on the U.S. mass media for your information about the world. Read various "alternative" media sources; consult the foreign press; read scholarly articles and reports; read books; think for yourself; then talk to other people about what you've learned and what you think.

Remember, these are just friendly suggestions. It's your life, and you may live it as you please. But I have high hopes for you. After all, you weren't content just to watch the *Matrix* movies. You then went out and got a book about them, and now you're reading it. You're well on your way out of the Matrix.

9

Music and *The Matrix*: *Where* Are We Hearing *When* We Hear the Future?

THEODORE GRACYK

The past is a foreign country; they do things differently there.
—LESLEY P. HARTLEY

When *Matrix Revolutions* appeared simultaneously on movie screens in 109 countries on November 5th, 2003, Egypt was not among them. The official state censorship board had not yet certified it as acceptable for Muslim viewers. Although the same government committee had initially banned *Matrix Reloaded* for being religiously offensive, they found almost nothing objectionable in the trilogy's final installment: a glimpse of a topless woman in the nightclub scene, and two lines of dialogue suggesting that Neo is divine. Rid of its overt obscenity and blasphemy, *Matrix Revolutions* was approved in April 2004 for release in Egyptian theaters.

But if the Egyptian censors cut the film intending to protect devout Muslims from exposure to problematic ideas and themes, they surely failed to cut enough. They did not remove any of the music from *Matrix Revolutions*. So they did not remove the complex religious statements that conclude the film and, with it, the whole trilogy.

The Visual and Auditory Streams

The Matrix envisions a world in which most of humanity is enslaved. The enslavement includes continuous manipulation by false sensory input. The film reflects the growing concern that increasing numbers of people live in a simulated reality, manipulated by mass media to accept a world that is very different from the real world. The co-directing Wachowski brothers signal their awareness of this growing concern in Morpheus' chilling line, "Welcome to the desert of the real," a description lifted from the writings of Jean Baudrillard.

The Wachowski brothers are filmmakers, artists whose very profession consists in enticing an audience to engage in an elaborate game of make-believe. But unlike many action films and thrillers, the *Matrix* trilogy surely has a philosophical side, and the three films do not exist simply to get us to part with our money and time in order to escape reality. The Wachowski brothers want to encourage us to think about our real lives. Ironically, their films employ the very techniques that they seem to criticize. The most memorable sequences of the *Matrix* films manipulate the audience's sensory input, using techniques designed to suppress conscious awareness of the manipulation we experience. I am not talking about visual effects. I am talking about the almost continuous presence of music in the three films.

A film is far more than a set of moving pictures. The experience of a film integrates two distinct experiences, one visual, and the other auditory. We can experience either of the two streams of information in isolation from the other. Viewers with visual or hearing impairment always do so, and many fans purchase and listen to the soundtracks of the films. However, perceiving one stream without the other is an impoverished experience, like reading every-other page of a novel or viewing only the left half of a famous painting. The visual and auditory streams are designed to interact with one another.

Diegetic and Non-Diegetic

Very little of the music in the Matrix trilogy is diegetic music. "Diegetic" indicates anything that exists within the narrative world of a story, such as dialogue between Neo and Morpheus or visual sequences showing what they are doing. But films supply some material to the audience without incorporating it into the world of the story. These materials are non-diegetic. For instance, we are presented with a title for each film and there are credits at the end. Neo and Morpheus have no access to these things. Many films offer non-diegetic elements *during* the film, such as place names or dates superimposed over a scene so that we'll understand where we are in the diegetic world.

A film's music is diegetic when it has a source in the story, so that the characters can hear it. When Trinity, Seraph and Morpheus enter the lobby of the Hel Nightclub in *Revolutions*, music accompanies the elaborate choreography of the ensuing shoot-out. But there is no reason to think that Trinity, Seraph, and Morpheus hear this music! Then they walk down the stairs into the nightclub. The crowd is dancing to music. We hear the music because the music is in the nightclub. (At Merovingian's command, we see the disc jockey hit the "start-stop" button.) We understand that Trinity, Seraph, and Morpheus hear the music, followed by silence. The fight in the lobby is set to non-diegetic music. The nightclub crowd dances to diegetic music.

Whose Music Do We Hear?

Don Davis composed most of the non-diegetic music for the *Matrix* films. Ben Watkins (credited as "Juno Reactor") assisted Davis for most of the "techno" sounding music. But this music was commissioned by and subject to the approval of Andy and Larry Wachowski. In the same way that the Wachowski brothers did not have to personally design every aspect of the city of Zion in order for us to treat Zion as their creation, we can talk about the music as part of *their* artistic vision. The vamping brass that accompanies the outdoor fight between Neo and the army of Agent Smiths in *Reloaded* sounds like a James Bond theme. This non-diegetic music tells us not to take this fight too seriously. The "Neodämmerung" theme that accompanies the fight between Neo and Agent Smith at the end of *Revolutions* has weight and solemnity, imparting a completely different message: this time, it is deadly serious.

Stylistic differences are only one of the musical resources influencing our understanding of a scene. Our judgment that music is diegetic rather than non-diegetic can also influence our interpretation of a scene or character. For example, the first time that Neo visits the Oracle in her apartment, we hear two different pieces of music. Typical film scoring accompanies the spoon-bending incident in the living room. The scene suddenly cuts to the kitchen, at which point different music takes over.

This new music is very faint. It is the music of Duke Ellington. Is this music diegetic, or non-diegetic? (Does the Oracle hear it or not?) If the music is diegetic, the choice of Duke Ellington is *the Oracle's* choice, as *her* background music for baking cookies. Since Ellington is one of America's greatest musicians, it demonstrates the Oracle's sophistication. However, if the music is non-diegetic, we know a little less about the Oracle. We don't know whether she is more likely to listen to funk or jazz. In that case, the choice of Ellington's song "I'm Beginning to See the Light" is an ironic joke on the part of the Wachowski brothers. But if it's diegetic, the Wachowski brothers have given the Oracle a sly sense of humor, for she is the one making the joke (a joke she repeats in *Revolutions*, when she is again baking cookies when Neo visits).

So how does "I'm Beginning to See the Light" function in the Oracle's apartment? Did she choose the music, or is it a non-diegetic joke by the Wachowski brothers? We don't see the sound source, yet the evidence suggests that the Duke Ellington music is diegetic—it is *in* the Oracle's kitchen. Notice that it is much, much fainter than the non-diegetic music that surrounds it in the film. Second, in both the first and third films, the soft jazz gives way to louder, orchestral scoring when the dialogue reaches a dramatic point (plot events that are dramatically inconsistent with the tone of "I'm Beginning to See the Light"). Third, when the film suddenly cuts from Neo in the kitchen to Neo with Morpheus, the music ceases at the precise moment when the scene cuts away from the kitchen. Fourth, we do not hear the same music when Neo visits the Oracle in *Reloaded*. Meeting out of doors, there is no music at all. The song is only heard where it is appropriate for the Oracle to be listening to music, and we don't hear it when it she has no reason to be hearing music. If Ellington's music were a non-diegetic comment on the Oracle's interactions with Neo, we'd expect to hear it all three times. So it appears to be music that the Oracle is listening to, and it seems to be a diegetic irony provided by the Oracle.

Notice something else about this use of music. The filmmakers have taken care to supply diegetic music that is appropriate to the characters and setting. It is plausible that such music would be found in the home of a mature, sophisticated African-American woman in 1999 (and so also in the Matrix world, in a simulation of 1999). When we return to the Oracle's kitchen in *Revolutions*, she isn't listening to Norah Jones singing "Don't Know Why," a jazzy performance with a similar tempo that would furnish an equally ironic commentary on Neo's struggles with fate and choice. Norah Jones released her performance in 2002, and it is still 1999 in the Oracle's kitchen. The Wachowski brothers had access to Norah Jones's music, but its inclusion would destroy the logic of the complete normality of events in the green-tinted world of the Matrix. Everything there is a computer program, and the "Norah Jones" program has not yet been unleashed into the Matrix.

Zion's Music

Diegetic music is prominently heard in Zion, the home of the quarter million humans outside the Matrix. As the final battle approaches, Morpheus rallies the populace with his stirring vision of their situation and of his faith in Neo. "For one hundred years we have fought these machines," intones Morpheus. It is time to send a message to the advancing machines: "We are still here!" The audience cheers. Morpheus gestures, and then we see that he is gesturing to a group of drummers. They begin to pound out a heavy rhythm, and the people of Zion erupt into a frenzy of dancing. Well, not quite everyone. Neo and Trinity slip away to their private quarters. As the masses dance, they begin to make love.

But the sound of this music violates the logic of the story. While Norah Jones would *sound* appropriate in the Oracle's kitchen, it is doubtful that the diegetic music played in Zion sounds anything like the music that would or could be played there. The problem is that Morpheus tells Neo that the "real" year is around 2199. Morpheus does not know that this is the sixth time that Zion has arisen, so it is "really" more like 3199. (Neo is upset to learn this new wrinkle in the story.) To those in Zion, however, 3199 is irrelevant. After five forgotten failures, their civilization has again progressed to a situation equivalent to 2199. So when the drumming starts in Zion, we are going to hear the music of the future. We are going to hear dance music as it will sound in 2199. But the dance music that we hear is very much dance music of 1999. (I predict that its repeated riff and steady pulse will sound very dated to anyone who watches the movie twenty years from now.) So music in Zion appears to violate the laws governing music everywhere else in the universe. For the music in Zion does not reflect stylistic change over time. Are we supposed to notice that the music does not fit the narrative? Or are we supposed to ignore this failure to match the music with the situation?

More Mixed Messages

When Neo sacrifices himself and dies at the end of *Revolutions*, he suddenly throws out his arms into the pose of the crucified Christ. Light steams from his body. For a brief moment, this light is in the shape of a cross. The non-diegetic music that accompanies this scene is unmistakably *religious* music, with a massed choir singing elongated vowels set to solemn chord progressions. To be more precise, this music is unmistakably religious if one is familiar with the majestic music that accompanies solemn religious events in Christian churches. Don Davis composed it to sound like the traditional chorale music that Bach, Haydn, and other early classical composers used for the setting of Christian texts. When Neo dies, both his pose and the accompanying music underscore the *Christian* significance of his sacrifice.

Egyptian censors removed two lines of dialogue suggesting that Neo is divine. They apparently missed the significance of his very brief pose and of the *style* of music playing during his death scene. I am puzzled that they did not object to the pose, however brief. The music is not brief, and provides considerable non-diegetic confirmation of the idea that Neo is a Christ-figure, simultaneously human *and* divine, whose self-sacrifice saves humankind. But the censorship board's failure to censor this music is not surprising. Without appropriate exposure, people have no ear for any music except that of their own time and place. Unless one of the censors listened regularly to the appropriate non-Egyptian music, there was no reason for Egyptian clerics to recognize the stylistic clues that identify the music as Christian. But the Egyptian censorship board represents the Sunni branch of Islam, and Sunnis prohibit certain uses of music, particularly when the music is of Western origin. The music might just as well have been played to deaf ears, because if the censors were devout Sunni Muslims, they had limited practical experience with Western music.

If you think that the musical clues would be impossible to miss—obvious even to Egyptian clerics who do not listen to Western music—consider the following experiment that I regularly conduct with college students. Playing both secular and religious music to a group of students, I find that most of them are unable to hear any differences along these lines when the music is not of European origin. Most of us make all kinds of fine discriminations with culturally familiar music, but we have no basis for noticing and understanding parallel differences in unfamiliar styles.

One way to think about the subtle messages communicated by musical style is to compare music with language. Different languages and musical styles have distinct "grammars," rules of phrase structure that must be learned. These rules change over time, more rapidly with music than language. The music of different generations is very different—we are not surprised that the Oracle likes Duke Ellington, but we would be surprised to find her listening to any of the contemporary rock music found on the *Matrix* soundtracks. And despite their similarities, music is very different from language. Although the same melody can be played in different styles, there is no such thing as *translating* a piece of music. If a listener does not comprehend a piece of music as it is presented, there is no alternative way to present it that will not result in a different piece of music. If the listener hasn't formed the associations that underlie the musical "language" of a film soundtrack, only the tempo and rhythm is likely to contribute to the experience of the visual scene. There is no reason to be surprised that Egyptian censors did not grasp the religious emphasis of the musical arrangement in Neo's death scene.

There is a second reason that the censors did not object to the music. Focusing on diegetic elements of the film, such as dialogue, most viewers forget that non-diegetic music contributes to the film's content. If you have previously associated some basic musical cues with Christian church services, you need not be *conscious* that the music sounds like church music in order for it to succeed in assigning a Christian connotation to Neo's death scene. Music guides viewers in their interpretation of a scene, yet most of the audience will claim that their interpretation is due to dialogue and visual information. For instance, suppose a movie scene lacks a satisfying narrative conclusion. If it is accompanied by music featuring a traditional resolution with a "perfect" cadence, more of the audience will feel that the scene has a satisfying conclusion than when viewing it with music that does not supply a musical resolution.

Viewers who "understand" a film's non-diegetic music have an enriched experience, for they incorporate an additional stream of information into their experience. They experience the narrative differently from viewers who lack the listening habits appropriate to the music. The audience needs to possess enough background experience to follow the music, but they need not do so consciously.[1]

Based on these principles, some of the music of *Revolutions* plays a strange game with its audience. The scrolling end-credits are a non-diegetic element. So is the music that accompanies those credits. One film convention is that the music playing with the end-credits expresses the film's overall theme, providing a musical resolution to the whole film. A love story, for instance, will place a love song with the credits. *Reloaded* ends with "When the World Ends." *Revolutions* concludes with a new version of the "Neodämmerung" music that accompanies the final confrontation between Neo and Agent Smith. Renamed "Navras," it now supports prominent percussion and vocal parts. Singers wail in a non-Western musical style, singing non-English lyrics. Massed voices chant Sanskrit words from Hindu religious texts, the *Upanishads*. During Neo's death scene, the choir sang some of this same text: "From darkness lead me to light/From death lead me to immortality."

So both Neo's death scene and the end-credit music of *Revolutions* invite us to interpret his sacrifice from a Hindu perspective. Neo's sacrifice is not really Christ-like, for it is not a personal sacrifice. Either Neo is fated to die in this way (it is his karma), or he has escaped the cycle of karma/fate and achieved immortality by transcending all personal desires.[2] If the latter,

---

[1] For more detailed discussion of this point see Theodore Gracyk, "Popular Music: The Very Idea of Listening to It," in Carlos Rodriguez, ed., *Bridging the Gap: Popular Music and Music Education* (Reston: MENC—The National Association for Music Education, 2004), pp. 51–70.

[2] Since Neo is promised immortality without practicing the required five pillars of Islam, these lyrics give the Egyptian censors another reason to object to Neo's death scene.

Neo has achieved peace by recognizing that Zion and the machine city are as unreal as the noodle shop he used to visit when he was at home in the Matrix simulation of 1999.

These interpretations assume that the music supporting the credits to *Revolutions* serves as a final comment by the Wachowski brothers, stipulating that a Hindu reading overrides all others. As such, they have provided a remarkable pair of musical jokes. First, they hid Hindu themes in a Christian chorale. Second, they conclude with a style of singing and a sung text that Western audiences cannot grasp when listening to the music. Except for its rhythms, Western audiences are as removed from the "Navras" music as the Egyptian censors are from the Christian choir at Neo's death. Movie music normally guides interpretation without requiring the audience to think about the music. But for most of its intended audience, the *Matrix* trilogy includes non-diegetic music that does not deliver its message unless it is consciously analyzed.

Zion Revisted

Reloaded also provides diegetic music that most viewers will not consciously think about, but should. The culture inhabited by the Oracle, Thomas Anderson, and Agent Smith is the dominant culture of the industrial world at the end of the twentieth century. The culture of Zion is notably multi-cultural in its origins, as if the wars between humans and machines obliterated industrial society, with non-Western cultures supplying much of Zion's population. Why, then, does the music of Zion sound so much like the dance music of the Hel Nightclub?

The diegetic music in Zion in *Reloaded* offers one of the most interesting *artistic* problems of the trilogy. Because it is in Zion and not in the green-tinted Matrix, it is the music of the future. The design of Morpheus's ship, the *Nebuchadnezzar*, poses a parallel visual problem. The ships are complex machines, reflecting two hundred years of technological innovation. Their design is recognizably advanced, but not too advanced (for the people of Zion have limited resources). Given similar constraints, how might their music sound? How can it sound futuristic and still sound musical?

If anyone does not understand why the music of Zion should sound strange to us, they might listen to some ragtime music by

Scott Joplin, popular at the start of the twentieth century. Then listen to the music of Duke Ellington, from mid-century, and then to the music of Dave Matthews and Rob Zombie featured in *Reloaded*. Each is a good representative of the popular music of its time. The passage of time ensures that they sound nothing alike. Since Zion has existed for some two hundred years when we hear its music, shouldn't the music of Zion be at least as far removed from the music of 1999 as the music of Rob Zombie and the Hel Club is from the music of Scott Joplin?

Some viewers will advance a simple explanation of why the music of Zion does not sound odd, like the music of a different time. The citizens of Zion are deliberately engaging in a neo-tribal ritual. Like most groups, they use traditional music for their public rituals and celebrations. The drumming is purposely dated from their perspective—just the way that J.S. Bach's *Matthäus-Passion* (*St. Matthew Passion*) is still performed during Easter rituals in some places, despite its having been composed more than two hundred years ago. Perhaps the dancers in Zion are doing something similar, preserving tradition as an important dimension of their communal ritual.

But listening to it again, I am afraid that the music used in the scene does not support this interpretation. Massed polyrhythmic drumming may suggest tribal roots. But the rhythms used do not feature the polymetrical complexities of real tribal drumming. The drumming in Zion is synchronized around a dominant metrical pulse. At predictable and frequent intervals, all the drums sound together to reinforce the basic dance beat. Tribal drumming does not work this way. While there will be a basic pulse, only one drummer plays it. Other drummers play "against" this main pulse, complicating the beat instead of reinforcing it. If the basic beat has groupings of four beats, the others will avoid groupings of four. Some drummers will adopt patterns that fit five or six beats into the same period, while others will launch patterns that only rarely synchronize with the main pulse. Some drummers will "solo," avoiding all synchronization with the main beat. In Zion, all the drums rein-force the basic pulse. If this music is a self-conscious preserva-tion of tradition, the tradition in question is commercial dance music of the late twentieth century! The rhythmic design of the music of Zion is just like that of the Hel Club back in the Matrix world.

So the music of Zion presents a dilemma. Either the music will sound strange to us, or it will sound familiar. If the music is stylistically distinct, as music will be in two hundred years, its strangeness will call attention to it, deflecting attention from the narrative. But if the music is familiar enough to be understood by most viewers, it cannot be stylistically removed enough to be the music of Zion.

Rasa

Let me suggest a sympathetic solution to the problem of the inappropriate diegetic music in Zion. The problem arises from the logic of the narrative, its time frame, and the laws of music. My solution depends on philosophizing about art. Taking my cue from the music and lyrics at the end of *Revolutions*, the solution draws on traditional Hindu philosophy.[3] The music preserves the *rasa* of the scene, which would be violated if the music were sufficiently futuristic to satisfy the requirements of the narrative.

To condense thousands of years of tradition into a few lines, Hindu philosophy of art emphasizes the concept of *rasa*, meaning "taste" or "flavor."[4] Each work of art should emphasize a specific emotion, which is the work's dominant mood or flavor. Each part of the work should also feature a specific *rasa*, as when different scenes in a play or film have different moods. Notice that the music at the end of *Revolutions* is "Navras," the traditional term for "the nine flavors" that are thought most basic and thus most suitable for art. The nine moods are the erotic, comic, pathetic, furious, heroic, terrible, odious, marvelous, and peaceful. Thus the final battle between Neo and Agent Smith is furious, while Neo's death is pathetic. Although artistic realism

---

[3] According to Ben Watkins, the music's co-composer, this music is meant "to tie together musically much of the philosophy expressed in the Matrix." Interview with Ben Watkins, Dynaudio Acoustics website, posted November 12th, 2003, and accessed June 8th, 2004, <http://www.dynaudioacoustics.com/Default.asp?Id=296&AjrNws=576&AjrNwsPg=4>.

[4] Introductions to *rasa* theory are available in Richard L. Anderson, *Calliope's Sisters: A Comparative Study of Philosophies of Art* (Englewood Cliffs: Prentice Hall, 1990), pp. 157–172, and V.C. Chari, "Rasa," in Michael Kelly, ed., *Encyclopedia of Aesthetics*, Volume 4 (Oxford University Press, 1998), pp. 103–06.

is important, realistic representations of events are far less important than the higher purpose of presenting a distinct *rasa*.

Hindu philosophy teaches that the goal of life is self-transcendence and liberation from the cycle of rebirth. Meditation is one path to this spiritual emancipation. But when art is properly saturated with *rasa*, it offers another path.

Tasting a grape and then a lemon, we experience distinct flavors. This difference is not just a fact about perceivers. We perceive something outside ourselves. According to *rasa* theory, successful art is similarly seasoned with emotion. But the desired effect does not involve manipulating the emotions of the audience. We do not have to feel sad to see that a scene is sad, any more than we have to become furious in order to recognize that the fight between Neo and Smith is furious. The mood of sadness or fury is *there*, in the construction of the scene.

Art is valuable because it encourages us to contemplate emotion that is rendered impersonal or depersonalized, distancing us from the relevant emotion. This distancing is desired because it opens a path to a higher spiritual level. Because it is not specific to any individual, *rasa* is an eternal emotion. So *rasa* presents an element of *Brahman* (the absolute). Furthermore, if we can observe emotions in art without being personally subjected to their fluctuating demands, we can do the same with our own emotions. By purifying consciousness of selfishness, we move toward a liberating union with *Brahman*. Finally, both intense aesthetic delight and immersion in the work of art are additional experiences of a higher reality of pure spirit.

What does *rasa* theory say about the diegetic music of Zion? If the music were sufficiently futuristic to reflect the logic of the narrative, the audience would be confused about its *rasa*. From a Hindu perspective, the scene would fail to satisfy its artistic purpose of immersing the audience in a non-personal emotion. By combining the dense percussion with slowed visuals of the dancing masses of citizens, the scene has a very distinct unifying flavor: it is one of the very few scenes in the *Matrix* trilogy with an erotic *rasa*. Futuristic sounding music would call attention to itself. It would dilute the scene's erotic mood.

Rasa liberates the audience by focusing attention on universalized, eternal emotions. The eroticism of the Zion celebration would not seem basic and eternal if we were aware of it as something of another time. Paradoxically, the music of Zion successfully reinforces the visual of the dancing mob because the music is so very clearly the music of *our* time, playing on our human tendency to treat the familiar as something universal. By violating the expectation of realism appropriate to diegetic music, *Reloaded* briefly embodies the Hindu philosophy expressed in the music that concludes *Revolutions*. In this respect, the music and erotic celebration of the "We Are Still Here" scene may be the *Matrix* trilogy's best fusion of artistic form and philosophical content.

Scene 3

Global Philosophy Unplugged

10

The Matrix and Vedanta: Journeying from the Unreal to the Real

ANNA LÄNNSTRÖM

The opening scenes of *The Matrix* layer dreams and wakeful-
ness, inviting confusion and questions about what is real and
what is merely dream. Neo wakes up three times. The first time,
he sees "Wake up Neo" on his computer screen. Then, he awakens sweating and trembling from a nightmare during which
Agent Smith has implanted a metal bug in him. Both Neo and
we quickly learn that it was not a nightmare; the bug was real.
But Neo is truly "asleep" until his third awakening when he is
roused from the dream that had been his life up to this point,
learning that what he had always thought was real is not. The
world he knew and loved, the place where he would eat really
good noodles, is a computer-generated illusion. His body is in
a tank, generating electricity, while his brain is tricked into
thinking that he is living an ordinary human existence. Like
countless others, Neo has been asleep for the first part of his life
and has come closest to encountering reality in dreams.

 The Matrix trilogy raises a series of deep philosophical questions, beginning with Neo's own about how we can know that
we really are awake: "You ever have that feeling where you're
not sure if you're awake or still dreaming?" Might what I experience as reality be an illusion; might I be dreaming right now?
How can I be sure that what I see is really there, and if it's an
illusion, how do I dispel it? Long before being brought to the
big screen by the Wachowski brothers, these questions occu-
pied philosophers. Descartes presented the ominous possibility
that the world around him, including his own body, might be

an illusion created by an all-powerful evil genius. Plato likened
the human condition to that of prisoners in a cave, tied down
and unable to move, looking at shadows of puppets cast upon
the wall and mistaking them for real living beings. Coming to
know, Plato suggested, is like being dragged out of the cave and
facing the blinding light of the sun outside. Vedanta (one of the
nine systems of Indian philosophy, and with the exception of
Buddhism the most well-known) tells us that the world as we
see it isn't real; it's *maya*, cosmic illusion.[1] Explanations for the
source of the illusion abound. The Vedanta philosopher
Shankara (*circa* A.D. 686–*circa* A.D. 718) argued that we can't
know what caused the illusion and that it doesn't matter. Rather,
the important question is: How do we dispel the illusion? If we
are trapped, how can we escape?[2]

A Splinter in the Mind

Shankara argues that since the problem is ignorance, the solution is knowledge, remembering who we truly are. The first step
is to distinguish between the self and not-self. Shankara con-
ceives the true self as covered by several layers, including the
body and the mind. In the grasp of illusion, we identify with
these superficial layers. At first, we identify with our bodies.
Slightly more advanced, we recognize that we aren't our bodies,
but we identify with our mind and ego. The goal is to go further inward still, peeling away the layers until only our true self
(*Atman*) remains. *Atman* isn't the mind or the ego; it's the still,
permanent witness that underlies all the fluctuations of the mind
and body and that was never born and will never die.

After distinguishing between self and not-self, the second
and final step towards liberation is to understand the relation
between the self and the world. For Shankara, this means that
we must recognize that all distinctions between you and me and

---

[1] Strictly speaking, saying that the world is unreal is incorrect because the
world can be experienced. For Vedanta, only Brahman is fully real and only
self-contradictory objects like square circles are unreal. The world falls in-
between these two categories; it's both real and unreal, less real than Brahman
and more real than the square circle.

[2] This chapter quotes from Shankara's *Crest-Jewel of Discrimination*
(*Viveka-Chudamani*) and assumes that the *Crest-Jewel* is indeed authored by
Shankara. Some scholars dispute this.

between Brahman and me are only apparent; they are not *really* real. *Atman* is identical to ultimate reality. We view the world as a multiplicity, filled with distinct objects, and we consider ourselves to be separate individuals. But our separateness is illusory: all is one. Shankara asks us to imagine immersing a glass filled with water into the ocean. We can distinguish between the ocean water and the glass water because the glass separates them. However, once we remove the glass, we remove the separation. There's no longer glass water and ocean water – there's just water. *Tat twam asi*—you are that—you are the Absolute; you are Brahman.

Shankara and his followers repeatedly speak about liberation as waking up from a dream. Our "reality" is a dream; our spiritual task is to recognize that we are dreaming and to wake up. Just as in *The Matrix*, the initial problem is that we don't understand that we are asleep. Like Neo, we make initial contact with reality when we are doubly asleep, when we are sleeping in our illusory existence. For Shankara, however, this happens not in dream sleep but rather in deep sleep because then, we lose our awareness of our selves as separate: "In dreamless sleep, when there is no object of experience, the joy of the *Atman* is felt."[3] But deep sleep isn't liberation; it's a state of oblivion. We must wake up from the dream which is our lives, and that can't be accomplished by going to sleep.

Although the illusion does a thorough job in making us forget our true selves, neither the *Matrix* nor Shankara present the illusion as perfect. Those who are suited for escape have felt a quiet discontent for a long time, noticing that something isn't right. In their first conversation, Morpheus tells Neo: "You're here [talking to me] because you know something. What you know, you can't explain, but you can feel it. You've felt it your entire life, that there's something wrong with the world, you don't know what it is but it's there like a splinter in your mind driving you mad." Without that splinter, Vedanta teaches, escape wouldn't be possible. If we don't long for liberation, we won't escape. Self-knowledge is the solution to a problem; one who doesn't recognize that he has a problem isn't ready for a solu-

---

[3] Shankara. *The Crest-Jewel of Discrimination*, translated by Swami Prabhavananda and Christopher Isherwood. Third edition (Hollywood: Vedanta, 1978), p. 49. Henceforth, *Crest-Jewel*.

tion. The spirit isn't mature enough yet. It needs to live a bit longer, journeying through more reincarnations, until it starts recognizing that the world around it is unsatisfactory. At any given time, the vast majority of people aren't yet ready. Similarly, Morpheus says: "Most of these people are not ready to be unplugged. And many of them are so inert, so hopelessly dependent on the system that they will fight to protect it."

"Lead Us from the Unreal to the Real"

Shankara and *The Matrix* agree that somebody must shake us awake. The task is too hard for us to accomplish on our own. The *Crest-Jewel* opens with reference to the difficulty of attaining liberation, and stresses that we can succeed only through "discipleship to an illuminated teacher" and with the help of scriptures (pp. 33–34). Even Neo needs a teacher at first. Morpheus is an invaluable guide as Neo first explores the possibility that the reality he has always known is illusory. Without Morpheus's guidance, he might never have known. Similarly, Shankara argues that liberation is impossible without the guidance of a teacher and sacred texts, the Vedas. Human reason is too weak. I can't by myself see through the illusion. Thus, using an ancient mantra from the *Upanishads*, the seeker prays for assistance: "Lead us from the unreal to the real, from darkness to light, from death to immortality" (*Brihadaranyaka Upanishad* 1.3.28).

A guide is crucial for another reason as well. When Morpheus first contacts Neo, he wonders if Neo is ready: "I don't know if you're ready to see what I want to show you, but unfortunately you and I have run out of time." Seeing reality melt and change shape, waking up in a tank plugged into electrodes can shatter a weaker mind, and will be terrifying for all. Apologizing, Morpheus tells Neo that they normally don't liberate adults: "We have a rule. We never liberate a mind once it has reached a certain age. It's dangerous, the mind has trouble letting go." The shock of seeing a multitude dissolve into a unity, all distinctions flickering and disappearing, must be equally terrifying. Swami Vivekananda (1863–1902), spiritual teacher and follower of Shankara, was terrified the first time he saw truly. He describes the experience as follows:

I saw with my eyes open that all the things of the room together
with the walls were rapidly whirling and receding into an unknown
region and my I-ness together with the whole universe was, as it
were, going to vanish in an all-devouring great void. I was then
overwhelmed with a terrible fear. I knew that the destruction of
I-ness was death, so I thought that death was before me, very near
at hand. Unable to control myself, I cried out loudly.[4]

"This self cannot be attained by one without strength" says the
Mundaka Upanishad (3.2.4) and perhaps that's for the best. The
idea of liberation is frightening enough even for the strong; the
weak won't even dare to pursue it, and it would destroy them.

Initially, we need to trust that the guide knows what he is
doing. "Please, Neo. You have to trust me," says Trinity. We
don't yet know that the guide knows reality better than we do.
Perhaps following her will lead to madness instead of knowledge. We have to assume that she means well and that she
knows what she is doing. Still, at least for Shankara, this does-
n't mean that others can save us. The guide is necessary but she
is not enough. One must begin by trusting scripture but end by
seeing for oneself. Our guide can help us see by pointing in the
right direction and describing what is there, but the final step is
our own: "The words of the scriptures, your own power of reasoning and the teaching of your master should all help to convince you—but the only absolute proof is direct and immediate
experience, within your own soul" (*Crest-Jewel*, 112). If you
don't see, my pointing will be in vain—I can't see for you. The
task of saving oneself belongs to each and every one of us,
because we are all Brahman, and none of us can be redeemed
except by our own efforts: "Children may free their father from
his debts, but no other person can free a man from his bondage:
he must do it himself"(*Crest-Jewel*, 40). *The Matrix* points in the
same direction. It's true that Neo is the one, a Christ-figure come
to redeem us. However, he resists the role as Savior. In
Reloaded when Michael Karl Popper, the kid from *Animatrix*,
thanks Neo for saving him, Neo denies having done so: "You

---

[4] Vivekananda's account is recorded in Saradananda's *Sri Ramakrishna The
Great Master*, translated by Swami Chetanananda (Hollywood: Vedanta, 1979),
p. 842. Vrajaprana drew my attention to this passage.

saved yourself." Morpheus's advice to Neo points in the same direction: "You have to see it for yourself." "I can only show you the door, you're the one who has to walk through it."

It's Not the Snake that Changes, but Your Perception of It

Once a person has seen through the illusion, it has no power over him any more. Shankara compares the illusion to mistaking a rope for a snake. If I see what I think is a snake, I'll be frightened. But once I notice that what I thought was a snake is just a rope, I won't be afraid anymore. The rope doesn't change. It is and remains a rope; it's just my perception that has changed. But, for me, this change in perception changes everything.

Even though the illusion loses power, the liberated one can still see it when he chooses to, and his body and mind will continue to exist in the illusory world because of *karma*. *Karma* means "action," and in this context it refers to the consequences of one's actions. Shankara and other Hindus believe that we accumulate good *karma* when we do good things and bad *karma* when we do bad things. In other words, we must reap what we sow, experiencing the results of our past actions, if not in this life then in the next one. Because the body and mind have accumulated *karma*, they will continue to exist (within the illusion) until they die. But this doesn't trap the *Atman*, because it no longer identifies with them and it does not accumulate *karma*. Consider becoming so captivated by a truly engrossing movie, like *The Matrix*, that you forget it's just a movie. If you identify with Trinity perhaps you suffer her pains as though you were her. But then, with a shift of focus, you realize that this is silly. You aren't in the movie; you aren't Trinity; you are a "calm, detached onlooker" outside it (*Crest-Jewel*, 124). After you distinguish between yourself and Trinity and recognize that she isn't real, her fate doesn't pain you anymore, and you know it won't affect you. But you can still see the movie. You might even stop watching for a while, ignoring the movie, maybe even leaving the room, but the DVD will play until the movie is over, available for you to watch if you so choose. In this way, the liberated one in Vedanta will alternate between the two perspectives available to him, seeing unity, multiplicity, and then unity again.

Being outside the illusion in this way gives the liberated one power within the illusion. Vivekananda writes that the aim of yoga is for the practitioner to "arrive at the point where what we call 'nature's laws' will have no influence over him, where he will be able to get beyond them all. He will be master of the whole of nature, internal and external."[5] Vivekananda continues:

> Suppose, for instance, a man understood the Prana perfectly, and could control it, what power on earth would not be his? He would be able to move the sun and stars out of their places, to control everything in the universe, from the atoms to the biggest suns, because he would control the Prana. This is the end and aim of Pranayama. When the Yogi becomes perfect, there will be nothing in nature not under his control. (CW 1:148)

But Vivekananda cautions his followers against placing too much emphasis on such feats because they can make us lose sight of the goal, forgetting that the goal is escaping and instead trying to perfect and control our prison cell. The liberated one may be able to dominate the illusion, but he sees that such dominance is pointless.

In contrast, dominating the Matrix is quite useful because that is where part of the battle against the machines takes place. Like the liberated ones in Vedanta, Neo and the others can weave in and out of the *Matrix*—entering the illusory world again and again. Because they know that it isn't real, they can bend and sometimes even break its rules. Trinity can hang suspended in midair, run on walls, and jump in a way that pursuing wide-eyed cops call "impossible." Most of the crew remain bound by some laws, however, due to the limits their insufficiently liberated minds impose. Thus, Trinity and Morpheus can run very fast, but they don't go through walls or floors, and while they can jump, they can't fly. They must run from the agents instead of fighting them. Neo goes further than the others in suspending the rules. He is a lightning quick fighter; he can jump from tall buildings, dodge bullets, fight many agents at once, and eventually fly like Superman.

---

[5] Vivekananda. *The Complete Works of Swami Vivekananda* (Kolkata, India: Advaita Ashrama, 1989), Volume 1, p. 133. Henceforth, CW 1:133.

Neo's ability to do all this has nothing to do with his body and everything to do with his mind. The fighting scenes are physical expressions of a mental struggle in which physical laws are transcended. The little boy in the Oracle's apartment is bending spoons with his mind, not with his hands, and he can do so because he understands that "there is no spoon." Once the mind is completely freed from its self-imposed limitations, it can do what previously seemed impossible. Thus, the task is clear: "Free your mind, Neo!" In the first movie, Neo gradually frees his mind, and his power inside the Matrix keeps increasing. He learns to fight and eventually can defeat the agents and even fly. Because he knows that the Matrix isn't real, Neo is able to defy its laws.

Beyond the Matrix of Dichotomies

While the similarities between Shankara's world and the Matrix are instructive, the differences are ultimately more suggestive. The central difference is that the two worlds in *The Matrix* are much more closely intertwined. The Vedantin will continue to exist in the apparent world until his *karma* has worked itself out. His body won't die before its time, but once it does die, he'll continue his true existence, unaffected by the death of the body, just as the viewer won't die because a character in a movie dies. This means that the liberated one is beyond fear because he recognizes that what truly matters can't be harmed. The *Atman* is "birthless and deathless. It neither grows nor decays. It's unchangeable, eternal. It doesn't dissolve when the body dissolves" (*Crest-Jewel*, 53). The men and women in *The Matrix* on the other hand are transient and mortal. Inside or outside the Matrix, they remain vulnerable, mortal beings. If they die inside the Matrix, they die outside it too. "Your mind makes it real," says Morpheus, implying that the mind could choose not to make it real. I suspect that's what happens when Neo pulls Trinity back to life at the end of *Reloaded*. Still, we remain vulnerable. Neo can't make Trinity immortal, and in *Revolutions* she can and does die outside the Matrix. Fear thus remains a sensible response to reality because what matters most to us, those we love and care about, can be killed, and this means that we lose them forever.

For Shankara, fear is misguided because the true self is invulnerable. Reality is completely unlike the illusory world and it's infinitely better. Indeed, Vedantins describe it as being, consciousness, and bliss. Simply put, reality is good and in it, we are free and happy. The desire to forget all about reality and to re-enter illusion is unimaginable because an Advaita red pill would offer bliss as well as truth. Picking the blue pill is unimaginable. In *The Matrix*, by contrast, truth and bliss are separated. Those who awaken find themselves in a horrific dystopia, a nightmare made even more frightening by the recognition that they won't wake up from it. Morpheus is honest when he tells Neo that "all I am offering is the truth." Consequently, while we may not like Cypher's decision to choose illusion over reality, we understand it. Going back to sleep, re-entering a world of sunshine, smiling people, and well prepared steak, isn't the courageous choice, but it's a tempting one especially if we, like Cypher, reenter the Matrix knowing that we won't remember the nightmarish reality outside. In the world of *The Matrix*, Cypher is right; ignorance is bliss. We might add that knowledge is suffering. We escape illusion at a high price when we exit the Matrix.

And do we in fact escape illusion? In Vedanta, once we're out, we know it. We're no longer taken in by appearance but see reality as it is. Knowledge dispels all possibility of doubt. A person who has seen reality will never be taken in by illusion again, and he'll never long for illusion again. In *The Matrix* trilogy, the situation is quite different. The trilogy often deals in rigid, either/or dichotomies—should I take the red or blue pill, this right door or the left? Should I choose a return to the safety of ignorance or a leap to the knowledge of a terrifying reality? Humans stand against machines, reality against illusion. In the final showdown of *Revolutions*, Neo faces Smith, and one of them will win. By contrast, Shankara teaches that true liberation can be found only by going beyond dichotomies. If we see black and white, reality and illusion, we don't see truly yet. True reality lies beyond the verbal distinction between reality and illusion, transcending our intellectual understanding of both.

What happens if we apply this Vedantic lesson to *The Matrix*? What happens if we question the trilogy's black and white surface? The trilogy itself points in this direction. Parts of Zion look pre-industrial—even primitive. There are torches, bare feet dancing to drumbeat, soft flowing clothing, and sweaty half-naked bodies. The images of Zion seem designed to illustrate the contrast between humans and machines. But *Reloaded* soon undermines this stark contrast. Zion is completely dependent on technology. At night in Zion, Neo has a quiet chat with Councilor Hamann, who says: "This city survives because of these machines. These machines are keeping us alive while other machines are coming to kill us. . . . I think about all those people still plugged into the Matrix and when I look at these machines, I . . . I can't help thinking that in a way, we are plugged into them." So what is the difference? Neo answers that they could shut off the machines. The difference, then, is choice. But, as the Councilor replies, while they certainly could turn off the machines, doing so would be suicide. Without the machines, the people of Zion would die; they would have no light, no heat, and no air. Similarly, the machines are dependent upon humans as a source of energy. They need each other.

The power of mind undermines the trilogy's dichotomies. At first, the metaphysics of *The Matrix* trilogy seems simple: There are two worlds—illusion and reality, the Matrix and the outside. A strong mind like Neo's can manipulate the Matrix because the Matrix is an illusion; it can't manipulate reality in the same way because reality is, well, real and thus has firm spatiotemporal laws. Neo can fly and fight multiple opponents in the Matrix and not in reality. Agent Smith is a program and consequently not real, so while he is immensely powerful inside the Matrix, he remains trapped there.

In *Reloaded* and especially *Revolutions*, it becomes clear that this is too simplistic. *Revolutions* introduces the possibility of being stuck in an in-between state, a world in between the Matrix and reality. The train station is "nowhere . . . [it's] between your world and our world," the program Rama-Kandra explains. If there are three worlds, surely there can be more. In particular, there could be something beyond these three worlds, and the movies suggest that this something is mind. In *Reloaded* and *Revolutions*, Neo's mind grows so powerful that he can enter the Matrix without being plugged in. He stops sentinels outside the Matrix simply by thinking it. He is blind during the last half of *Revolutions*, but still he can see. In short, he becomes increasingly able to control reality outside the Matrix in the same way that he can control the Matrix. Similarly, Agent Smith, a pro-

gram who ought to be confined to the Matrix, is able to tran-
scend it. Smith himself says that "there's nowhere I can't go."
The power of the mind extends beyond the Matrix. Smith can
destroy the Matrix and he won't stop there. He won't stop until
there's nothing left at all. A powerful mind can break the rules
in the real world too.

The mind's ability to control the real world, bending and
breaking its rules, suggests that the real world isn't as real as we
have been led to believe. Neo can control the Matrix because he
understands that it isn't real. His ability to control the outside
suggests that he has gained the same insight about it, recognizing that just as the world inside the Matrix is an illusion created
by a mind (the Architect); the world outside is yet another illusion, created by another mind. Early in the first *Matrix* movie,
Neo is doubly asleep. At the end, he finally is fully awake, having recognized the full power of the mind and his own true
nature. *Tat twam asi*—you are that—you are the Absolute; you
are Brahman.[6]

So what about you? You've slept for too long. Are you finally
ready to wake up?

---

[6] I have learned much about Vedanta from Swami Tyagananda at the Vedanta
Center in Boston. I also owe great thanks to my dear friends Shannon Hartzler,
Pravrajika Vrajaprana, and Stefan Kalt for offering helpful comments on drafts
of this paper and especially to Shannon for suggesting that mind may be what
is most real in the *Matrix* trilogy.

11

The Cosmological Journey of Neo: An Islāmic Matrix

IDRIS SAMAWI HAMID

KUMAYL: What is Reality?
ᶜALĪ: A light that illuminates from the dawn of pre-eternity, and whose imprints shine upon the *matrices* of oneness.
—From a conversation between ᶜAlī ibn Abī Ṭālib and his disciple Kumayl

The *Matrix* trilogy provides an interesting smörgåsbord of philosophical questions and issues. Yet underlying the metaphysical questions (What is real? What is the nature of reality?), the epistemological questions (How do I know what is real?), and the ethical questions (what am I really supposed to do?) there lies the larger context of the cosmology of the Matrix. Cosmology seeks the mutual and consistent integration of the answers to particular philosophical and scientific questions with a view to providing a model that, as comprehensively as possible, explains

the origin of the world and humanity,
the purpose of the world and humanity, and
the destiny of the world and humanity.

Plato's *Timaeus* is the classic Western archetype of philosophical cosmology. Whitehead's *Process and Reality* is perhaps the last comprehensive work in this field in the West.[1] Today, in the

---

[1] Alfred North Whitehead, *Process and Reality*. Corrected Edition (New York: Free Press, 1978).

136

wake of the present separation of philosophy and physics (formerly natural philosophy), cosmology has largely been left to the astrophysicists, and its domain restricted to the physical universe.[2]

Islāmic Philosophy

The *Matrix* trilogy addresses cosmological questions, but it does not provide a comprehensive or consistent cosmological system. Instead it provides elements that may be woven into a larger cosmological scheme. Yet the trilogy does offer a solid foundation in which all the cosmological questions can be rooted, namely Neo's journey, from his first leap of faith (in the first film) to his return to the Source in *Revolutions*. I believe that, more than anything else, the story of the *Matrix* trilogy is first and foremost the story of the cosmological journey of Neo.

Placing the cosmology of *The Matrix* in the context of Neo's journey also allows us to compare aspects of that journey with some of the cosmological themes of Islāmic philosophy. In watching the trilogy I was amazed at how many philosophical motifs in the series could be seen as expressions of themes in traditional Islāmic philosophical cosmology, particularly its late period (the sixteenth century through the nineteenth).[3]

For the rest of this chapter we will consider some aspects of Neo's journey from the perspective of the cosmology of Shaykh Aḥmad (died 1826 C.E.). The last of the great and original philosophers of traditional Muslim civilization, Shaykh Aḥmad was at once mystic, scientist, philosopher, and cosmologist.

An important feature of Shaykh Aḥmad's system is that it represents the most ambitious attempt, in the context of late Islāmic philosophy, to systematize primordial Islāmic philosophy, a strand that goes right back to the time of the Prophet of Islām,

---

[2] But see William Desmond, *Being and the Between* (Albany: State University of New York Press, 1995).

[3] This period is marked by both an integration and analysis of the phenomenology of mysticism, as well as an integration of that primordial prophetic philosophy that goes back to the Prophet himself and to his successor and son-in-law, ᶜAlī ibn Abī Ṭālib (died 661). Imâm ᶜAlī is buried in Najaf, Iraq, and his tomb is one of the holiest sites in Islām. For more on these two relatively unknown phases of Islâmic philosophy, see Henry Corbin, *History of Islamic Philosophy* (London: Kegan Paul, 1993).

his successor ᶜAlī ibn Abī Ṭālib, and the latter's successors. This provides an opportunity to connect some themes of the *Matrix* trilogy with something of the essence of Islām itself.

In what follows, we will consider Neo's cosmological journey from the following aspects

the Source as origin (and the dialectic of determinism and choice);

the Matrix as illusion (and the universe of *Dunyā*);

the Matrix as higher matter (and the universe of *Hūrqalyā*);

and

the Source as destination.

From the Source

We are all from Allâh and to Him shall we return.
—The Qurᵓān (2:156)

Everything that has a beginning has an end.
—The Oracle

Although Neo is a flesh-and-blood human being, the ultimate origin of his being is the Source, that principle upon which is predicated the entire universe of the Matrix and the machines that made it. The Source is thus the origin of the Matrix, the machines, and of Neo. In the Neoplatonic cosmology of Plotinus (died 270 C.E.) and his Hellenic successors—a system which was adopted and extended in classical Islāmic philosophy—the Source corresponds to the *Universal Intellect*, the first emanation of the One that is *beyond substance* or *being* (*hyperousia*).

The Universal Intellect is a pure immaterial consciousness containing the general principles of all things. It emanates the next immaterial sub-realm (such as the Soul or the Second Intellect). Through emanation all sub-realms are ordered in a strict *vertical* hierarchy from the highest (the Universal Intellect) to the lowest (the material world). The expression 'vertical' refers to the non-temporal nature of this hierarchy.

In its pure form, Neoplatonic cosmology cannot adequately accommodate one very important sub-context of the *Matrix* trilogy. Whatever a complete cosmology of the Matrix entails, one of the key elements it must contain is a fundamental role for choice. Indeed, the dialectic of freedom versus control, choice versus determinism, constitutes the major sub-context of the entire trilogy.

The problem with the traditional Neoplatonic model in this regard is that the emanation scheme has no place for choice; it is absolutely deterministic, rooted as that model is on the principles of logical and mathematical precision. Emanation is not a process at all. Giving birth is a process; cooking food is a process; producing a diamond is a process. Emanation, rather, is analogous to the relation of implication in logic. The proposition "Two is even and prime" implies the proposition "Two is even." There is no choice or process here, only a necessary relationship between two (abstract) objects. "Two is even and prime" cannot choose to not imply "Two is even." Whatever "Two is even and prime" implies it must imply. Whatever the Neoplatonic One emanates it must emanate. Whatever the Universal Intellect emanates it must emanate, right down to every detail of the material world. The Neoplatonic system does not provide a counterweight to this.

In *Reloaded* we are introduced to the Architect, that manifestation of the Source who reveals to Neo the history of the Matrix along with Neo's own role in that history.[4] If the Architect had his way, so to speak, the world of the Matrix would exactly mirror a Neoplatonic cosmology:

> THE ARCHITECT: You [Neo] are the eventuality of an anomaly which, despite my sincerest efforts, I've been unable to eliminate from what is otherwise a harmony of mathematical precision. . . . .
> The first Matrix I designed was quite naturally perfect; it was a work of art. Flawless, sublime. A triumph equaled only by its monumental failure.

The problem, of course, is choice, as Neo points out. The Architect's words illustrate the fundamental flaw of Neoplatonic philosophy in this regard. For the Matrix to work, it needed a fundamental place for choice. This is where the cosmological role of the Oracle enters. As the Architect says, "If I am the father of the Matrix, she would undoubtedly be its mother."

---

[4] The Architect is like the Second Intellect—the first emanation of the Universal Intellect—in the system of Fārābī (died 950).

Thus the Oracle fills in a major gap in the Neoplatonic scheme. Yet the way this is handled in the trilogy itself is somewhat unsatisfactory. On the one hand the Oracle is the mother of the Matrix. On the other hand she is just another program created by the Architect, a child of the Architect, so to speak. So the Oracle is both complementary to the Architect and derivative from the Architect, while the Architect is not in any way derivative from the Oracle. This is somewhat inconsistent given the overall thrust of the trilogy. The source (no pun intended) of this tension in the plot is related to the dual nature of Neo in the trilogy as both human and derived from the Source, as I'll explain below.

The needed symmetry is provided in a major modification of the Neoplatonic scheme offered by Shaykh Aḥmad al-Aḥsāʾī. Up to his time virtually all Islāmic cosmologies, whether systematic and Aristotelian or mystical, were unable to escape the deterministic parameters of Plotinus's original scheme. Shaykh Aḥmad introduced into Neoplatonic thought a major *dialectical* element that made choice, not merely a subjective or derivative feature of the world (as in the traditional scheme), but rather an essential feature—indeed, *the* essential feature.

Consistent with both primordial Islâmic philosophy and Plotinian thought, the essence of God or the One is beyond the beyond. From here the emanationist scheme is completely subverted. The first creation or emanation of the One is a process, the immaterial Absolute Existence. This now precedes the Universal Intellect as the source of all things. According to Shaykh Aḥmad, *Absolute Existence* is at once pure activity (or matter) and pure receptivity (or form); a unity and coincidence of opposites. Matter is the principle of willing, ordering, and determining; form is the principle of permissibility, receiving, and choosing. Everything that exists flows from the inner tension or dialectic that constitutes Absolute Existence:

> The meaning of the proposition that all things come from it [Absolute Existence] through marriage and procreation is that matter is the father [the active principle] and form is the mother [the receptive principle], as we will elucidate for you later. So matter "married" form . . .; so form gave birth to the thing. The Willing is the First Adam. His Eve is Permissibility and she is his equal; she does not surpass him, nor is she deficient with respect to him, as we alluded to previously. So understand! And this is the "fire"

alluded to in His saying (may He be Exalted!): the oil well nigh shines, though no fire touches it! (The Qurʾān (2:156)[5]

That is, the oil of choice and permissibility—although essentially receptive and actualized through the fire of willing, ordering and determining—almost has actuality even before it is actualized. That is, choice is not merely a derivative feature of reality, even though it is in essence receptive according to Shaykh Aḥmad. Indeed, both the cosmological Adam and the cosmological Eve are each derived from the other, much like the variables of a non-linear differential equation. The two cannot be decoupled: neither choice nor determinism is an independent variable in the world. Conceptually we may decouple them, as we can conceptually decouple the north and south poles of a magnet. In reality however, choosing and determining are coupled in the dynamic field of reality, just as the north and south poles of a magnet are modes of a dynamic electromagnetic field.

The *Matrix* trilogy identifies choice with a woman (the Oracle), and determinism with a man (the Architect). This is quite consistent with Shaykh Aḥmad's approach. The main difference—as I alluded to above—is that *The Matrix* gives a definite metaphysical priority to determinism in the construction of the Matrix.

This throws into relief two aspects of Neo's relationship with the Matrix. On the one hand Neo (along with all of humankind) stands in an antagonistic relationship with the Machines. In this context the Machines are attempting to achieve absolute control of the human psyche and introduce the Oracle only as a grudging acceptance that choice must be taken into consideration as a factor of control. As the Architect says, "While it [the anomaly of choice] remains a burden assiduously avoided, it is not unexpected and thus not beyond a measure of control." On the other hand and on a deeper level, however, Neo is a manifestation of the Source of those very machines and beyond being a mere human. His purpose is ultimately to return to the Source, which is what happens at the end of *Revolutions*.

This dual nature of Neo is a fundamental tension within the trilogy that gives rise to a number of inconsistencies. From the

---

[5] For an introduction to the thought of Shaykh Aḥmad, see my doctoral thesis, *The Metaphysics and Cosmotology of Shaykh Aḥmad al-Aḥsāʾī* (Buffalo: SUNY Buffalo, 1998. For this quotation, see p. 291.

perspective of Neo's cosmological journey it is the second perspective that is more interesting, not the battle with the Machines *per se*. From the latter perspective: Since the essence of Neo comes from the Source, and since choice is a part of Neo's essence, it seems that the Source should also reflect the origin of choice. Shaykh Aḥmad's scheme in many ways provides a more consistent model for Neo's relationship with the Source.

In Shaykh Aḥmad's cosmology, the primordial Adam-Eve of Absolute existence produces delimited existence, which immediately bifurcates into the Universal Intellect and the *Arid Earth*, a field of receptivities like a soil that receives rain and seeds. The Universal Intellect is the Second Adam, the second father. The Arid Earth is the Second Eve, the second mother. So emanation has been subverted into a process, at each level of which there is both father and mother. The Architect is the Universal Intellect; the Oracle is the Arid Earth. The Arid Earth is the container of all possibilities and choices seeking actualization through the "rain" of the Universal Intellect. The Universal Intellect provides direction and order; the Arid Earth provides choice and possibilities.

In her conversations with Neo, the Oracle explains her complementary role *vis-à-vis* the Architect:

> ORACLE: . . . that man [the Architect] can't see past any choice.
> NEO: Why not?
> ORACLE: He doesn't understand them. He can't. To him they are variables in an equation. One at a time, each variable must be solved, then countered. That's his purpose: to balance the equation.
> NEO: And what's your purpose?
> ORACLE: To unbalance it.

The Oracle and the Architect here play complementary roles, with a symmetry between them. In this conversation it is clear that she cannot be a mere creation of the Architect. The Oracle provides a limitless source of possibilities that defies any one equation, one structure. In both Permissibility and the Barren Earth—the first and second Eves—this is called "the Great Depths" in Shaykh Aḥmad's cosmology.

At each level, Adam and Eve are not in conflict but rather complement one another. Similarly, the Architect and Oracle are not at war; they complement each other. Indeed, in *Revolutions* the Oracle works (through Neo) to save the very world the Architect had built. Despite being the torch-bearer of choice, she is no nihilist or anarchist. While she subverts order locally, she seeks to preserve order globally. Similarly, in Shaykh Aḥmad the exercise of choice may lead to evil consequences in the world but part of the responsibility of choice involves the preservation of order, both personally and otherwise.

From the rain of the Universal Intellect upon the Arid Earth droplets of choice are actualized. Thus, according to Shaykh Aḥmad, every person ultimately comes into existence through his own choice, beginning his downward descent to our world of lower matter. And this is where Neo begins his search to answer the question, "What is the Matrix?"

Illusion and Dunyā

In the cosmological journey of Neo the Matrix plays two roles. First, it is a world of illusions and control. We will look at this role in this section. Second, it is an intermediary realm between Neo's earthly existence and the source that is his cosmological origin. We will discuss this second role in the next section.

The Matrix in the first sense corresponds to the world of *Dunyā* or the immediate world in Islāmic terminology. It is the realm of which we are immediately conscious. It is a phenomenal world wherein lie our immediate desires and attachments. It is an ephemeral world whose objects of desire do not last. It is a universe where one is not free except as a slave to one's own desires. It is a place where the initial choice that brought us into existence has been forgotten and buried very deep in the recesses of consciousness. Yet most of us accept this world as ultimately real and are completely enslaved by it.

The founder of primordial Islāmic philosophy, ᶜAlī ibn Abī Ṭālib, was famous for his countless exhortations about the dangers of the phenomenal world of Dunyā and the need to wake up from it. For example:

> I hereby caution you about Dunyā! It is apparently sweet and green, surrounded by desires, loved for its immediate pleasures. It excites wonder through that which is small, big hopes are attached to it, and it is adorned with illusions. Its joys do not last and no one is secure from its harm. It is full of illusions and harmful . . .

The Dunyā is not the world of matter per se but rather the illusions that we attach to the world of matter. ᶜAlī ibn Abī Ṭālib was not a recluse from the world as a physical object; rather he only sought refuge from attaching any ultimate importance to the world of sensible matter. According to Islām, the matrix of illusions, desires, and ultimate significance that we attach to this life is the Matrix from which we must wake up. Hence the saying of the Prophet of Islām: "Die before you die!," which Imām ᶜAlī explains in his saying, "The people are asleep; only when they die do they wake up."

The *Matrix* trilogy presents the Matrix as primarily a structure of control. In primordial Islāmic philosophy, especially as systematized by Shaykh Aḥmad, it is about more than mere oppression from the outside but oppression from the inside. As the Qur ān says (7:160): "They did not do us any harm; rather they only oppress themselves." Thus one may escape the structure of external control and still be enslaved by the structure of internal control. The Qur ān gives the example of the people of Moses. He rescued them from the matrix of Pharaoh. But it was not long before his people complained about the better food and drink they had back in Egypt, compared to the stuff they had to eat as a free people in the wilderness.

Thus "waking up" from the Matrix is more than just escaping from a place or location; it refers to an awareness of Dunyā and all of the illusions that one attaches to it. This perspective gives context to Cypher's betrayal. He never really left the Matrix in the full sense. Yes, there was a transfer of physical location, like the Hebrews from physical captivity in Egypt. But real knowledge and awareness escapes Cypher. Consider this exchange in a famous tradition of the prophet often quoted by Shaykh Aḥmad and other mystics:

> THE PROPHET: Knowledge is a light that Allāh casts in the heart of one that he loves. He then becomes at ease so that he sees the unseen. He opens up so that he can carry trial and tribulation.
>
> SOMEONE ASKED: Is there a sign of that?
>
> THE PROPHET: Withdrawal from the house of illusions. . . .

Cypher never attained awareness. He was not ready for the trials and tribulations entailed by freedom because he never really freed himself from the Matrix and "the house of illusions" to begin with. When one attains true knowledge and awareness one becomes capable of carrying the trial and tribulations that accompany a higher degree of knowledge. Morpheus gives an excellent description of the state of those who, like Cypher, are still trapped in Dunyā, saying to Neo, "You have to understand . . . most of these people are not ready to be unplugged. And many of them are so inert, so hopelessly dependent on the system, that they will fight to protect it."

There are degrees of knowledge and awareness. To each degree there corresponds choice, hardship, and trial. In primordial Islāmic philosophy there are three general degrees of consciousness, choice, and action. This first is *faith (īmān)*. At this stage, one has the sense that there is more to reality than meets the eye and makes a leap of faith. Neo meets Morpheus, makes a choice, and takes the red pill on nothing but faith that truth lies on the other side.

This stage is also marked by questions: "Who is Morpheus?" is the first question. But that's not the real question, as Trinity points out, "You're looking for him (Morpheus). I know because I was once looking for the same thing. And when he found me, he told me I wasn't really looking for him. . . . I was looking for an answer. It's the question that drives us, Neo." Neo realizes the question is "What is the Matrix?"

This is the first stage of knowledge, obtained by Neo's first choice and based on faith. In primordial Islāmic philosophy, the word 'Īmān' signifies both faith and action equally, and thus entails choice. Faith produces choice, then choice produces action. This is the field of Īmān;

Next is *awareness (taqwā)*. Upon waking in the *Nebuchadnezzar*, Neo recognizes that he had been a prisoner his entire life. Life has become more difficult. The nature of the Matrix is no longer the question. There is a more important question now: Who is Neo and what is the choice that he has made? In *Reloaded* the Oracle guides Neo further:

NEO: But if you already know, how can I make a choice?
ORACLE: Because you didn't come here to make the choice. You've already made it. You're here to try to understand why you made it.

Neo made a choice at the very onset of his existence that he is now trying to understand. "Know thyself," the Oracle urges. Neo asks if he is "the One" whom Morpheus is expecting. The Oracle responds, "Being the One is just like being in love. No one can tell you you're in love; you just know it. . . ." No one can tell Neo he's "the One." He has to become aware of it himself through the journey of self-knowledge. And that involves a choice, to save or not to save Morpheus. As the Oracle warns, "One of you is going to die. Which one . . . will be up to you." By choosing to save Morpheus "the One" within Neo moves from inner potential to outer realization and manifestation. Based upon his faith, first he saves Morpheus. Then he takes on Agent Smith, something previously thought impossible. Then, analogous to his rebirth and awakening after taking the red pill, he awakens again, defeats Smith, and is now aware of himself as the One.

Analogous to 'īmān', 'taqwā' equally signifies awareness and action. Awareness gives rise to choice, and choice produces action. Continual application of this leads to the next level, *certainty (Yaqīn)*. This is the stage where one actually sees and witnesses the realities of things removed from the veils that generally separate things. To reach this level, Neo had to make yet another very difficult choice. The Oracle hints at it and Neo resists, for this choice will be a more difficult trial than the first. This time he has to navigate the apparently mutually exclusive and jointly exhaustive choice between saving Trinity or saving humanity, in the face of the heavy intimidation of the Architect.

Rending this veil, the distinction between the Matrix and the material world begins to disappear for Neo. He begins to travel the Matrix without even being plugged in.

These three levels are actually mentioned in an off-hand and inverse manner in the *The Matrix*. Morpheus says, "You have to let it all go, Neo: fear, doubt, and disbelief."

Upon rearrangement and inversion of the three things mentioned by Morpheus we can say that

> Letting go of disbelief produces faith (īmān). Letting go of fear produces awareness (taqwā). Letting go of doubt produces certainty (yaqīn).

A descendant of Imām ᶜAlī, Jaᶜfar Ṣādiq—one of the most important figures in primordial Islāmic philosophy—made the following general point that captures the entire process described above: "Through wisdom the depths of consciousness are fathomed; through consciousness the depths of wisdom are fathomed." Shaykh Aḥmad interprets this as meaning that one must apply whatever level of consciousness one has to wise action commensurate to that state of consciousness. Continual application will deepen that consciousness, which will deepen the wisdom of actions and choices, which will feed back into deeper consciousness, and so forth. At each level, consciousness produces a wise choice, which produces a wise action, which leads to a deeper consciousness. This process is the engine of the cosmological journey.

Looking back at the *Matrix* trilogy, we can say that the first film marks Neo's journey from faith to awareness (*īmān* to *taqwā*); *Reloaded* marks his journey from awareness to certainty (*taqwā* to *yaqīn*); and *Revolutions* marks the final leg of Neo's journey from certainty to his final destination, that of *bayān* or clarity, where yet another choice had to be made. We will return to this in the final section.

Subtle Matter and Hūrqalyā

One of the interesting things about the Matrix is that, on the one hand, it starts off as a prison of control. But for Neo and his unplugged cohorts, it is also a platform for spiritual development that is more subtle than the outside world of matter and physics. In *Reloaded*, it is inside of the Matrix that Neo undergoes further awareness and development.

Put another way, for those who are "plugged in," the Matrix corresponds to Dunyā. But for those who are unplugged, the Matrix corresponds to the higher realm of Hūrqalyā. But what is Hūrqalyā?

Originally, Neoplatonic cosmology postulated two general realms. First, the purely intelligible, non-spatial, atemporal realm. Here one finds the intellects, the soul, and so forth. Second, the purely sensible realm of matter, time, and space. Suhrawardī (died 1191) and later philosophers of Muslim civilization argued that reality—and hence the journey from the material world to Absolute Existence in Shaykh Aḥmad's cosmology—is analogically graded from the material to the immaterial and therefore an intermediary between the two had to exist. This is the world of Hūrqalyā. There are two corollaries of this principle. First, every level of reality contains features of the level immediately beneath it, but in a more sublime way. Second, every level of reality contains features of the level immediately above it, but in a more coarse way.

With these principles Shaykh Aḥmad turns Aristotelian hylomorphism on its head. Here matter is the active, actualizing principle; form is the receptive, potential principle. This goes against the very grain of traditional Neoplatonism, which saw matter as something low, evil, and even non-existent in itself.

Shaykh Aḥmad goes even further: active matter is in constant movement through the receptivity and reflexivity of forms and states. The matter of a given thing or substance is what identifies that particular substance, but the forms, both essential and accidental, of that substance are always in flux. This provides for a kind of substantial movement—that is, motion in the category of substance—something generally considered impossible in traditional Aristotelian metaphysics.

Hūrqalyā is a universe corresponding to a set of states of matter that are more subtle than those of the sensible world. Space and time are also more subtle. The topological possibilities for the configuration and manipulation of matter are much richer in Hūrqalyā than in the material world. Indeed, if Shaykh Aḥmad saw *The Matrix* he would almost certainly say that the Matrix is really nothing but one of the many sub-realms of Hūrqalyā. Doors that open to different regions of a subtle space-time depending on which key is used are quite consistent with the nature of Hūrqalyā.

Full access to Hūrqalyā from the sensible world requires a particular kind of cognitive vision, though a low level of access is obtained just by looking at an image in a mirror. Virtual reality, advanced video games; these worlds are all low levels of Hūrqalyā.

Hūrqalyā is also important to spiritual and cosmological development. According to Shaykh Aḥmad each of us has a subtle physical body that belongs to Hūrqalyā. It's not a mere "residual self-image" as Morpheus put it in the first film, but rather it is more "real" than the outer sensible body. Actually it is the same body as the outer sensible body, containing matter in a more subtle state of which we are not normally aware. Shaykh Aḥmad often says that the relationship of the outer sensible body to the body in Hūrqalyā is like the relationship of sand to glass. The matter of the transparent glass is the matter of the opaque sand, but the glass is a more subtle state of that very sand.[6]

In his journey through Hūrqalyā, Neo learns more about who he really is. He is no longer limited as he was in the sensible world. Shaykh Aḥmad says in this regard:

> When these bodies of the immediate world (Dunyā) are purified of those accidents that are really foreign to them, then the way of those who are lower join the way of those who are above. . . . Similarly, when the spirits which are presently connected to these bodies are purified of the disobedience and forgetfulness [of their primordial choice at the beginning of their cosmological journey], they perceive—in and of their essences—the [purified] bodies and all that pertains to them. This is because their bodies may become spiritualized just by wishing it; their spirits can become bodies and renewed just by wishing it.[7]

Hūrqalyā also has levels and degrees:

> NEO: What are you trying to tell me? That I can dodge bullets?
> MORPHEUS: No, Neo. I'm trying to tell you that when you're ready. . . . you won't have to.

For Neo, the first degree corresponds to being able to "dodge bullets." This also corresponds to the level of īmām or faith. Then he dies in Hūrqalyā and is reborn in Hūrqalyā with taqwâ and awareness. Now he is no longer like his friends. He can see the structure of the Matrix. He can now fly high like a spirit and

---

[6] In primordial Islâmic philosophy two "cities" of Hūrqalyā are mentioned. These are Jābalqā and Jābarsā. Jābalqā in particular can be something of a hellish place, according to Shaykh Aḥmad; maybe we can assimilate it to the machine city. Yet ultimately even the inhabitants of Jābalqā "do only what we are meant to do," to quote the Keymaker, just like the non-human inhabitants of the Matrix all do what they are meant to do (at least until Smith gets unplugged). Jābarsā is more paradisal; needless to say this is *not* where the Matrix is located.

[7] For more on Hūrqalyā, Jābarsā, and Jābalqā, see Henry Corbin, *Spiritual Body and Celestial Earth: From Mazdean Iran to Shi'ite Iran* (Princeton: Princeton University Press, 1977). Page 208 contains an alternate translation of this passage.

walk on the ground.[8] He no longer needs to "dodge bullets." As he continues to grow, he finally begins to outgrow the need to be physically "jacked in" to access the Matrix. He is now permanently aware of his subtle body; the worlds have collapsed into one; he is always in Hūrqalyā.

Back to the Source

O Allāh! Show me things the way they really are!

—Muḥammad

KUMAYL: What is Reality?

ᶜALĪ: The unveiling of the auroras of majesty independent of direction.

KUMAYL: Increase me in *clarity (bayān)!*

ᶜALĪ: A light that illuminates from the dawn of pre-eternity, and whose imprints shine upon the matrices of oneness.

—From a conversation between ᶜAlī and his disciple Kumayl

According to a famous tradition of the Prophet of Islām, between our sensible level of consciousness and God there are 70,000 veils of darkness and light. Accordingly, the spiritual journey involves piercing these veils until one reaches back to the source of Absolute Existence:

> ORACLE: The power of the One extends beyond this world. It reaches from here all the way back to where it came from [the Source]. . . . That's what you felt when you touched those sentinels, but you weren't ready for it.

In *The Matrix* and in most of *Reloaded*, Neo's journey consists mainly of penetrating the veils of darkness. He travels through many doors and visits many places. But then Neo is led to a special portal. The Keymaker informs him, "One door is special. One door leads to the Source." When Neo passes through that door, he is embraced by light. But it is just the first of the veils of light. For this first encounter with the light does not bring a final answer or resolution. Neo is disappointed, not realizing

---

[8] Death and rebirth in Hūrqalyā is interpreted by Shaykh Aḥmad as corresponding to the "Day of Resurrection."

that in passing through these first veils of light he has crossed a major threshold and milestone in his journey. This is part of what the Oracle meant when she said, "That's what you felt when you touched those sentinels, but you weren't ready for it." That is, "You did not realize that you had penetrated some of the veils of light; thus you did not fully grasp the power that thereby manifested itself in you." Neo has more questions, then the following exchange takes place:

> ORACLE: If there's an answer, there's only one place you're going to find it.
> NEO: Where?
> ORACLE: You know where.

With the knowledge and eye of yaqīn, Neo must now face the most difficult choice of all, the most arduous leg of his long, hard journey. Yaqīn has placed him on the threshold of the penultimate choice, the final answer, the point and moment of final and certain truth.[9]

During the journey, Neo is physically blinded by Smith, who has managed to install a copy of himself into a human cerebrum. But this apparent setback opens Neo to yet another field of light. Continuing his journey, he encounters more sentinels, appearing to him as more veils of light. Finally Neo reaches the center of the machine city. In his physical blindness his vision is clear and penetrating. He has reached the final veils of light, the last auroras of majesty. As he describes it, "It's unbelievable, Trin. . . . Light everywhere. Like the whole thing was built of light. I wish you could see what I see."[10] Neo moves on and encounters a manifestation of the gatekeeper to the Source. The gatekeeper tests Neo, then allows him to enter the Matrix one last time. Here Neo faces the final test.

---

[9] There are three degrees of yaqīn: knowledge of certainty, eye of certainty, and truth of certainty, the highest. The above paragraph plays on these three.

[10] One of the more poignant scenes in *Revolutions* is the final dash above the clouds Trinity makes, culminating in her vision of the Sun and sky. At this point Neo cannot see what she sees, making this phenomenon a unique gift for Trinity. Given her quite serene and content death immediately thereafter I see this as a symbol of the culmination of her own cosmological journey, and a satisfying complement to Neo's journey.

Throughout his travels and battles, Neo has always held onto one thing: his own self-identity. While trapped in the intermediary region (*barzakh* in Islāmic terminology) between the sensible world and the Matrix, between Dunyā and Hūrqalyā, Neo tries to bully his way onto the train to Jābalqā, and the Trainman just laughs at him, pushes him aside, and drives away. Neo does not quite get what's needed to overcome the Trainman. Neo's self-identity, the essence that says, "I," this is the last thing to go in the cosmological journey. It is one of the highest veils of light, one of the "auroras of majesty" referred to by Imām ᶜAlī above. Letting that go marks the end of the journey. As Imām ᶜAlī says in a poem:

> You think you are nothing but a little germ
> Yet within you the Greater World is enfolded!

After fruitlessly fighting an out-of-control Smith for what must have felt like an eternity, Neo finally understands. He lets go of himself and completely gives up his self-identity. At this point he exemplifies the most fundamental axiom of primordial Islāmic cosmology and that of Shaykh Aḥmad's cosmology as well (first enunciated—as far as we know—by the aforementioned Jaᶜfar Ṣādiq):

> Servitude is a jewel whose inner reality is lordship. That which is missing in servitude is found in lordship. That which is hidden in lordship is attained in servitude.

By letting go and turning himself over, Neo has now annihilated his self-identity in the Source and becomes its manifestation so that he now easily destroy Smith. Neo has now attained the final cosmological stage of *bayān* (clarity). His journey has now come full circle from the Source, to the Source.

The first definition in *Merriam Webster's Dictionary* of "matrix" is, "something within or from which something else originates develops, or takes form." The very essence of Neo's being is now itself a matrix, a matrix of oneness that reflects the one light of the One Source, the light of Absolute Existence. This points to the final answer to the question that has been driving Neo's cosmological journey from the opening lines of the first film. And the questions, "What is the Matrix?", "Who is Neo?"

and "What is Reality?" are really all the same question. We will let Imām ꜥAlī articulate the final answer:

KUMAYL: Increase me in clarity (*bayān*)!

ꜥALĪ: A light that illuminates from the dawn of pre-eternity, and whose imprints shine upon the matrices of oneness.

KUMAYL: Increase me in clarity!

ꜥALĪ: Turn off the lamp, for the Dawn has arisen!

12

Faith, Understanding, and the Hidden God of *The Matrix*

WILLIAM JAWORSKI

The Matrix Reloaded and *Revolutions* highlight a notion that plays a central, perhaps *the* central role in traditional revealed religions, the notion of faith. The prophecy, Neo, and Morpheus and Lock going head to head over the legitimacy of the Oracle are a metaphor for the centuries-old philosophical struggle to understand what faith is, and what legitimate place it has—if any—in human life.

Faith and Revealed Religion

The struggle to understand what faith is and how it relates to other forms of human experience goes back at least to the Middle Ages when Jewish, Christian, and Muslim philosophers tried to assimilate the wisdom of the pagan philosopher Aristotle. Aristotle's philosophical system was wide-ranging and rigorous. He seemed right about . . . well . . . just about *everything*, and he had arguments purporting to prove there must be a divine being. The problem was that the divine being whose existence he claimed to prove seemed quite different from the being Jews, Christians, and Muslims claimed to worship. According to Aristotle, for instance, God was ceaselessly engaged in contemplating his own being, and hence had neither knowledge of nor love for individual human beings, something at odds with the beliefs of Jews, Christians, and Muslims.

If Aristotle was right about the nature of God, their entire way of life, their entire way of understanding themselves in relation to God, the universe, and each other was misguided. What many Jews, Christians, and Muslims claimed, therefore, was that Aristotle was only *partially* right. Aristotle had gotten things right as far as he went; he saw rightly that God exists and has certain extraordinary features, but he didn't go far enough. He didn't see, and indeed *couldn't* see God's "personal" features, for those features, they claimed, were knowable only with the help of God's *revelation*, something to which Aristotle had no access.

According to Jews, Christians, and Muslims, God is a divine, extraordinary, "other-worldly" being whose special nature exceeds our human ability to understand it. The only way humans can come to know God (and know that God knows and cares about them) is if God *reveals* himself to them through, say, the words and deeds of a prophet or prophets (as Judaism and Islam claim) or by becoming a human being and revealing himself in person (as Christianity claims). This notion of God's self-*revelation* lies at the heart of *revealed* religions: God is a "hidden" God whose extraordinary nature makes it difficult for humans to know, yet God very much wants to be known, and will take extraordinary steps to insure that he is.

Why does God want to be known? Jews, Christians, and Muslims all share a conviction that knowing God is in our best interests, and that God wants to insure we have what is best for us. If, for instance, nothing would be better for us than to share in the unending peace and joy of God's own divine life, and we could share in this life only with the help of revelation, we could count on God to reveal to us everything we needed in order to have it.

In the context of revealed religion, *faith* is the human response to God's efforts on our behalf; most fundamentally it consists in *trusting in God*, and doing so by trusting in his revelation, accepting it, living in accordance with it. It is the sort of attitude exemplified in the *Matrix* most clearly by Morpheus. The Oracle communicates a message to Morpheus, a revelation: he will find the One who will return to the Source and end the war. The encounter changes his life: he dedicates himself to finding the One and doing his part to bring the prophecy to fulfillment.

Trusting the prophecy earns Morpheus misunderstanding and contempt from people like Commander Lock who have no such trust. From Lock's perspective, Morpheus's decisions seem the epitome of foolishness, a waste of precious time and resources. Similarly, the efforts of many Jews, Christians, and Muslims seem a complete waste to people who have no particular religious commitments. Are critics of revealed religion right? Is Lock right about Morpheus? The answer given in the film is "No!". The trilogy vindicates the perspective of people of faith: Morpheus is right; Lock is wrong; Neo is in fact the only one who can save Zion.

But is *The Matrix* right to vindicate that perspective? Or would a more realistic plot line have vindicated Lock instead? Would it have included, say, a final scene in which Morpheus is proven a fool, his faith in vain: there are no prophecies; there is no deliverance; there is only darkness and death? Should the trilogy have ended that way? Is faith foolishness? Are people who claim to have it fools? To try to answer these questions we first need to consider more carefully what faith is supposed to be.

Faith ≠ Belief ≠ Knowledge

Faith is not the same as belief. Belief in general consists in accepting a certain statement or claim, in thinking that it is true. People believe many things that are not matters of faith. You probably believe, for instance, that $2 + 2 = 4$, that elephants are larger than ants, and that water is wet. You think these claims are true, but you don't think they're true on the basis of faith. Most fundamentally, faith consists in trusting God; it consists in believing *in* something, you might say, not believing *that* something—as when we say, "Believe in yourself": we mean *trust* yourself, *have confidence* in yourself. When we speak of Jews, Christians, and Muslims having faith we are speaking most fundamentally about them having trust or confidence in God—in his power and goodness, in his concern for what is in our best interests.

If faith is not the same thing as belief, however, it might nevertheless involve having certain beliefs, for one of the ways people might trust in God is by accepting God's revelation. Because they trust God, in other words, Jews, Christians, and Muslims are willing to accept the things God reveals—the same way you might accept the claims of a good friend because you trust her knowledge and experience. This brings us to another point

about the notion of faith: faith does not involve believing something in the absence of evidence, but rather believing something
in the *presence* of evidence of a certain sort, namely God's say-
so, and one's trust in God. Hence, in the Christian scriptures, for
instance, the apostle Paul calls faith, "the evidence of things
unseen" (*Hebrews* 11:1).[1]

If faith involves evidence, however, it should be clear it's not
the sort of evidence that could, say, convince atheists they're
wrong, for atheists deny there is any evidence of this sort. If
there is no God, as they claim, then obviously there can be no
trust in God, and hence no basis for accepting the claims Jews,
Christians, and Muslims in fact accept. From the point of view
of these religions, atheists seem like people who ask for proof
that colors exist, but won't accept eyewitness testimony about
what other people see. From the atheistic point of view, on the
other hand, people who accept things based on faith seem to
accept things with no evidential basis at all, to think, feel, and
act in ways that are completely groundless.

It's not just atheists who might think this either, but anyone
who would deny that faith has evidential value. The seventeenth-
century philosopher John Locke, for instance, was not an athe-
ist. He nevertheless claimed that all beliefs had to be evaluated
by standards independent of faith, that faith had no evidential
standing of its own, but was always subject to the "superior"
judgment of faith-independent forms of evidence—faith-
independent standards. Like John Locke, Jason Lock doesn't
think faith is a distinctive form of evidence. He wants Morpheus
to provide faith-independent reasons to support his claims: "I
don't care about oracles, or prophecies, or messiahs," he says,
"I care about one thing: stopping that army from destroying this
city!" "With all due respect, Commander," Morpheus replies,
"there is only one way to save our city: Neo!" "Goddammit,
Morpheus!" Lock retorts, "Not everyone believes what you
believe!" From Lock's perspective, Morpheus's beliefs appear to
have no "real" evidential backing, no backing of a faith-independent sort, which is the only sort he acknowledges. To him,
therefore, Morpheus's beliefs seem no more than opinion, con-
jecture, or superstition.

---

[1] The Greek word translated "evidence" here is ʼελεγχος. It's sometimes used
to designate an argument or proof.

Because of their divergent views on the nature of faith, there is nothing Morpheus and Lock could say to each other that would convince the other he is wrong. Morpheus's claims seem groundless to Lock because Lock denies the evidential value of prophecies and the like. Lock's claims, on the other hand, seem misguided to Morpheus since Lock denies the legitimacy of a very important, perhaps the most important prophecies source of information about the salvation of Zion.

Morpheus and Lock are not alone in thinking as they do. Captain Roland, for instance, would appear to share Lock's mindset. He thinks Neo is "totally out of his goddamn mind," and that Niobe is a fool for lending him her ship. Councilor Hamann, on the other hand, would appear to share Morpheus's understanding of faith. His attitude (and name) recall the eighteenth-century philosopher Johann Georg Hamann.

Hamann criticized Enlightenment thinkers like John Locke for what he took to be their uncritical insistence on the alleged "superiority" of faith-independent forms of evidence. According to Hamann, the evidence of faith, although different from that of, say, mathematics or natural science, is nevertheless equally legitimate within its sphere. Consequently, he said, to insist with Locke that beliefs based on faith be discounted unless supported by faith-independent forms of evidence is to insist on an unduly narrow conception of what evidence is. Like Hamann the philosopher, Hamann the councilor refuses to accept what he takes to be Lock's narrow-minded dismissal of oracles, prophecies, and the like, and says as much when Lock demands to know why he's cleared the *Nebuchadnezzar* for take off: "I believe I need every ship we have if we're going to survive this attack . . ." Lock cries, "Why did you allow the *Nebuchadnezzar* to leave?!" "Because," says Councilor Hamann, "I believe our survival depends on more than how many ships we have."

Despite their differences, Morpheus, Lock, and Hamann could agree about at least one thing: having faith is not the same as having knowledge. Knowledge involves being able to grasp or articulate the reasons why something is the case. I know all bachelors are unmarried, for instance, because I know a bachelor is by definition an unmarried man. Likewise, I know the hypotenuse of a right triangle with opposing sides of three and four inches, respectively, must be five inches since this follows directly from the Pythagorean theorem: $3^2 + 4^2 = 5^2$. Faith, by contrast, does not involve the ability to say why something is the case, since faith is fundamentally about God, a being whose nature we can only imperfectly understand. We can't grasp God's nature the way we can grasp the Pythagorean theorem, and hence we can't derive conclusions about God from the principles of a divine science the way we can derive conclusions about triangles from the principles of Euclidean geometry.

Because having faith doesn't amount to having knowledge, and yet because it's not totally groundless, Medieval philosophers such as Thomas Aquinas claimed faith was "half way" between knowledge and mere opinion. We see this sort of thing in *The Matrix*: no one who accepts the prophecy *knows* how things will turn out, not even the Oracle: "Did you always know?" Seraph asks her; "Oh no," she says, "no, I didn't. But I *believed*." Yet if Morpheus, Trinity, and the other "believers" lack knowledge, their beliefs and actions are nevertheless not completely groundless, but are based on a certain groping confidence or conviction that reaches for something it can't "see" but nevertheless feels certain is within reach. As Aquinas says in the *Summa Theologica*, "the act of faith is firmly attached to [something] and in this respect the person of faith is in the same state of mind as one who has knowledge or understanding. Yet the believer's knowledge is not completed by a clear vision, and in this respect he is like one having a doubt, a suspicion, or an opinion" (2a.2ae.2.1).

Growing in Faith:
Understanding the Erotic God

I've so far talked about the *attitude* of faith and how it differs from knowledge and belief. We now need to consider the *object* of faith, what faith is *about*. I've already said that faith is most fundamentally trusting in God, so this is the object of faith; it is what people have faith *in*.

Jews, Christians, and Muslims claim God's nature exceeds our understanding, and hence faith could never amount to knowing God or grasping God's nature in a "clear vision." Focusing on this aspect of faith, the nineteenth-century philosopher Søren Kierkegaard (echoing the third-century African Church Father, Tertullian) declared *credo quia absurdam*! I believe *because* it is absurd, *because* it is impossible to understand. Lack of understanding is not a problem for Captain Soren of the *Vigilant* either, who is the first to answer the Council's call to aid the *Nebuchadnezzar*. His actions in *Reloaded* defy a pessimism Lock attributes to lack of understanding: "Be hard for any man," says Lock, "to risk his life—especially if he doesn't understand the reason!" But lack of understanding doesn't stop Captain Soren, and it didn't stop Søren Kierkegaard. He saw lack of understanding not as an impediment to faith, but as an inspiration.

Lack of understanding is not the last word, however, but only the first. Kierkegaard's statement was meant to recall an earlier statement by the fourth-century philosopher Augustine of Hippo who said *credo ut intelligam*: I believe in order that I might understand. Augustine's point was that any lack of understanding in matters of faith was a product of our limited cognitive abilities and not the subject matter itself, a point that recalls Councilor Hamann's words to Neo as the two overlook the engineering level of Zion: "There is so much in this world that I do not understand. See that machine . . . I have absolutely no idea how it works, but I do understand the *reason* for it to work. I have absolutely no idea how you're able to do some of the things you're able to do, but I believe there's a reason for that as well." God's revelation is fully intelligible and fully rational even if we can't fully understand or discern its rationality. Consequently, it's possible for people of faith to grow in their understanding of it, to come by degrees to understand God more fully than they did before.

The fact that humans can never fully understand God, in other words, doesn't mean they can't *grow* in their understanding of God. Indeed some philosophers have claimed that striving to understand the God in whom we have faith is precisely the way we deepen our relationship with him. Aristotle had claimed that humans by nature desire to understand, that our enjoyment of life is enhanced or perfected through understanding. Some Jewish, Christian, and Muslim philosophers extended this idea, and concluded that in seeking to grow in our understanding of God, we seek to enjoy more fully our relationship with him; to grow in understanding, in other words, is to grow in love.

Considerations of this sort led the eleventh-century philosopher Anselm of Canterbury to characterize theology (the "science" or "study" of God), as *fides quaerens intellectum*: faith seeking understanding. The notion of *seeking* here is key. Faith is not something static, but a dynamic source of growth and adventure. It is accepting God's invitation to have an intimate relationship with him, a relationship the Jewish scriptures characterize in explicitly erotic terms (see, for instance, *The Song of Songs*). Various creeds and doctrines are only so many invitations to deepen one's relationship with God. Their meanings are not visible on the surface, but lie concealed in the beautiful, mysterious depths of our own being and God's, depths which, according to Jews, Christians, and Muslims, God invites us to explore together with him.

Similarly, the prophecy communicated to Morpheus in *The Matrix* doesn't wear its meaning on its sleeve; that meaning has to be discovered gradually, in the course of a journey with many pitfalls. Morpheus realizes this only after Neo's encounter with the Architect. When Neo claims the prophecy was a fraud meant to conceal yet another level of machine control, Morpheus's faith reaches a crisis:

"I don't understand it," he says, "everything was done as it was supposed to be done: once the One reaches the Source the war should be over."

"It was a lie," says Neo, "the One was never meant to end anything. It was all another system of control."

"I don't believe that!" says Morpheus.

"But you said it yourself," Neo responds coolly, "How can the prophecy be true if the war isn't over?"

Faced with this crisis Morpheus doesn't lose his faith; he merely reinterprets it. He recognizes he didn't understand the real meaning of the prophecy. What its real meaning is he doesn't yet know; he nevertheless continues to act with that groping confidence characteristic of faith, a humble confidence wedded to a recognition of ignorance and limitation. His faith is challenged and subsequently reinterpreted, but certainly not lost. In the end the prophecy is fulfilled: Neo returns to the Source and ends the war. The way this happens, however, is not the way Morpheus, the Oracle, or anybody else anticipated.

Faith and Human Striving

The prophetic revelation that occurs in *The Matrix* is an invitation to embark on a journey of discovery, the meaning of which is understood only gradually. The salvation of Zion is part of that meaning, but only a part since it marks the beginning of a new chapter in the lives of the characters, human and machine, who are invited to explore the possibilities of the new peace. Similarly, the claim of revealed religions is that our relationship with God is ever surprising, ever new, that the joy and excitement of new discovery never ends as we grow in our understanding of what God's revelation means—like falling in love for the first time only every day. This brings out another aspect of faith.

Because faith is the way humans have a relationship with God, it is a way humans strive for the extraordinary. Faith seeks liberation from the dullness of human frailty, from the petty, repressive ugliness that can damage and disfigure human life, and that has often asserted itself in human history as a force of fear, misery, devastation, and decay, a force personified in *The Matrix* by Smith, who poses a threat to both humans and machines. He represents the power of death, the threat of ultimate endings, the loss of everything that is lovable, everything that is beautiful, everything that makes life worth living. Faith is a striving against death and for life, a striving for freedom from the oppressive darkness of the evil, the ugly, the dull—the freedom to create and appreciate beauty, the beauty in ourselves that seeks to express itself the way Sati, in the final scene of the trilogy, expresses her creative spirit in the beauty of the sunrise. Faith is a striving for the freedom to explore, to utilize and enjoy all those things that Jews, Christians, and Muslims identify as gifts from God, things that God has created precisely for our enjoyment.

Jews, Christians, and Muslims all affirm the hope that death is not the end of the story, a message affirmed in *Revolutions* as well when Smith recognizes, much to his chagrin, that everything that has a beginning has an end, even his power, even death itself. Faith is a striving for something beyond death, an expression of the deepest desire of the human heart for life, for peace, for beauty, for love. It affirms that our deepest desires extend beyond a reality in which murder, corruption, exploitation, and injustice are daily news, in which death and decay are commonplace. Faith reaches for a life liberated from the constraints of this mundane reality, a life of extraordinary joy not cut short or compromised. Jews, Christians, and Muslims claim that we share in such a life here and now through faith, through having a dynamic relationship of trust with God.

But What If It's All Bullshit?

Are Jews, Christians, and Muslims right? And what if they're wrong? This is precisely Niobe's worry: "I can't help thinking," she says to Morpheus, "What if you're wrong, what if all this, the prophecy . . . everything, is just bullshit?"

Morpheus's answer is reminiscent of the answer given by the seventeenth-century philosopher Blaise Pascal: "Then tomorrow," Morpheus says, "we may all be dead. But how would that be different from any other day? . . . Death can come for us at any time. Now consider the alternative: What if I am right? What if the prophecy is true? What if tomorrow the war could be over? Isn't that worth fighting for? Isn't that worth dying for?" According to Morpheus, what he and Niobe, Trinity, Neo, and everyone else stand to gain if they're right far outweighs what they stand to lose if they're wrong; it therefore makes better sense for them to believe in the prophecy than not to. Likewise, Pascal reckoned that each of us faces a choice to accept the gift of faith or not. What we stand to gain in accepting it, a life of immeasurable joy, is of infinite value, he said, and therefore outweighs any cost that might be incurred along the way. If, on the other hand, we're wrong, then we're no worse off than anybody else: We die, just like everybody else.

If Jews, Christians, and Muslims are wrong, they stand to lose the same things they would lose if they lacked faith. If the mundane reality we see around us is all there is, if death is the end of the story, then human life is a wash for everyone whether they have faith or not: everyone loses; everyone and everything eventually dies. But if Jews, Christians, and Muslims are right, if faith is what they claim it is, then persons of faith look to gain a lot more than persons without it, for they embark on a journey of joy and discovery that begins the moment they accept God's invitation and that promises never to end. Isn't the promise of such a life, the promise of the freedom, the beauty, the joy, the love we so desperately desire worth fighting for? Isn't it worth the risk we might be wrong? This is how Pascal sought to address someone in Niobe's position, someone afraid to make a "leap" of faith.

But we still haven't answered the original question: Is faith really just foolishness, and are people who claim to have it really just fools? To find an answer we needed to understand more clearly what faith was supposed to be. But now that we know, it's going to be difficult if not impossible to answer the question. The reason is that there is no "neutral" perspective from which we can answer it. If faith is supposed to consist in having a relationship with God, then people with faith and people without it won't be able to evaluate it the same way. Those with faith will claim those without it can't really evaluate it because they don't really know what it is. How could they, the faithful will say, they've never experienced it? Those without faith, on the other hand, will claim there's nothing there to experience, that the claims of the faithful are totally groundless. We reach an impasse, just like Morpheus and Lock.

We haven't been able to answer the original question, but hopefully considering it has been worthwhile. Philosophy, like faith, is a journey, and I hope I've given you some ideas to start a journey of your own.

13

Neo-Orthodoxy: Tales Of The Reluctant Messiah, Or "Your Own Personal Jesus"

BEN WITHERINGTON III

Postmodern life has acquainted us with the manipulation of ideas and images. In such syncretism, like sampling in hip-hop, bits and pieces of ideas are taken from a myriad of sources and all blended or morphed together into a new whole. So it is hardly a surprise that the religious substance of the *Matrix* trilogy is one part Gnosticism, one part Christianity, one part Indian religion, and one part Kung Fu.

Neo himself is a composite or, better said, a distillation of various religious essences from a variety of sources. The cross of Neo's sacrifice in *Revolutions* left no doubt that the Wachowskis intended messianic connections. But what sort of Christ figure is Neo?

While Neo does in some respects resemble Jesus, the religion he proffers has more to do with mere believing in one's own powers than it has to do with being saved from one's sins, and the rescue he offers is rescue from runaway technology and computer programs rather than from specifically human flaws and sins. Liberation in this vision has more to do with liberation from Big Brother than from the enemy or flaws within or from some supernatural evil. *Deus ex machina* has been exchanged for *Deus as machina*, or at least Devil as *machina*.

As Chris Seay and Greg Garrett have pointed out in *The Gospel Reloaded*[1] there is an obvious attempt to associate Neo

---

[1] (Colorado Springs: Pinon, 2003).

with Jesus in various ways in the *Matrix* trilogy. It's not just the resurrection beyond death towards the end of the first movie and then again the hint of his resurrection (or reincarnation?) beyond Neo's death (triumphing through self-sacrifice) at the end of the third. Nor is it just because of the "divine" nature or spirit of Neo. Nor is it even because Morpheus, Neo, and Trinity make up something of a Trinity, with Cypher as a Judas figure, and Bane/Smith as the Devil or a major demon. Seay and Garrett note in addition that when the name Christ is used as a swear word in these movies, it is always used in connection with Neo. They also point out that his name, Thomas A. Anderson, has echoes of the Gospel of John. Thomas as in doubting Thomas, and Anderson (Swedish for Andrew's son) as in son of andros (Greek for man), thus etymologically "son of man."[2]

But this Thomas doubts himself, rather than someone else. Indeed he states clearly that he is "not the One" towards the end of the first movie:

> NEO: I'm not the one, Trinity. The Oracle hit me with that too.
> TRINITY: No. You have to be.
> NEO: Sorry, I'm not. I'm just another guy.

only to prove himself wrong a bit later as he is resurrected and defeats Smith. Even once he realizes he is the One, Neo is plagued with self-doubt. In *Reloaded* Neo worries: "I just wish . . . I wish I knew what I'm supposed to do. That's all. I just wish I knew." Trinity responds, "She's gonna call. Don't worry." Apparently, this messiah needs an Oracle to tell him what to do. Once he ultimately knows what to do in *Revolutions*, Neo still doesn't truly know how it will turn out, whether his mission will succeed or whether he will survive. As he says, "Trinity . . . There's something I have to say. Something you need to understand. I know I'm supposed to go. But beyond that—I don't know . . ." She responds, "I know. You don't think you're coming back. I knew it the moment you said you had to leave. I could see it in your face. Just like you knew the moment you looked at me that I was coming with you."

---

[2] For more detail on the Christian elements of the first film see Gregory Bassham, "The Religion of *The Matrix* and the Problems of Pluralism" in William Irwin ed., *The Matrix and Philosophy: Welcome to the Desert of the Real* (Chicago: Open Court, 2002), pp. 111–125.

Portrait of Neo as the New Man

Near the outset of the first movie Choi calls Neo "my own personal Jesus Christ." Trinity says to him that he is looking for the answer to the question "What is the Matrix?" But in fact the real question turns out to be, "Who will save us from the Matrix?" and the answer is Neo. Like the old canard, "If Jesus is the answer, what is the question?," these movies ask, "If the Matrix is the problem, what is the solution?" Neo is the solution more than he is the Answer (indeed he is seeking the answer), he is the stopgap more than he is the Truth. Yet there are more things messianic in the trilogy than is apparent on a surface examination of the story.

Neo is, of course, a more vulnerable and more fallible son of man than Jesus, one who even falls in love, but then he lives in a far more complex and dark world in which the machines have taken over. Not only does he fall in love, but he is also a self-serving messianic figure when, at the end of *Reloaded*, he chooses to try to save Trinity rather than rescue Zion, when the Architect gives him a choice in the matter.

Since the figure of Jesus is only one source of the portrayal of Neo in the *Matrix* trilogy it is difficult to know how seriously we are to take the echoes of the life of Jesus and also the contrasts. Neo is a profoundly violent person, unlike the historical Jesus. Jesus's cleansing of the temple hardly bears comparison to all the shooting and destruction unleashed by Neo. He is more akin to Christ the warrior of Revelation 19 than to the Jesus of the Gospels. In Revelation 19 Jesus is depicted as a warrior riding a white horse into battle coming to "judge with justice and make war" (19:11). He is dressed in a robe dipped in blood and is followed by the armies of heaven. Out of his mouth comes a sharp sword with which to strike down the nations, and it is said he will rule them with an iron hand. This Jesus "treads the winepress of the fury of the wrath of God" (verse 15). Even here Christ does not conquer by actually fighting, only by speaking judgment on the nations. His Word is the sword that effectively accomplishes what it announces.[3] Clearly Neo does not merely speak judgment but actually fights for justice.

---

[3] Notice how even in the so called battle of Armagedon in Revelation 20:7–10 there is no actual fight, only a raining down of fire from heaven putting an end to the combatants' warlike activities.

It would, however, make for an interesting exercise in comparison to reflect on the huge amount of violence done to Jesus in Mel Gibson's movie *The Passion of the Christ*, and the huge amount of violence Neo both suffers and inflicts in these *Matrix* movies.[4] The theme or motif of violence is an important one in postmodern movies (witness Quentin Tarantino's *Pulp Fiction* and *Kill Bill*), and both Mel Gibson's movie and *The Matrix* movies support the thesis that our culture is so saturated in violence that it will only be affected or moved by a portrayal of Jesus that involves extreme violence. One might object, since most of the fighting is done in the Matrix, that "real" or "physical" violence is not involved, only mental or spiritual battles. But in fact there is a physical battle between Smith and Neo in the third movie. We are not merely to think that it is all mental or spiritual warfare.

If we examine the portrait of Jesus in the Gospels there are certain salient features which characterize Jesus which certainly don't characterize Neo. While there are times that Jesus is ignorant of some things (see Mark 13:32), on the whole Jesus is portrayed as not only in the know, but as a teacher. This can hardly be said of Neo. Near the beginning of the first movie, Neo, the computer hacker, has to be told by Morpheus that he is the One, whom Morpheus has been seeking all his life. He must also rely on the Oracle to learn important things about himself, the Matrix, and the future. While others believe in Neo, they do not follow him really, but Jesus clearly chooses and trains disciples to be his followers. Neo has a singular mission, and while he has allies and companions (Morpheus, Trinity), these are not really his followers.

Jesus on the other hand knows who he is from the outset of his ministry, if not before, as the baptismal scene in Mark 1/Matthew 3/Luke 3 makes clear. He has been told he is the Son of God, and he goes forth to overcome temptation and do ministry in the light of that knowledge. Neo on the other hand keeps correcting people as to whether he is the One. The difference is that Jesus knows who he is and proceeds to help bring in the divine saving reign of God upon the earth by deliberate design

---

[4] See William Irwin, "Gibson's Sublime *Passion*: In Defense of the Violence," in Jorge J.E. Gracia, ed., *Mel Gibson's Passion and Philosophy* (Chicago: Open Court, 2004), pp. 51–61.

and understanding of the divine plan. When Neo accomplishes something marvelous, it is a wonder even to Neo himself. Whoa.

But Neo does not merely need to be informed. He must be transformed to begin to see on his own and to see the Matrix for what it is. There is thus an unpleasant birthing process he has to go through, and instead of a Holy Spirit landing on him gently like a dove, a machine unplugs him from the Matrix. This is more a matter of enlightenment than empowerment. The Matrix, as it turns out, is a computer-generated dream world, which was built to delude and keep humans under control so they in turn could be used as energy sources for the machines. Neo must be reborn, retooled, and retrained.

Jesus is regularly portrayed as a miracle worker in the Gospels, and while Neo's revivification of Trinity through fixing both her Matrix form and her physical form could be said to be a miracle, on the whole Neo's mission is not to heal people, but rather to combat evil, in particular evil rogue programs and the Matrix run amuck. A scene in *Reloaded* has people in Zion come to Neo for healing, but he is not in fact depicted as healing them, though it appears he may have done so. They come to him with gifts as Neo comes into the city of Zion. Though Neo wants to have a tryst with Trinity, she leaves him with the needy. Later in *Reloaded* we see gifts and food items left at Neo's door in gratitude for what he apparently had accomplished by way of help and healing. Yet there is no depiction or emphasis on Neo's powers in this regard, unlike what we find in the depiction of Jesus in all four canonical Gospels.

First Encounters of a Close Kind

One way to figure out who Neo is in these movies is to analyze how he relates to the other major characters. The relationship of Neo to Morpheus is important in this regard. Morpheus is far more than just a friend or ally to Neo; he is very much a mentor. He knows far more than Neo about the Matrix, and informs Neo of his own importance. Morpheus tells Neo, "What you know you can't explain. But you feel it. You've felt it your entire life. That there's something wrong with the world. You don't know what it is but it's there, like a splinter in your mind driving you mad." Morpheus already knows that it is the Matrix, the very virtual environment in which Neo and all others live, that is the problem. Morpheus thus plays the role of the father figure who educates Neo in the first movie. But there is something even more remarkable about Morpheus.

Like the Jesus of Matthew's Gospel, Neo could say to Morpheus: "I thank you Father . . . because you have hidden these things from the wise and learned [read the agents and the Architect], and revealed them to the little children. . . . All things have been committed to me by my Father" (Matthew 11:25–27). In fact as they are about to pull the plug on Morpheus, Tank says: "Morpheus, you're more than a leader to us. You're our father. We'll miss you always." While Neo is the Savior, Morpheus is his spiritual Father.

An equally important dialogue, that reveals something of Neo's identity, takes place in the first movie between Neo and Cypher, the Judas figure. The dialogue begins by Cypher saying that when Neo slipped up behind him, he scared the "bejeezus" out of him. Cypher seeks to plant a seed of doubt in Neo's mind, so he will not believe his press clippings as read to him by Morpheus. Cypher seeks to discredit the idea that Neo is the savior of the world. Cypher suggests that Neo is thinking the same thing as he had been thinking, namely why hadn't he taken the blue pill which led back into the illusory virtual world and blissful ignorance of reality, rather than the red pill which only promises the truth, however unpleasant. If Cypher is Judas, then Neo is the one whom he is trying to lead down the garden path to destruction.

But perhaps the most important first encounter in the first movie is between Neo and the Oracle, who has a placard in her kitchen which says in Latin "Know thyself." She applies it to Neo, in an indirect way. When she asks Neo if he thinks he is the One, he tells her quite honestly he does not know. The key is for Neo to trust and believe in himself and who he really is. Christology is reduced to anthropology, just as in Gnosticism, and Jesus's dictum "Know God and Know the Truth" is reduced to "Know thyself."

In the waiting room at the Oracle's house are various *Wunderkinder*, called potentials, potential messiahs who can bend spoons and levitate blocks. One child who is bending spoons instructs Neo that it's a matter of the mind bending, not the spoon being bent by the mind. But such is the logic one would expect in a purely mental world. In this same scene we realize that Neo is only "Messiah in training" for most of the first movie. As the Oracle says, "You got the gift, but it looks like you are waiting for something."

Neo, unlike Jesus, does not have a messianic image of himself. Indeed he has a hard time believing in himself and his ability to complete his mission. In both the second and the third movies he says repeatedly, "I wish I knew what I was supposed to do" and in *Reloaded* he denies saving the kid from *Animatrix* who is prepared to see him as his Savior. Instead he says "You saved yourself." Such self-doubt and angst is not a characteristic of the Biblical Jesus, and seeing salvation as a human self-help program is more Gnostic in character, or even narcissistic, than like the Good News of Jesus. The Neo-Gospel is more in tune with the cultural flow of our narcissistic postmodern Western culture.

The only Gospel story that tells us anything about what Jesus knew about himself prior to adulthood and his baptism, Luke 2:41–52, tells us that as a child he already had a sense of vocation and mission (he must be about his Father's business), yet ends by telling us Jesus grew in wisdom as he grew in age. This means that he gained knowledge over time about who he was and what God required of him.[5] This is quite different from Morpheus's remark about Neo at the end of the first movie, "He's beginning to believe." We do not find Jesus having some sort of identity crisis or conversion experience where he becomes someone he was not, or would not have viewed himself as before.

The baptism scene in the canonical Gospels seems to be a moment of confirmation of what Jesus has known in part all along. Jesus, in our earliest Gospel, Mark, does not speak about a mission to die for others before the encounter at Caesarea Philippi in Mark 8, which we are apparently meant to think takes place about half way through the ministry period. Once the who question is answered by Peter in regard to Jesus's identity, it is only then, in three straight chapters (Mark 8–10) that Jesus reveals he must suffer many things, be killed, and on the

---

[5] For more on Jesus's self-knowledge as both God and man see Richard Swinburne, *The Resurrection of God Incarnate* (Oxford: Oxford University Press, 2003), pp. 51–54.

third day arise. These sorts of Passion and Resurrection predictions climax in Mark 10:45 when Jesus even says his death will be a ransom for many. Interestingly though, in none of these Passion predictions does Jesus ever mention crucifixion specifically. Perhaps he did not foresee that is how he would meet his untimely end until later. But clearly he expected a sacrificial and atoning death, well before his last trip to Jerusalem. Neo lacks this clear a picture of the coming events in his life. He exhibits less courage all along, since he doesn't know what is coming until it happens.

Marching to Zion Without a Prayer

Neo rescues the city of Zion and its inhabitants by his self-sacrifice in the battle with Smith. But rescues them from what? The city does not go forward into a different kind of life. The citizens do not become "new creatures in Christ." They breathe a sigh of relief, and desire and plan to go back to life as it was before the machines tried to eliminate them. The *Matrix* movies do not end with the new Jerusalem coming down from above and the corporate merger of heaven and earth.

Revolutions ends with a beautiful city scene, but, as Sati tells the Oracle, it's all generated by a computer program. It is ultimately a pleasant illusion. Rather than the lion lying down with the lamb, we simply have a truce in the end. Neo's sacrifice doesn't provide a permanent solution to the human dilemma. His act of redemption has a limited warranty. This brings us to another feature of the trilogy that differs from the Gospel portrait of Jesus and the life of his followers.

Dualism, body/mind or body/spirit, or body/soul dualism is an essential feature of the *Matrix* trilogy. In this regard the films are far more like Platonic and Gnostic speculation than the vision of Jesus and other New Testament figures who look forward to new life by means of a bodily resurrection. It is also in another respect like Gnosticism, namely that the life of the mind and being in the know seems to be what both good and evil essentially are about. Mind games are the essence of the matter, and virtual reality often supplants reality in the *Matrix* trilogy.

Nevertheless, there are certain human qualities of the human figures in the movie, including Neo, that are highlighted and stressed. These qualities involve action and human relationships at their best: faith, hope, and love. As in the Bible, the greatest of these is love. This certainly fits with Jesus's teaching (love God and love others with all one's heart). Yet, by contrast, note that while Link and others have good luck charms or some belief in destiny, none of the central human characters pray.

When the residents of Zion meet in the temple we hear that the opening prayer is being offered by a member of the Council. But in fact the Councilor simply speaks to the congregation, not God, and then he introduces Morpheus who gives a brief sermon. There is indeed a profound lack of talking to God in these movies, even when the protagonists are in dire straits.

While the light of revelation occasionally breaks through by means of the Oracle (who in the end is just another program), there is no personal relationship with a God who transcends the Matrix, and God is not called upon to intervene. Humans, even if messianic like Neo, are still humans. Indeed, we are informed that there have been five or six previous Neo's. Neo is just the latest Marvel or DC action figure here to save the day.

Instead of stressing Neo's capacity to heal and redeem *Reloaded* contents itself with portraying him as Superman flying around. The exclusive claims made for Jesus in the New Testament, and the highlighting of his divinity distinguish the portraits of Jesus from the portrait of Neo in these movies. Neo is a man with juice or current running through him, who has some powers of flight, and strength, and prescience. The scene that most clearly reveals Neo's spiritual sight is paradoxically the scene in which he is physically blinded, and yet continues to be able to see auras of his enemy, and so is able to continue to do battle. But such spiritual sight does not make Neo part of a Trinitarian divine being. Rather he is in love with Trinity who, like Neo, is all too human.

At the end of *Revolutions* we have a nice pastoral scene involving the Oracle and Sati—two of the more pleasant programs. Sati asks whether Neo will be seen again. The Oracle can only say "I suspect so." This is a far cry from stories about resurrection appearances of Jesus. Jesus has been seen again by many real humans in the real Gospel. The "Neo"-orthodox can only hope to see their Savior figure again.

The *Matrix* movies tap into a culture whose spiritual birth certificate is from Missouri. Such postmodern people say "Show me." Characters believe in Neo largely because of what they have seen him do, not because of what he promised to do in the future. Those who dwell in Zion hope only for truce on earth, not truth on earth. No one in these movies would be caught dead saying "Now faith is the assurance of things hoped for, the conviction of things not seen." It is true that there is one possible exception to this conclusion—Morpheus, who seems to believe from the outset, and before there is any concrete evidence that Neo is the one. But then Morpheus is not just another human being nor is he Neo's disciple. Rather he is that unique father figure in the movie who mentors Neo. His belief in Neo is rather like God the Father's belief in Jesus in the Gospel of John, not like the faith of ordinary mortals in that Gospel.

What the *Matrix* movies offer is a faith not grounded in historical realities but in virtual realities, a believable message for the computer generation which has indeed been effectively sucked into the matrix of the Internet, a generation which has more hope in changing the virtual world through better programs than the real world either by being better people, or by trusting in the one who was truly the New Man, the eschatological Adam-Jesus. To put the matter bluntly, Jesus not only is definitely said to have a future in the Gospels, and to be returning later to earth; the risen Jesus, unlike Neo, promises to be with his followers always even in the interim (Matthew 28). As for Neo, while one may suspect he will reappear, he does not become an object of a living hope, or the basis of a living relationship, nor the one about whom it can eventually be said: "The kingdoms of this world have become the kingdoms of God and of his Christ."

Scene 4

We're Not Living
in Zion: Social
and Political Issues
in *The Matrix*

14

Race Matters in *The Matrix*: Is Morpheus Black? Is Race Real?

JORGE J.E. GRACIA and WILLIAM IRWIN

Not a word is said about race in *The Matrix* trilogy, but much is shown. The principal bad guys Smith, the Architect, and the Merovingian are all white. Members of the oppressive power structure are all white: the Agents, the Trainman, the cops, the security guards, Anderson's boss. Hell, the evil twins are albinos! Many, though not quite all, of the good guys are black or Asian: Morpheus, Tank, the Oracle, Seraph, Niobe, the Keymaker, and Mifune, for example. Indeed, blacks and Asians make up a far higher percentage of the population in Zion than they do in 1999 America.[1] Why? Are minorities more sensitive to injustice, making them less likely to be deceived by the Matrix and more likely to be among the one percent who do not accept the program? It would be easy enough to ignore the issues, but "race matters," as Councilor West might say. The Councilor was, of course, played by the author of *Race Matters*, Cornel West, the professor who got dissed by the president of Harvard for his hip-hop endeavor. Now he's "keepin' it real" at Princeton.[2]

Race raises at least three philosophical questions in the context of *The Matrix*. How can we tell what race someone is? Is race real? What should we do about race?

---

[1] 'Though the world of Zion does not just represent America. Still, the blacks in Zion seem to be African Americans.

[2] Stay tuned for Derrick Darby and Tommie Shelby eds., *Hip Hop and Philosophy* (Open Court, forthcoming).

Can We Know It When We See It?

In the first movie, Morpheus tells Smith, "You all look the same to me." Of course he is referring to Agents, but the irony of a black man saying this to a white man is not lost on us. In truth, not only do members of the same race not all look alike, we often can't even tell what race someone belongs to. In the beginning of the first film Choi tells Neo, who has just had a bizarre interaction with his computer, "You look whiter than usual." Neo really does look pale when we hear this, but Keanu Reeves, who plays Neo, is in fact half Asian (as his father is part Hawaiian and part Chinese). When you reflect on the fact that Neo/Keanu is half Asian, doesn't his skin have a yellow tinge to it? Doesn't his hair take on the qualities of typical Asian hair?

Lenny Kravitz, the great black hope for rock and roll, is actually half white—his father is Jewish. What about Morpheus? He doesn't look all that black next to Link. It probably never occurred to you to wonder whether he was really black, but maybe he's not, at least not completely. Indeed, the story goes that a leader of the black community, who shall remain nameless, recently had a genetic test done to learn about his ancestry. He found the results devastating: half of his ancestors were European. The fact is that a large proportion of American "whites" have African ancestry, and a large proportion of American "blacks" have European ancestry. So how can we tell who's what?

This question is explored in epistemology, the branch of philosophy concerned with the nature of knowledge. Maybe there are definite features we can look for, such as skin color, in coming to know what race someone belongs to. But are these features independent of or dependent on what people think? Is dark skin an objective quality, independent of how the skin appears to me? Don't thoughts about skin color change from person to person? There is plenty of evidence that people have different views with respect to how a particular feature is interpreted.

Consider our experiences. Those Americans who know that Jorge is Cuban tend to think of him as dark. But someone who does not know, when first told he is Cuban, often reacts by saying that Jorge does not look Cuban, because he is not dark. An avid Yankees' fan as a boy, Bill could not believe that Reggie Jackson was black. Mickey Rivers and Willie Randolph were black. How could Jackson be black?

So where is the color, in the skin or in the mind? And where is the race, in the body or in the psyche? Add to this that the features associated with particular races change from place to place. Color, of course, is most pervasive, but other features count also in places, such as frizzy hair, and body shape, particularly of the nose, lips, and buttocks, to name just a few. Yet, these features cut across all racial lines. Proof: Many people considered white in Cuba are taken as black in the U.S., and many people taken as black in the U.S. are considered white in Cuba.

Steve Martin's character, Navin, believes he was "born a poor black child in the deep South." When his family finally reveals to him that he was adopted, he replies in horror, "you mean I'm gonna stay this color?" Maybe he wasn't such a "Jerk" after all. Just looking at the way "the code" is expressed, you can't necessarily tell if someone is black or white. There are plenty of recorded cases of "blacks" who have "white" skin, red hair, and blue eyes.

Is Race Real?

Metaphysics is the branch of philosophy concerned with the nature of reality. To better address the epistemological question of how can we know what race someone belongs to, we may first have to address the metaphysical question, "Is race real?" Why does the spoon bend? Because there is no spoon. It is only the mind that bends. Could it be that there is no race, but only a mind that bends reality? Or, could it be that "your mind makes it real"?

If we can't always tell with the naked eye what race someone belongs to, maybe a microscope would help. Maybe the melanin and pigment have an underlying "code" that will allow us to put people into racial categories. After all, we can generally do this with sex. Men and women are biologically different. As it turns out, though, science and its microscopes can't help metaphysics here. There is no clear genetic difference between races. Genetic studies suggest that all human beings descend from the same mother and that the number of characteristics common to humans is extraordinary; we are fundamentally the same biologically.[3] In fact, if DNA were the only "code" to con-

---

[3] Masatoshi Nei and A.K. Roychoudhury, "Genetic Relationship and Evolution

sider, we might well come to the conclusion that there is no such thing as race.

So what is a race? As the famous black philosopher W.E.B. Du Bois suggested at the beginning of the twentieth century, a race is a group of individual persons organized as a family. The bases of its unity, however, are different from those of other kinds of families. They consist in a descent link and a set of persceptible and genetically transmittable physical features, selected from a socially constructed list, generally associated with the race. Such features may include skin color, hair texture, and nose shape.

For Morpheus to be "black," he must be dark skinned, or have curly hair, or a flat broad nose. It is not necessary that Morpheus have all the features generally associated with the black race, but he must have some. If he has some of them and is related by descent to other members of the black race, then Morpheus is black.

Having a feature associated with a certain race does not automatically make a person a member of the race or serve effectively to identify the person as such. For example, Rama-Kandra is nearly as dark as Morpheus. But Indians are not generally regarded as "black" and they do not consider themselves to be "black." People from southern Italy are frequently as dark, and have some features that satisfy the non-descent conditions of membership in the "black" race. Yet, because they do not satisfy the descent condition, no one thinks of them as "black." Of course, there will be cases in which membership is disputed, and indeed with reason, but in the majority of cases membership will not be disputed or be seriously disputable.

What Should We Do with and about Race?

Ethics is the branch of philosophy that asks: What should I do? So what should we do about race? One common answer these days is that we should forget it. There is nothing biological that justifies the notion of different human races, and so we should just drop the concept. Indeed, many of those who make this

---

of Human Races," *Evolutionary Biology* 14 (1982), pp. 1–59 and Paul Hoffman, "The Science of Race," *Discover* 15 (November 1994), p. 4.

claim argue that race is a social construct, and as such can, and because of its pernicious effects should, be eliminated.[4]

Yet, whatever its biological or metaphysical status, clearly race is a social reality. Like the Matrix, we are immersed in it, whether we know it or not, and it affects many things we do and think. As Try Duster says, "It's there. It's often buried. But I assure you, it's alive."[5] So, unless we play the ostrich game, we need racial categories, for racial categories allow us to understand certain social realities that would otherwise escape us.[6] Racial concepts allow us to grasp aspects of human experience that would otherwise be missed, in part because the conceptual frameworks we use are either too broad or too narrow. A racial concept is a unique window through which we can look at a section of human history and social reality. But like any frame, it reveals something by excluding something else. The use of racial concepts and terms, then, uncovers something unique by simultaneously narrowing and widening our perspective.

But this is not all. The paradox of race is that it appears to be socially constructed, and perhaps even invented, and yet it is real insofar as it has had and continues to have enormous historical and social effects.[7] The mind makes it real in this sense. Much in the history of African slavery cannot be explained without reference to race. The American Civil War cannot be adequately grasped without it; and the present condition of many members of American society, or other societies for that matter, cannot be understood without recourse to it.

The Matrix of Race

Race has been the source of much oppression and abuse. To correct this requires not only that we refer to race, but also that

---

[4] K. Anthony Appiah, "The Uncompleted Argument: Du Bois and the Illusion of Race," *Critical Inquiry* 12 (1985), pp. 21–37; and L.L. Cavalli-Sforza, *et al.,* *The History and Geography of Human Genes* (Princeton: Princeton University Press, 1994).

[5] Quoted in Sheryl Gay Stolberg, "Shouldn't a Pill Be Color Blind?" *The New York Times*, Section 4 (2001), p. 3.

[6] Frantz Fanon, "The Lived Experience of the Black," in Robert Bemasconi, ed., *Race* (Oxford: Blackwell, 2001), pp. 184–202.

[7] Michael Omi and Howard Winant, *Racial Formation in the United States: From the 1960s to the 1990s*, Second edition (New York: Routledge, 1994), p. 55.

we have an appropriate understanding of it. Without a concept of race, we cannot fight the ghosts that populate our social consciousness or overturn the oppressive, racist structures that are embedded in our social institutions. Without an understanding of race—just like awareness of the Matrix—we cannot set right much that is wrong in our society.[8] Consciousness of race is a condition of liberation from racial oppression.[9] Of course, no wrong can be set right with another wrong. So we need an appropriate and adequate understanding of race to understand the root of much evil and conflict in society. And this is where philosophy can help.

In the first film Trinity informs Neo that, "The Matrix cannot tell you who you are." We might add that your race cannot tell you who you are. Race, like gender, can be a trap that "has you," "a prison for your mind." We become imprisoned by our own acceptance of the suppositions and expectations placed on us by others because of our race. Although race matters in dealing with social reality, race can also be a trap.

The Matrix of race is a structure that has replicated like a virus. It is an idea born not of metaphysical or biological necessity, but largely of fear and ignorance. Worse, those who are victimized by racial prejudice are commonly complicit in their own caging. Let's focus on blacks since their racial trap is currently the most malignant. Like a person plugged into the Matrix, who seemingly resists the choice to wake up and fights to stay dependent on the system, some blacks aid their oppressors. Young black men who speak English properly and pursue education are sometimes accused by their peers of "acting white." They may be accused of not really being black, of instead being an Oreo, black on the outside but white on the inside. As long as this mentality remains, the Matrix of race will have these men.

Remember, the Architect of the Matrix is a silver-back white male. Like the Architect, the people who benefit most from black youth's complicity in its own imprisonment are not black. So why help them? There are too many African American men going to jail, not enough to Yale; too many caught in the Matrix

---

[8] Linda M. Alcoff, "Toward a Phenomenology of Racial Enbodiment," in Bemasconi, ed., *Race*, pp. 267–283; and Lucius T. Outlaw, Jr., *On Race and Philosophy* (New York: Routledge, 1996), p. 157.

[9] Jean-Paul Sartre, "Black Orpheus," in Bemasconi, ed., *Race*, p. 118.

of the state pen and exploited on the field at Penn State. Literacy and education, as Fredrick Douglass taught, are the keys to unlock the cage. The too cool attitude and the "acting white" accusations simply make African Americans unwitting collaborators in their own imprisonment. Well-meaning whites who would balk at the idea that they are prejudiced are also nonetheless often unwittingly complicit, guilty of the soft bigotry of low expectations. Consider the person who remarks that "Colin Powell speaks so well." The implication is "for a black man" or "and you wouldn't expect it from a black man."

Sports and entertainment sometimes seem the only way out of poverty for blacks, but this is another trap, another Matrix. Not everyone can be Michael Jordan or Puff Daddy. And how much good do these stars really do? How many blacks did Michael Jordan and the Bulls typically play before at a home game in Chicago? Does buying a pair of Air Jordans do anything to help break out of bondage? Isn't Bill Cosby closer to the truth in suggesting that expensive sneakers keep blacks in chains? Far more young black men and women could become doctors, lawyers, teachers, leaders, and role models. Michael Jordan, like Oprah, could endorse a book instead of sneakers and fast food.

Is there an alternative? Sex can be the great equalizer. Race doesn't matter when you're aroused. Why else would segregationist Strom Thurmond have a child with his family's black domestic servant? And what red-blooded white male would mind making it with Niobe?[10] The (biracial) nurse from the *Curb Your Enthusiasm* episode "The Surrogate," suggests, "But if we all keep fucking each other, then we're gonna be the same race sooner or later, anyway." Larry David responds, crossing his fingers, **"Let's pray for that!"** "I do!" says the nurse. This exchange may be funny, but its insight is hardly a solution in the short run.

What wisdom does the *Matrix* trilogy offer? By all appearances there is a racial harmony in Zion.[11] But when one prejudice is overcome we often see it replaced by another. Without race you cannot have racism, but you can still have discrimina-

---

[10] Of course sexism remains a problem in society. A white woman who finds Morpheus/Laurence Fishburne sexually attractive will not as easily find social validation for her feelings.

[11] But see "Matriculated" from the *Animatrix* which indicates a kind of racist repulsion toward becoming intimate with a machine in virtual reality.

tion of others kinds. We might expect some friction between the free-born of Zion and the pod-born of the Matrix, but aside from Mifune's passing putdown of the kid as "a pod-born pencil-neck," there is none. So what's the secret of Zion's harmony? Is it a common enemy? The scarce few times the word "race" is used at all in the *Matrix* trilogy it is used to refer to the "human race" and the "race of machines." Differences among humans seem to matter not at all. Do we really need to wait for Artificial Intelligence to take over the world and enslave us? Can't we just get past the differences now? "Can't we all just get along?"[12]

---

[12] Thanks to all those who provided helpful feedback and criticism including Greg Bassham, Joe Kraus, Jim Lawler, Megan Lloyd, and Abby Myers.

15

Pissin' Metal: Columbine, Malvo, and the Matrix of Violence

HENRY NARDONE and GREGORY BASSHAM

The *Matrix* films are whup-ass, shoot-'em-up action films, but so are *Die Hard*, *Blackhawk Down*, and a ton of other movies nobody picks on. So why do the *Matrix* films get singled out so often by critics of media violence? Are they really any different from any number of other big-budget, heavy-caliber flicks anybody could name?

Actually, yeah, they are different.

Why Don't You Sample This Instead?

Like Paris Hilton's dates, violent films come in many varieties, from the mostly antiseptic techno-violence of *Star Wars*, to the graphic sadism of *The Passion*, to the endless-ammo-belt fantasy of *Rambo*, to the gruesome horror-junkie violence of *Friday the 13th*, to the blood-splattered, shell-shocked realism of *Saving Private Ryan*. Two things are different about the violence in the *Matrix* trilogy: its "coolness" and its "funness."

From the opening scene of *The Matrix* we know we're in for some serious coolness when a hot babe dressed in sleek, black leather (Trinity) does some serious ass-kicking wearing some seriously cool shades. And the coolness quotient just builds from there. The clothes, the weapons, the high-speed kung-fu fighting, the slow-motion "bullet time," the impossible acrobatics, the slowly ejecting cartridges, the gadgets, the memorable one-liners ("Dodge this"), the eclectic New Age spiritualism and "deep" philosophical conundrums: all cutting-edge cool. Clearly, the *Matrix* films glamorize violence in a way that very few other films have.

Moreover, much of the violence in the *Matrix* movies is also *damn fun*. All the films have a definite video-game feel to them. What gamer wouldn't love to be dodging squiddies, steering through a supply line, hauling ass on a motorcycle down the wrong side of a freeway, or pissin' metal from a belt-fed bio-mechanical APU? And the best part is, the creatures you're blowing away are either soulless machines, bad guys, or evil computer programs,[1] so it's all good, clean guiltless fun.

Consider the scene from *Revolutions* in which Trinity, Morpheus, and Seraph (motto: "You do not truly know someone until you fight them") fight their way into the Merovingian's Hel Club. Heavily armed and oh-so-stylishly dressed, the multicultural trio is looking good as they confront some of the Merovingian's henchmen in the Club garage:

> Q-BALL GANG MEMBER #1: You've got to be kidding.
> Q-BALL GANG MEMBER #2: Holy shit, it's Wingless.
> Q-BALL GANG MEMBER #1: I get it. You must be ready to die.
> SERAPH: I need to speak to him.
> Q-BALL GANG MEMBER #1: The only way you're getting through this door is over my big dead ass.
> SERAPH: So be it.

And so it is, as the stylish trio proceed to kick the crap out of the goons and then step over their big dead asses into the garage elevator. When they get off the elevator, there's another burly brawl, this time with some serious gun-play and cool acrobatics. At last the trio fights their way into the club itself and are escorted to the equally stylish and cool Merovingian (Motto: "American teenie boppers love it when I curse in French"). He offers them a deal—Neo in exchange for the eyes of the Oracle—and then goes off on his usual spiel about universal causality. Trinity (speaking for audiences everywhere) says, "I don't have time for this shit," and there's more ass-kicking and gun play. Finally, Trinity grabs a pistol and points it at the Merovingian's forehead:

---

[1] Never mind the innocent cops and security guards who die in the real world when their cyber selves bite it in the Matrix.

TRINITY: You want to make a deal, how about this? You give me Neo, or we all die, right here, right now.
MEROVINGIAN: Interesting deal. You are really ready to die for this man?
TRINITY: [cocks gun] Believe it.
PERSEPHONE: She'll do it. If she has to, she'll kill every one of us. She's in love. . . .
TRINITY: Time's up. What's it going to be, Merv?

It's all there. The glamour. The stylishness. The romance. The adolescent vulgarity and clever repartee. The very cool violence.

It's this potent linkage of violence with fun and coolness that makes the *Matrix* films a prime target of media-violence critics. Do they have a point, or are they shooting blanks?

Guns, Lots of Guns

The United States has one of the highest levels of violent crime in the developed world, and its citizens are exposed to extremely high levels of media violence. Estimates are that by age eighteen an average American has witnessed 200,000 acts of violence on television, including 16,000 murders. And the problem, of course, isn't limited to TV: video games, music lyrics, and the Internet are also becoming increasingly more violent. It's natural to wonder whether there's a connection. Does media violence contribute to real-world violence? If so, how should we respond to it?

The research findings are surprisingly clear. Hundreds of studies have been done on the effects of media violence, and virtually all have found a link with increased aggressive behavior. So clear is this emerging consensus that in 2000 the American Medical Association, the American Academy of Pediatrics, the American Psychological Association, and the American Academy of Child and Adolescent Psychiatry issued a rare joint report warning that the anti-social effects of media violence are "measurable and long lasting" and that "prolonged viewing of media violence can lead to emotional desensitization toward violence in real life."[2]

---

[2] Stanley J. Baran, *Introduction to Mass Communication*, third edition (New York: McGraw-Hill, 2004), p. 444. Critics often claim that media violence can't

How exactly does media violence contribute to real-world violence? Researchers point to four primary effects:

First, people with heavy exposure to media violence tend to be more fearful, pessimistic, and suspicious. Seeing increasing amounts of violence and corruption in the media, they assume (often wrongly) that society itself must be getting more dangerous and corrupt. Though they may actually live in safe, friendly neighborhoods, they imagine that they're living in gloomy, crime-ridden Gotham Cities.

Second, media violence can cause reduced sensitivity to real-life violence, a loss of empathy or "compassion fatigue" in which violence and the suffering it can cause no longer evoke a strong emotional response. Like the Roman citizens who could look calmly on the savageries of war because death and gore was their daily fare in the Coliseum, we can become numb to the real physical and psychic costs of violence. Brought up on a steady diet of nobody-gets-hurt electronic violence, real-life violence increasingly comes to be seen as "no big deal."

Third, media violence can produce an appetite for more violence. Like the junkie who needs ever more potent doses to get him high, or the smut addict who finds *Playboy* lame and tame after sampling the higher-octane fare of the Internet, violence can become an appetite that feeds on itself. Nearly forty years ago, many Americans were shocked by the bloody shootouts in the film *Bonnie and Clyde* (1967). Today the movie might not even receive a PG-13 rating. Indeed, many criminologists speak of a growing "video violence" generation gap today. As many older academics discovered when they spoke to students about Mel Gibson's film, *The Passion of the Christ*, what shocks one generation may leave another unmoved.

---

be a major cause of real-world violence because many countries have nearly as much exposure to media violence as Americans do but have far lower rates of violent crime. This is like arguing that high-fat diets can't be a major cause of heart disease because the French, who typically have high-fat diets, have low rates of heart disease. What the argument ignores is that the French may do things (such as drink lots of red wine) that counteract the effects of eating high-fat foods. The argument does not show that high-fat diets are not a major contributing cause of heart disease *for Americans*. A similar point can be made about media violence. People in Japan, for instance, may be exposed to high levels of media violence, but there may be cultural factors (such as having no guns) that neutralize many of the anti-social effects of this violence.

What things are over the edge for today's students that will seem ho-hum to tomorrow's?

This ratcheting effect of violence is evident in the *Matrix* films themselves. The violence in the first film, while intense, was not particularly graphic or over-the-top. Except for the "guns, lots of guns" scene in which Neo and Trinity rescue Morpheus, most of the violence involved martial arts combat and simple (if abundant) firearms. In *Reloaded* the violence ramps up a notch. Semis explode in head-on crashes, Neo carves up a roomful of the Merovingian's henchmen with ancient weapons and whups multiple Smiths in a "burly brawl," albino shape-shifting twins wield razor weapons like 9/11 terrorists, and Trinity is shot in a spectacular scene in which she and an Agent are falling from a building. By *Revolutions*, the violence builds to a kind of grand fireworks finale. Heads are knocked off with crowbars, Neo is blinded by hot plasma, Trinity is skewered by cables, the skies are filled with calamari, APU's spurt rivers of hot lead, many of the leading characters are killed, and Neo and Smith—now Supermen[3]—engage in a final climactic battle (the "super burly brawl") in, over, and under the now-darkened, Smith-controlled City. It's what viewers expect. Bigger, louder, faster, bloodier.

The fourth effect of media violence is an increase in aggressive behavior. According to expert consensus, heavy exposure to media violence has both short-term and long-term effects on real-world crime and violence.[4] In one leading study, Al Austin and Leonard Eron tracked 835 third graders in Hudson, New York from 1960 to 1993. They found that those who had been heavy consumers of TV violence as children were consistently more aggressive from childhood to middle age. They logged more arrests and convictions, were more aggressive in their homes, and had more aggressive children. Numerous studies have found a similar effect with sexual violence in pornography. As Cass Sunstein notes,

---

[3] Indeed, the whole scene is strongly reminiscent of scenes in *Superman II*, where Superman battles the three equally powerful Kryptonians: General Zod, Ursa, and Non.

[4] Brad J. Bushman and Craig A. Anderson, "Media Violence and the American Public: Scientific Facts versus Media Misinformation," *American Psychologist*, Volume 56 (June–July 2001), pp. 477–489.

Some laboratory studies show a reduced sensitivity to sexual violence on the part of men who have been exposed to pornography. Men questioned after such exposure seem more prepared to accept rape and other forms of violence against women, to believe that women derive pleasure from violence, to associate sex with violence; they also report a greater likelihood of committing rape themselves.[5]

This is the cultural and research backdrop critics of media violence have in mind when they criticize violent films, and particularly highly popular movies like the *Matrix* trilogy, which glamorize violence and can achieve iconic status for a whole generation of young movie-goers.[6] Indeed, as we see in the next section, the *Matrix* films can have an exceptionally powerful effect on people's lives, some of whom, unfortunately, are not very stable.

Tales of Whoa: The Matrix Defense?

Since 1999, when the first *Matrix* film was released, several criminal defendants have offered a novel plea: not guilty by reason of *The Matrix*. Their claim: At the time they committed their crimes they were so obsessed with *The Matrix* that they were either legally insane or not fully responsible for their conduct.

Lee Boyd Malvo, the eighteen-year-old shooter in the 2002 Washington, D.C.-area sniper killings, used this plea (along with other exculpatory claims) to successfully avoid the death penalty

---

[5] Cass R. Sunstein, "Pornography and the First Amendment," *Duke Law Journal* (1986), p. 598.

[6] Not all depictions of violence in the media or in great literature glamorize violence. Like glamorized or pornographic displays of sex or death, depersonalized violence cuts violence off from its normal connections with other important emotions, such as the sorrow and grief that accompany real loss and injury to human life. Violence properly portrayed has the power to teach empathy and compassion and to show the consequent damage of injury or death to human life, even when it may be justified. Think, for example, of the rape and shotgun killing scenes in the film *Dead Man Walking*, as well as the film's concluding footage of the state-sanctioned lethal injection of one of the murderers. These acts of violence are shocking but instructive: rather than glamorize violence they reveal its tragic consequences and confirm the respect and dignity that should be accorded to human life.

(he was sentenced instead to life in prison without the possibility of parole).

In February 2003 nineteen-year-old Josh Cooke, of Oakton, Virginia, who played violent video games six hours a day and claimed he sometimes believed he lived inside the Matrix, used a twelve-gauge shotgun to shoot his parents. A noted expert on media violence testified at his trial about the effects of violent movies on susceptible individuals, and Cooke received the relatively lenient sentence of forty years in prison.

In May 2000, Vadim Mieseges, a twenty-seven-year-old Swiss exchange student, confessed to dismembering his landlady and depositing her torso in a dumpster in San Francisco's Golden Gate Park. He did it, he said, because she was emitting "evil vibes" and he was afraid of being "sucked into the Matrix." He successfully pled not guilty by reason of insanity.[7]

Eric Harris and Dylan Klebold, who committed the Columbine massacre only weeks after the *Matrix* was released, were avid *Matrix* fans and were known for wearing long black trench coats similar to the one Neo wears in the films.

In July 2003, eighteen-year-old Matthew Lovett was arrested before he and his two teenaged accomplices could follow through with their plan to kill three high school "enemies," then engage in random killing in their hometown of Oaklyn, New Jersey. When arrested after a foiled carjacking, the teens were found to have "rifles and shotguns strapped to their back and handguns tucked into their waistbands, and carried 3-foot-long swords, knives, and more than 2,000 rounds of ammunition."[8] Fond of calling himself Neo, Lovett, after watching *The Matrix Reloaded*, wrote in his diary, "I have a whole new reason to do this now."[9]

"Bull*merd*!" we hear Matrix bloggers everywhere saying. "*The Matrix* doesn't kill people, people kill people!" Warner Brothers certainly would agree. In May 2003 they issued a press release denying any connection between the movie and any

---

[7] Mark Schone, "The Matrix Defense," www.boston.com/news/globe/ideas/articles/20003/11/09/the_matrix_defense.

[8] "Police: Arrests Foil Teens' Killing Spree Plot," www.cnn.com/2003/US/Northeast/ 07/07/teen.arrested

[9] Schone, "The Matrix Defense."

killings, and saying "any attempt to link these crimes with a motion picture . . . is disturbing and irresponsible."[10]

But Warner Brothers, wethinks, doth protest too much. There clearly is a connection, and it's the Merovingian's favorite: "Causality. Action. Reaction. Cause and effect." It's what philosophers call "but-for" causality. But for the sun's energy, there would be no life on earth. But for the 9/11 terrorist attacks, the United States would not have invaded Afghanistan and Iraq. But for *The Matrix*, it's unlikely that at least some of these crimes would have been committed. This doesn't justify or excuse the conduct (so calm down, bloggers), but it does raise two interesting questions: Should those who can show that they have been injured by film-inspired violence be able to sue filmmakers to recover damages? Do those responsible for producing such films—and the *Matrix* trilogy in particular—bear any moral responsibility for the crimes of those disturbed individuals who may be inspired by the films to act violently?

Suing Violent Filmmakers?

Americans love to sue, so it probably won't surprise you that many lawsuits have been filed against makers of violent films and video games. Families of the victims of the Columbine massacre sued creators and publishers of the video game *Doom*. Parents of a girl who committed suicide sued makers of the *Dungeons and Dragons* game. Lawsuits have also been filed by victims' families against the video games *Grand Theft Auto* and *Mortal Kombat*, as well as against violent films such as *Natural Born Killers* and *The Basketball Diaries*. The result? The film and video game makers always win.

The legal basis for these court decisions was stated succinctly by the Sixth Circuit Court of Appeals in *James v. Meow Media, Inc.*[11] The case involved a fourteen-year-old boy, Michael Carneal, who on December 1st, 1997 walked into the lobby of a Padukah, Kentucky, high school and shot several students, killing three and wounding five. The victims' families sued a host of video game makers, movie production companies, and

---

[10] *Ibid.*

[11] 300 F.3d 683 (6th Cir. 2002). Available online at http://caselaw.lp.findlaw. com/cgi-bin/getcase.pl?court=6th&navby=case&no=02a0270p.

Internet Web sites, claiming that the violent media Carneal was exposed to "desensitized" him to violence and "caused" him to commit the shootings. The suit alleged that these media producers were negligent in permitting such potentially harmful material to be distributed to impressionable youths like Carneal.

In order to win, the Court said, the victims' families had to prove that it was "reasonably foreseeable" that the media in question might inspire some impressionable youths—not necessarily Carneal himself—to commit crimes of this nature.

The court noted, however, that "forseeability" is a thorny issue in the law. Often the relevant issue isn't whether an event is actually foreseeable but whether as a matter of "public policy" courts should *treat* it as foreseeable. And this is a case, the Court ruled, where there are clear public policy reasons for declaring that crimes like Carneal's are not sufficiently foreseeable to hold producers of violent media liable for them.[12]

What sorts of public policy reasons? The Court mentions several but the two most important are (1) the law's general emphasis on personal responsibility for criminal acts and (2) constitutional guarantees of freedom of speech.

Both reasons are—no sick pun intended—right on target. As a general matter, Americans are highly suspicious of "twinkie defenses" that pass the buck of personal accountability. Sadly, there are so many impressionable, disturbed individuals in our society that almost any book, film, or video game is "reasonably foreseeable" to provoke at least some of them to commit acts of violence. (Think of the Stay Puft Marshmallow Man in *Ghostbusters*.) To hold authors and media producers liable for such acts seems fundamentally unfair and would clearly have a chilling effect on the arts. Artistic decisions would increasingly be made by lawyers, not by the artists themselves.

Equally important is the First Amendment issue of free speech. Whatever you may think about the current spate of lawsuits against tobacco companies, gun manufacturers, and now

---

[12] The legal issues presented in the case are more complicated than our brief summary suggests. Other important issues raised by the case include whether the violent media was a "proximate cause" of Carneal's actions (the court didn't rule on the issue but was clearly skeptical of such a claim) and whether the media were "defective products" under Kentucky product liability law (the court ruled that they weren't).

even fast food franchises, constitutionally speaking, lawsuits against makers of violent movies are in a whole different ball-game. Freedom of artistic expression has long been regarded by courts as a core First Amendment value. However we may sympathize with the victims of movie-inspired violence, there is no way courts will, or should, permit private lawsuits from a few individuals to determine the sorts of movie entertainment the rest of us may enjoy.

The Issue of Moral Responsibility

A harder question is whether filmmakers like the Wachowski brothers, who wrote and directed the *Matrix* films, bear any moral responsibility for the violent acts their films inspired. We've seen that the *Matrix* films glamorize violence—make it seem "cool" and "fun"—to a degree that few other films have. Did the makers of the films know, or have reason to know, that some disturbed or impressionable individuals would become so obsessed with the films that they would be moved to act out their violent fantasies? If so, do they share any measure of responsibility for these individuals' crimes?

First, did the Wachowski brothers know? Almost surely they did. Columbine, the Mieseges murder, and several other well-publicized *Matrix*-inspired killings occurred before the release of the second and third films. Indeed, the publicity surrounding these events is what prompted Warner Brothers' disavowal of responsibility in May 2003. Even if the Wachowski brothers didn't know, they should have known. The first *Matrix* was carefully crafted to appeal to disaffected, alienated youth. The clothes, the music, the video game-quality of the violence, the sexy rebel-with-a-cause heroes and heroines, the vulgarity, the quest for freedom and self-awareness, the suspicion of authority structures—all were clearly intended to appeal to a certain type of youth. Quite predictably, not a few of these youths became obsessed with the film.

Let's assume, then, that the Wachowski brothers should have known that their films might well incite a few disturbed individuals to violence. Does this show that they bear some responsibility for these violent acts? Not necessarily, because they might have been justified in making the films even if they knew it would have some tragic effects.

We live in a morally complicated world, a world in which good actions often have predictable but unintended bad consequences. Companies manufacture glues, knowing that some foolish souls will use them to get high. Judges send felons to prison, knowing that often their innocent families will suffer. Or consider this all-too-topical example: You're holding fifty notorious terrorists in your jail. Their terrorist compatriots threaten to execute a hostage unless you release the terrorists. You know that if you release the terrorists, many innocent people will die. You refuse, and the hostage is executed. You have, in some sense, "caused" something bad to happen. If you had acted differently, the hostage would be alive. But are you to blame? No. *The terrorists are to blame.* The death of the hostage was a foreseen but unintended effect of a morally justified action. You did the right thing, despite the tragic unintended death of the hostage.

How should we think about moral dilemmas like these? When is it ethical to do something that we know will have bad unintended side effects?

One of the best and most systematic attempts to think through issues like this is the doctrine of "double effect." Developed in the Middle Ages and still widely employed by Catholic ethicists today, the theory offers several criteria for evaluating the ethics of actions that have both good and bad effects. For our purposes, the two most relevant criteria are (1) that the act itself must not be intrinsically wrong (that is, wrong by its very nature, regardless of one's motivations or justifications), and (2) that the action be for a proportionately good end.

Some ethicists (for instance, utilitarians and moral relativists) would deny that there are any intrinsically wrong acts, but such a view is not widely shared. (Most of us would agree, for example, that torturing an innocent baby just for the fun of it is intrinsically wrong.) And of course if an act is intrinsically wrong it cannot be justified, regardless of its effects. For example, suppose a bank robber plans a heist with two foreseen effects. One foreseen effect is good (he will donate a million dollars to charity), and the other is bad (a bank guard will be shot by a fellow robber). Would committing the bank robbery be ethical? No, because the robbery is intrinsically wrong.

The second condition—that the act have a proportionately good end—also makes good sense. Suppose you're a bomber pilot in a just war. You've been ordered to blow up a bridge just as an important enemy convoy is crossing it. As you're about to drop your bombs, you notice that there's an innocent civilian crossing the bridge. Should you bomb the bridge as ordered? According to the double effect principle, yes. The civilian will be killed. But his death is an unwanted and unintended consequence of the act of destroying the convoy and the bridge. In a just war, the good of destroying the bridge and convoy outweighs the tragic incidental death of the civilian. By contrast, it would not be justifiable for a pilot to drop a bomb on a lone jeep if he or she knew that the bomb would kill a whole busload of children.

Assuming that these two criteria of the double effect principle are sound, what implications do they have for the production of violent films like the *Matrix*? Were the makers of the films justified in producing the movies, even though it was likely that some violent acts might result from it?

Fans of the films may think this is a no-brainer. "They're *great* movies!" we can hear them say. "Of course they should have been made! Sure there's plenty of violence, but it's not particularly gory or graphic violence. And it's not pointless Jean-Claude Van Damme-type violence, either. These are movies with *substance*. They raise important issues of faith, self-knowledge, courage, loyalty, self-identity, and sacrifice. You don't pack teens into theaters with films featuring boring talking heads. The violence is essential to the films' impact. They're *terrific* films (especially the first). Hundreds of millions of people have watched and enjoyed these movies. How can anyone claim that it was somehow "unethical" for these films to be made?"

Sorry, but we beg to differ. We enjoyed the *Matrix* films too, but the bottom line remains that these incredibly popular movies glamorize violence in a way that few other films have. We live in a culture of violence, a violence fueled by increasingly more violent media. The message of the films is that we have the free will to resist "the Matrix," whatever metaphorically that may mean, but most of us will not resist, being too weak or preferring comforting illusions to harsh realities. Ours is a media-saturated society, a society in which "millions of children, in their formative years, grow up decade after decade bombarded with very powerful visual and verbal messages that demonstrate violence as the preferred way to solve problems and normalizing fear and violence as 'the ways things are.'"[13] The research shows clearly that many children believe these messages, and all too frequently act upon them. It is irresponsible in such an environment to make films, such as the *Matrix* trilogy, that add, not merely stones, but boulders to this avalanche of media violence. We're not saying just make films with boring talking heads. Keep the cool stuff about faith, self-knowledge, courage, and the like. Keep the cool special effects and action sequences. Just please don't glamorize the violence.

---

[13] Elizabeth Thoman, Center for Media Literacy, http://www.medialit.org/reading_room/article208.html

16
Reloaded Revolutions

SLAVOJ ŽIŽEK

There is something inherently stupid and naïve in taking the *philosophical* underpinning of the *Matrix* trilogy seriously and discussing its implications. The Wachowski brothers are obviously *not* philosophers. They are just two guys who superficially flirt with and exploit in a confused way some postmodern and New Age notions.

The Matrix is one of those films which function as a kind of Rorschach inkblot test, setting in motion the universalized process of recognition. Like the proverbial picture of Jesus which seems always to stare directly at you, from wherever you look at it—practically every orientation seems to recognize itself in it. My Lacanian friends are telling me that the authors must have read Lacan; the Frankfurt School partisans see in the Matrix the extrapolated embodiment of *Kulturindustrie*, the alienated-reified social Substance (of Capital) directly taking over, colonizing our inner life itself, using us as the source of energy; New Agers see a source of speculations on how our world is just a mirage generated by a global Mind embodied in the World Wide Web; not to mention the all-pervasive presence of Jean Baudrillard . . . This series goes back to Plato's *Republic*: Does *The Matrix* not repeat exactly Plato's *dispositif* of the cave (ordinary humans as prisoners, tied firmly to their seats and compelled to watch the shadowy performance of (what they falsely consider to be) reality—in short, the position of the cinema spectators themselves?

This search for the philosophical content of *The Matrix* is therefore a lure, a trap to be avoided. Such pseudo-sophisticated readings which project onto the film refined philosophical or psychoanalytic conceptual distinctions are effectively much inferior to a naïve immersion that I witnessed when I saw *The Matrix* at a local theatre in Slovenia. I had the unique opportunity of sitting close to the ideal spectator of the film—namely, an idiot. A man in his late twenties at my right was so immersed in the film that he all the time disturbed other spectators with loud exclamations, like "My God, wow, so there is no reality! So we are all puppets!"

The Big Other

What *is* interesting is to read The *Matrix* movies not as containing a consistent philosophical discourse, but as rendering, in their very inconsistencies, the antagonisms of our ideological and social predicament. What, then, is the Matrix? Simply what Lacan called the "big Other," the virtual symbolic order, the network that structures reality for us. This dimension of the "big Other" is that of the constitutive alienation of the subject in the symbolic order: the big Other pulls the strings, the subject doesn't speak, he "is spoken" by the symbolic structure. The paradox, the "infinite judgment," of *The Matrix* is the co-dependence of the two aspects: the total artificiality (the constructed nature) of reality, and the triumphant return of the body in the sense of the ballet-like quality of fights with slow motions and defiance of the laws of ordinary physical reality.

Recall a wonderful scene in which Cypher, the traitor, the agent of the Matrix among the rebels, who is located in reality, kills one after the other rebels (who are immersed in the VR of the Matrix) by simply unplugging them from the connection to the machine. While the rebels are experiencing themselves as fully immersed in ordinary reality, they are effectively, in the "desert of the real," immobilized on the chair on which they are connected to the Matrix: Cypher has the direct physical approach to them the way they "really are," helpless creatures just sitting on a chair as if under narcotics at the dentist, who can be mishandled in any way the torturer wants. Cypher communicates with them via the phone, which serves as the communicating link between virtual reality and the "desert of the

real," and the horror of the situation is that, while the rebels feel
like normal human beings freely walking around in reality, they
know that, at the Other Scene of the "desert of the real," a simple unplugging of the cable will cause then to drop dead in both
universes, virtual and real.

This situation, while parallel to that of all humans who are
plugged into the Matrix, is worse insofar as here, humans are
fully aware not only of their true situation, but also of the
threat posed in reality by the evil agent who intends to kill
them shortly. It is as if the subjects obtain here the impossible
direct link with the Real of their situation, the Real in all its
threatening dimensions. *The Matrix* is much more precise than
one would expect with regard to the distinction between the
Real and reality: Morpheus's famous "Welcome to the desert of
the real!" does not refer to the real world outside the Matrix,
but to the purely formal digital universe of the Matrix itself.
When Morpheus confronts Neo with the image of the ruins of
Chicago, he simply says "This is the real world!", that is, what
remains of our reality outside the Matrix after the catastrophe,
while the "desert of the real" refers to the grayness of the
purely formal digital universe which generates the false
"wealth of experience" of humans caught in the Matrix. In
short, this "big Other" is the name for the social Substance, for
all that on account of which the subject never fully dominates
the effects of his acts, on account of which the final outcome
of his activity is always something other than what he aimed
at or anticipated.

And the inconsistencies of the film's narrative perfectly
mirror the difficulties of our breaking out of the constraints of
the social substance. When Morpheus tries to explain to the
still perplexed Neo what the Matrix is, he links it to a failure
in the structure of the universe: "You've felt it all your life.
That there's something wrong with the world. You don't know
what it is but it's there, like a splinter in your mind, driving
you mad." Here the film encounters its ultimate inconsistency:
the experience of the lack/inconsistency/obstacle is supposed
to bear witness of the fact that what we experience as reality
is a fake. However, towards the end of the film, Smith, the
agent of the Matrix, gives a different, much more Freudian
explanation:

> Did you know that the first Matrix was designed to be a perfect human world? Where none suffered, where everyone would be happy? It was a disaster. *No* one would accept the program. . . . as a species, human beings define their reality through suffering and misery.

The imperfection of our world is thus at the same time the sign of its virtuality *and* the sign of its reality. One could effectively claim that Agent Smith (let us not forget: not a human being as others, but a computer program) is the stand-in for the figure of the analyst within the universe of the film: his lesson is that the experience of an insurmountable obstacle is the positive condition for us, humans, to perceive something as reality—reality is ultimately that which resists.

Linked to this inconsistency is the ambiguous status of the liberation of humanity announced by Neo in the last scene of *The Matrix*. As the result of Neo's intervention, there is a "SYSTEM FAILURE" in the Matrix; at the same time, Neo addresses people still caught in the Matrix, as the Savior who will teach them how to liberate themselves from the constraints of the Matrix—they will be able to break the physical laws, bend metals, fly in the air . . . However, the problem is that all these "miracles" are possible only if we remain within the VR sustained by the Matrix and merely bend or change its rules: our "real" status is still that of the slaves of the Matrix. We are, as it were, merely gaining additional power to change our mental prison rules. So what about exiting from the Matrix altogether and entering the "real reality" in which we are miserable creatures living on the destroyed earth surface? Is then the solution a postmodern strategy of "resistance," of endlessly "subverting" or "displacing" the power system, or a more radical attempt at annihilating it?

Recall another memorable scene in which Neo has to choose between the red and blue pill. His choice is that between Truth and Pleasure: either the traumatic awakening into the Real or persisting in the illusion regulated by the Matrix. He chooses Truth, in contrast to the most despicable character in the movie, the informer-agent of the Matrix among the rebels, who, in the memorable scene of the dialogue with Smith, the agent of the Matrix, picks up with his fork a juicy red bit of a steak and says in effect: I know it is just a virtual illusion, but I do not care about that, since it tastes real. In short, he follows the pleasure principle which tells him that it's preferable to stay within the illusion, even if one knows that it's only an illusion.

However, the choice of the Matrix is not as simple as that. What, exactly, does Neo offer to humanity at the film's end? Not a direct awakening into the "desert of the real," but a free floating between the multitude of virtual universes: instead of being simply enslaved by the Matrix, one can liberate oneself by way of learning to bend its rules—one can change the rules of our physical universe and thus learn to fly freely and violate other physical laws. In short, the choice is not between bitter truth and pleasurable illusion, but rather between the two modes of illusion: the traitor is bound to the illusion of our "reality," dominated and manipulated by the Matrix, while Neo offers to humanity the experience of the universe as the playground in which we can play a multitude of games, freely passing from one to another, reshaping the rules which fix our experience of reality.

Jouissance

In an Adornian way, one should claim that these inconsistencies are the film's moment of truth: they signal the antagonisms of our late-capitalist social experience, antagonisms concerning basic ontological couples like reality and pain (reality as that which disturbs the reign of the pleasure-principle), freedom and system (freedom is only possible within the system that hinders its full deployment). However, the ultimate strength of the film is nonetheless to be located at a different level.

The unique impact of *The Matrix* resides not so much in its central thesis (what we experience as reality is an artificial virtual reality generated by the "Matrix," the mega-computer directly attached to all our minds), but in its central image of the millions of human beings leading a claustrophobic life in water-filled cradles, kept alive in order to generate the energy (electricity) for the Matrix. So when (some of the) people "awaken" from their immersion into the Matrix-controlled virtual reality, this awakening is not the opening into the wide space of the external reality, but first the horrible realization of this enclosure, where each of us is effectively just a fetus-like organism, immersed in the pre-natal fluid . . .

This utter passivity is the foreclosed fantasy that sustains our conscious experience as active, self-positing subjects—it is the ultimate perverse fantasy, the notion that we are ultimately instruments of the Other's (Matrix's) *jouissance*, sucked out of our life-substance like batteries. This brings us to the true libidinal enigma: *Why* does the Matrix need human energy? The purely energetic solution is, of course, meaningless: the Matrix could have easily found another, more reliable, source of energy which would have not demanded the extremely complex arrangement of virtual reality co-ordinated for millions of human units. The only consistent answer is: The Matrix feeds on the human's *jouissance*—so we are here back at the fundamental Lacanian thesis that the big Other itself, far from being an anonymous machine, needs the constant influx of *jouissance*.

Therein resides the correct insight of *The Matrix*: in its juxtaposition of the two aspects of perversion—on the one hand, reduction of reality to a virtual domain regulated by arbitrary rules that can be suspended; on the other hand, the concealed truth of this freedom, the reduction of the subject to an utterly instrumentalized passivity. And the ultimate proof of the decline in quality of the following installments of the *Matrix* trilogy is that this central aspect is left totally unexploited: A true revolution would have been a change in how humans and the Matrix itself relate to *jouissance* and its appropriation. What about, say, individuals sabotaging the Matrix by refusing to secrete *jouissance*?

Back in the 1970s, there was a charmingly vulgar Italian sex-comedy set in a near future in which the world had run out of energy. Luckily, scientists made the discovery that a tremendous amount of energy is released by a human body during the sexual act, on condition that the couple is not in love. So, in the interest of humanity's survival, the Church is convinced to invert its stance: love is sinful, and sex is okay only if done without love. So we get people confessing to their priest: "Sorry, father, I've sinned, I fell in love with my wife!" To generate energy, couples are ordered twice a week to make love in large collective halls, controlled by a supervisor who admonishes them: "The couple in the second row to the left, move faster!" . . . The similarity with *The Matrix* is striking. The truth of both films is that, in today's late capitalism, politics is more and more the politics of *jouissance*, concerned with ways of soliciting or controlling and regulating *jouissance* (abortion, gay marriages, divorce . . .).

Inconsistencies Reloaded

The Matrix Reloaded proposes—or, rather, plays with—a series of ways to overcome the inconsistencies of the first movie. But in doing so, it gets entangled in *new* inconsistencies of its own. *Reloaded*'s end is open and undecided not only narratively, but also with regard to its underlying vision of the universe. The basic tone is that of additional complications and suspicions which render problematic the simple and clear ideology of liberation from the Matrix that underpins the first movie.

The ecstatic community ritual of the people in Zion cannot but recall a fundamentalist religious gathering. Doubts are cast upon the two key prophetic figures. Are Morpheus's visions true or is he a paranoiac madman ruthlessly imposing his hallucinations? Neo also doesn't know if he can trust the Oracle, a woman who foresees the future. Is she manipulating Neo with her prophecies? Is she a representative of the *good* aspect of the Matrix, in contrast to agent Smith who, in *Reloaded*, turns into an excess of the Matrix, a virus run amok, trying to avoid being deleted by multiplying itself?

And what about the cryptic pronouncements of the Architect of the Matrix, its software writer, its God? He informs Neo that he is actually living in the sixth upgraded version of the Matrix: in each, a savior figure has arisen, but his attempt to liberate humanity ended in a large-scale catastrophe. Is then Neo's rebellion, far from being a unique event, just part of a larger cycle of the disturbance and restitution of the Order? By the end of *Reloaded*, everything is put in doubt: the question is not only whether any revolutions against the Matrix can accomplish what they claim or whether they have to end in an orgy of destruction, but whether they are in fact taken into account, even planned, by the Matrix.

Are then even those who are liberated from the Matrix free to make a choice at all? Is the solution to nonetheless risk the outright rebellion, to resign oneself to play the local games of "resistance," while remaining within the Matrix, or even engage in a trans-class collaboration with the "good" forces in the Matrix? This is where *Reloaded* ends: in a failure of "cognitive mapping" which perfectly mirrors the sad predicament of today's Left and its struggle against the System.

A supplementary twist is provided by the very end of the movie, when Neo magically stops the bad squid-like machines attacking the humans by merely raising his hand—how was he able to accomplish this in the "desert of the real," *not* within the Matrix where, of course, he can do wonders, freeze the flow of time, defy the laws of gravity, and so forth? Does this unexplained inconsistency point towards the solution that "all there is is generated by the Matrix," that there is *no* ultimate reality? Although such a postmodern temptation to find an easy way out of the confusions by proclaiming that all there is is the infinite series of virtual realities mirroring themselves in each other is to be rejected, there is a correct insight in this complication of the simple and straight division between the "real reality" and the Matrix-generated universe: Even if the struggle takes place in the "real reality," the key fight is to be won in the Matrix, which is why one should (re)enter its virtual fictional universe. If the struggle were to take place solely in the "desert of the real," The Matrix would have been another boring dystopia about the remnants of humanity fighting evil machines.

To put it in the terms of the good old Marxist dichotomy of infrastructure and superstructure: One should take into account the irreducible duality of, on the one hand, the "objective" material socio-economic processes taking place in reality as well as, on the other hand, the politico-ideological process proper. What if the domain of politics is inherently "sterile," a theatre of shadows, but nonetheless crucial in transforming reality? So, although economy is the real site and politics a theater of shadows, the main fight is to be fought in politics and ideology.

Take the disintegration of the Communist power in the late 1980s. Although the main event was the actual loss of state power by the Communists, the crucial break occurred at a different level—in those magic moments when, although formally Communists were still in power, people all of a sudden lost their fear and no longer took the threat seriously. So, even if "real" battles with the police continued, everyone somehow knew that "The game is over" . . . The title *The Matrix Reloaded*, is thus quite appropriate: If the first movie was dominated by the impetus to exit the Matrix, to liberate oneself from its hold, the second film makes it clear that the battle has to be won *within* the Matrix, that one has to return to it.

No Solutions, Just Revolutions

In *Reloaded*, the Wachowski brothers thus consciously raised the stakes, confronting us with all the complications and confusions of the process of liberation. In this way, they put themselves in a difficult spot. They confronted an almost impossible task. If *The Matrix Revolutions* were to succeed, it would have to produce nothing less than the appropriate answer to the dilemmas of revolutionary politics today, a blueprint for the political act the Left is desperately looking for. No wonder, then, that it failed miserably—and this failure provides a nice case for a simple Marxist analysis: the narrative failure, the impossibility of constructing a "good story," which signals a more fundamental social failure.

The first sign of this failure is the broken contract with the audience. The ontological premise of *The Matrix* (Part One) is a straightforward realistic one: there is the "real reality" and the virtual universe of the Matrix which can be entirely explained in the terms of what went on in reality. *Matrix Revolutions* break these rules: in it, the "magic" powers of Neo and Smith extend into "real reality" itself (Neo can stop bullets there also). Is this not like a detective novel in which, after a series of complex clues, the proposed solution would be that the murderer has magic capacities and was able to commit his crime violating laws of our reality? The reader would feel cheated. The same is true of *Revolutions*, in which the predominant tone is one of faith, not knowledge.

But even within this new space there are inconsistencies. In the film's final scene, the meeting of the couple who makes the deal, the (feminine) Oracle and the (masculine) Architect, takes place within the virtual reality of the Matrix—why? They are both mere Computer programs, and the virtual interface is here only for the human gaze—computers themselves do not communicate through the screen of the virtual imaginary, they directly exchange digital bites . . . For which gaze is then this scene staged? Here, the film "cheats" and is taken over by the imaginary logic.

The third failure is a more narrative one: the simplicity of the proposed solution. Things are not really explained, so that the final solution is more like the proverbial cutting of the Gordian knot. This is especially deplorable with regard to the many interesting dark hints in *Matrix Reloaded* (Morpheus as a dangerous paranoiac, the corruption of the ruling elite of Zion) which are left unexplored in *Revolutions*. The only interesting new aspect of *Revolutions*—the focus on interworld, neither Matrix nor reality—is also underdeveloped.

The key feature of the entire *Matrix* series is the progressive need to elevate Smith into the principal negative hero, a threat to the universe, a kind of negative of Neo. Who effectively is Smith? A kind of allegory of Fascist forces: a bad program gone wild, autonomized, threatening the Matrix. So the lesson of the film is, at its best, that of an anti-Fascist struggle. The brutal thugs, Fascists developed by Capital to control workers (by the Matrix to control humans), run out of control, and the Matrix has to enlist the help of humans to crush them in the same way liberal capital had to enlist the help of Communists, its mortal enemy, to defeat Fascism. (Perhaps, from today's political perspective, a more appropriate model would have been to imagine Israel on the verge of destroying Arafat and the PLO, and then making a deal with them for a truce if the PLO destroys Hamas who have run out of control . . .) However, Revolutions colors this anti-Fascist logic with potentially Fascist elements: although the (feminine) Oracle and the (masculine) Architect are both just programs, their difference is sexualized, so that the film's end is inscribed into the logic of the balance between the feminine and the masculine "principles."

When, at the end of *Reloaded*, a miracle occurs in reality itself, there are only two ways out: either postmodern gnosticism or Christianity. That is to say, either we shall learn, in Part Three, that "real reality" itself is just another matrix-generated spectacle, there being no last "real" reality, or we enter the domain of divine magic. However, in *Revolutions*, is Neo really a Christ figure? It may look so. At the very end of his duel with Smith, he turns into (another) Smith so that, when he dies, Smith (all the Smiths) is (are) also destroyed. . . . However, a closer look renders visible a key difference: Smith is a proto-Jewish figure, an obscene intruder who multiplies like rats, who runs amok and disturbs the harmony of Humans and Matrix-

Machines, so that his destruction enables a (temporary) class truce. What dies with Neo is this Jewish intruder who brings conflict and imbalance. In Christ, on the contrary, God himself becomes man so that, with the death of Christ, this man (ecce homo), God (of beyond) himself also dies. The true "Christological" version of the *Matrix* trilogy would thus entail a radically different scenario: Neo should have been a Matrix program rendered human, a direct human embodiment of the Matrix, so that, when he dies, the Matrix destroys itself.

The final pact is ridiculous. The Architect has to promise the Oracle not only that the machines will no longer fight men who are outside the Matrix, but that those humans who want to be set free from the Matrix will be allowed to do it—how will they be given the choice? So, at the end, nothing is really resolved: the Matrix is here, continuing to exploit humans, with no guarantee that another Smith will not emerge; the majority of humans will continue their slavery. What leads to this deadlock is that, in a typical ideological short-circuit, the Matrix functions as a double allegory: for Capital (machines sucking energy out of us) and for the Other, the symbolic order as such.

Perhaps, however—and this would be the only way to (partially, at least) redeem *Revolutions*—there is a sobering message in this very failure of the conclusion of the *Matrix* series. There is no final solution on the horizon today. Capital is here to stay: all we can hope for is a temporary truce. Which is to say that a pseudo-Deleuzian celebration of the successful revolt of the multitude would undoubtedly have been worse than the actual ending of deadlock.

From *The Book of the Machines* (1872)

There is no security against the ultimate development of mechanical consciousness, in the fact of machines possessing little consciousness now. A mollusk has not much consciousness. Reflect upon the extraordinary advance which machines have made during the last few hundred years, and note how slowly the animal and vegetable kingdoms are advancing. The more highly organized machines are creatures not so much of yesterday, as of the last five minutes, so to speak, in comparison with past time. Assume for the sake of argument that conscious beings have existed for some twenty million years; see what strides machines have made in the last thousand! May not the world last twenty million years longer? If so, what will they not in the end become? Is it not safer to nip the mischief in the bud and to forbid them further progress?

But who can say that the vapour engine has not a kind of consciousness? Where does consciousness begin, and where end? Who can draw the line? Who can draw any line? Is not everything interwoven with everything? Is not machinery linked with animal life in an infinite variety of ways? The shell of a hen's egg is made of a delicate white ware and is a machine as much as an egg-cup is: the shell is a device for holding the egg, as much as the egg-cup for holding the shell: both are phases of the same function; the hen makes the shell in her inside, but it is pure pottery. She makes her nest outside of herself for convenience' sake, but the nest is not more of a machine than the egg-shell is. A 'machine' is only a 'device'. . . .

But it may be said that the plant is devoid of reason, because the growth of a plant is an involuntary growth. Given earth, air, and due temperature, the plant must grow: it is like a clock, which being once wound up will go till it is stopped or run down: it is like the wind blowing on the sails of a ship—the ship must go when the wind blows it. But can a healthy boy help growing if he have good meat and drink and clothing? Can anything help going as long as it is wound up, or go on after it is run down? Is there not a winding up process everywhere?

Even a potato in a dark cellar has a certain low cunning about him which serves him in excellent stead. He knows perfectly well what he wants and how to get it. He sees the light coming from the cellar window and sends his shoots crawling straight thereto: they will crawl along the floor and up the wall and out at the cellar window; if there be a little earth anywhere on the journey he will find it and use it for his own ends. . . .

If it be urged that the action of the potato is chemical and mechanical only, and that it is due to the chemical and mechanical effects of light and heat, the answer would seem to lie in an inquiry whether every sensation is not chemical and mechanical in its operation? Whether those things which we deem most purely spiritual are anything but disturbances of equilibrium in an infinite series of levers, beginning with those that are too small for microscopic detection, and going up to the human arm and the appliances which it makes use of? Whether there be not a molecular action of thought, whence a dynamical theory of the passions shall be deducible? Whether strictly speaking we should not ask what kind of levers a man is made of rather than what is his temperament? How are they balanced? How much of such and such will it take to weigh them down so as to make him do so and so? . . .

Either a great deal of action that has been called purely mechanical and unconscious must be admitted to contain more elements of consciousness than has been allowed hitherto (and in this case germs of consciousness will be found in the actions of the higher machines)—or (assuming the theory of evolution but at the same time denying the consciousness of vegetable and crystalline action) the race of man has descended from things which had no consciousness at all. In this case there is no *a priori* improbability in the descent of conscious (and more than conscious) machines from those which now exist, except that which is suggested by the apparent absence of anything like a reproductive system in the mechanical kingdom. This absence however is only apparent, as I shall presently show.

Do not let me be misunderstood as living in fear of any actually existing machine; there is probably no known machine which is more than a prototype of future mechanical life. The present machines are to the future as the early Saurians to man. The largest of them will probably greatly diminish in size. Some of the lowest vertebra attained a much greater bulk than has descended to their more highly organized living representatives, and in like manner a diminution in the size of machines has often attended their development and progress.

Take the watch, for example; examine its beautiful structure; observe the intelligent play of the minute members which compose it: yet this little creature is but a development of the cumbrous clocks that preceded it; it is no deterioration from them. . . .

I fear none of the existing machines; what I fear is the extraordinary rapidity with which they are becoming something very different to what they are at present. No class of beings have in any time past made so rapid a movement forward. Should not that movement be jealously watched, and checked while we can still check it? And is it not necessary for this end to destroy the more advanced of the machines which are in use at present, though it is admitted that they are in themselves harmless?

As yet the machines receive their impressions through the agency of man's senses: one travelling machine calls to another in a shrill accent of alarm and the other instantly retires; but it is through the ears of the driver that the voice of the one has acted upon the other. Had there been no driver, the callee would have been deaf to the caller. There was a time when it must have seemed highly improbable that machines should learn to make their wants known by sound, even through the ears of man; may we not conceive, then, that a day will come when those ears will no longer be needed, and the hearing will be done by the delicacy of the machine's own construction?— when its language shall have been developed from the cry of animals to a speech as intricate as our own? . . .

But other questions come upon us. What is a man's eye but a machine for the little creature that sits behind in his brain to look through? A dead eye is nearly as good as a living one for some time after the man is dead. It is not the eye that cannot see, but the restless one that cannot see through it. Is it man's eyes, or is it the big seeing-engine which has revealed to us the existence of worlds beyond worlds into infinity? What has made man familiar with the scenery of the moon, the spots on the sun, or the geography of the planets? He is at the mercy of the see-ing-engine for these things, and is powerless unless he tack it on to his own identity, and make it part and parcel of himself. Or, again, is it the eye or the little seeing-engine which has shown us the existence of infinitely minute organisms which swarm unsuspected around us?

And take man's vaunted power of calculation. Have we not engines which can do all manner of sums more quickly and cor-rectly than we can? What prizeman in hypothetics at any of our Colleges of Unreason can compare with some of these machines in their own line? In fact, wherever precision is required man flies to the machine at once, as far preferable to himself. Our sum-engines never drop a figure, nor our looms a stitch; the machine is brisk and active, when the man is weary; it is clear-headed and collected, when the man is stupid and dull; it needs no slumber, when man must sleep or drop; ever at its post, ever ready for work, its alacrity never flags, its patience never gives in; its might is stronger than combined hundreds, and swifter than the flight of birds; it can burrow beneath the earth, and walk upon the largest rivers and sink not. . . .

Who shall say that a man does see or hear? He is such a hive and swarm of parasites that it is doubtful whether his body is not more theirs than his, and whether he is anything but another kind of ant-heap after all. May not man himself become a sort of parasite upon the machines? An affectionate, machine-tickling aphid? . . .

It can be answered that even though machines should hear never so well and speak never so wisely, they will still always do the one or the other for our advantage, not their own; that man will be the ruling spirit and the machine the servant; that as soon as a machine fails to discharge the service which man expects from it, it is doomed to extinction; that the machines stand to man simply in the relation of lower animals, the vapour-engine itself being only a more economical kind of horse; so that instead of being likely to be developed into a higher kind of life than man's, they owe their very existence and progress to their power of ministering to human wants, and must therefore both now and ever be man's inferiors.

This is all very well. But the servant glides by imperceptible approaches into the master; and we have come to such a pass that, even now, man must suffer terribly on ceasing to benefit the machines. If all machines were to be annihilated at one moment, so that not a knife nor lever nor rag of clothing nor anything whatsoever were left to man but his bare body alone that he was born with, and if all knowledge of mechanical laws were taken from him so that he could make no more machines, and all machine-made food destroyed so that the race of man should be left as it were naked upon a desert island, we should become extinct in six weeks. A few miserable individuals might linger, but even these in a year or two would become worse than monkeys. Man's very soul is due to the machines; it is a machine-made thing: he thinks as he thinks, and feels as he feels, through the work that machines have wrought upon him, and their existence is quite as much a sine qua non for his, as his for theirs. This fact precludes us from proposing the complete annihilation of machinery, but surely it indicates that we should destroy as many of them as we can possibly dispense with, lest they should tyrannize over us even more completely. . . .

They have preyed upon man's grovelling preference for his material over his spiritual interests, and have betrayed him into supplying that element of struggle and warfare without which no race can advance. The lower animals progress because they struggle with one another; the weaker die, the stronger breed and transmit their strength. The machines being of themselves unable to struggle, have got man to do their struggling for them: as long as he fulfils this function duly, all goes well with him— at least he thinks so; but the moment he fails to do his best for the advancement of machinery by encouraging the good and destroying the bad, he is left behind in the race of competition; and this means that he will be made uncomfortable in a variety of ways, and perhaps die.

So that even now the machines will only serve on condition of being served, and that too upon their own terms; the moment their terms are not complied with, they jib, and either smash both themselves and all whom they can reach, or turn churlish and refuse to work at all. How many men at this hour are living in a state of bondage to the machines? How many spend their whole lives, from the cradle to the grave, in tending them by night and day? Is it not plain that the machines are gaining ground upon us, when we reflect on the increasing number of those who are bound down to them as slaves, and of those who devote their whole souls to the advancement of the mechanical kingdom?

The vapour-engine must be fed with food and consume it by fire even as man consumes it; it supports its combustion by air as man supports it; it has a pulse and circulation as man has. It may be granted that man's body is as yet the more versatile of the two, but then man's body is an older thing: give the vapour-engine but half the time that man has had, give it also a continuance of our present infatuation, and what may it not ere long attain to? . . . The comparison of similarities is endless: I only make it because some may say that since the vapour-engine is not likely to be improved in the main particulars, it is unlikely to be henceforward extensively modified at all. This is too good to be true: it will be modified and suited for an infinite variety of purposes, as much as man has been modified so as to exceed the brutes in skill.

In the meantime the stoker is almost as much a cook for his engine as our own cooks for themselves. Consider also the colliers and pitmen and coal merchants and coal trains, and the men who drive them, and the ships that carry coals—what an army of servants do the machines thus employ! Are there not probably more men engaged in tending machinery than in tending men? Do not machines eat as it were by mannery? Are we not ourselves creating our successors in the supremacy of the earth? Daily adding to the beauty and delicacy of their organization, daily giving them greater skill and supplying more and more of that self-regulating, self-acting power which will be better than any intellect? . . .

The main point, however, to be observed as affording cause for alarm is that whereas animals were formerly the only stomachs of the machines, there are now many which have stomachs of their own, and consume their food themselves. This is a great step towards their becoming, if not animate, yet something so near akin to it as not to differ more widely from our own life than animals do from vegetables. And though man should remain, in some respects, the higher creature, is not this in accordance with the practice of nature, which allows superiority in some things to animals which have, on the whole, been long surpassed? Has she not allowed the ant and the bee to retain superiority over man in the organization of their communities and social arrangements, the bird in traversing the air, the fish in swimming, the horse in strength and fleetness, and the dog in self-sacrifice?

It is said by some with whom I have conversed upon this subject that the machines can never be developed into animate or quasi-animate existences, inasmuch as they have no reproductive system, nor seem ever likely to possess one. If this be taken to mean that they cannot marry, and that we are never likely to see a fertile union between two vapour-engines, with the young ones playing about the door of the shed, however greatly we might desire to do so, I will readily grant it. But the objection is not a very profound one. No one expects that all the features of the now existing organizations will be absolutely repeated in an entirely new class of life. The reproductive system of animals differs widely from that of plants, but both are reproductive systems. Has nature exhausted her phases of this power?

Surely if a machine is able to reproduce another machine systematically, we may say that it has a reproductive system. What is a reproductive system, if it be not a system for reproduction? And how few of the machines are there which have not been produced systematically by other machines? But it is man that makes them do so. Yes; but is it not insects that make many of the plants reproductive, and would not whole families of plants die out if their fertilization was not effected by a class of agents utterly foreign to themselves? Does anyone say that the red clover has no reproductive system because the humble bee (and the humble bee only) must aid and abet it before it can reproduce? No one. The humble bee is a part of the reproductive system of the clover. Each one of ourselves has sprung from minute animalcules whose entity was entirely distinct from our own, and which acted after their kind with no thought or heed of what we might think about it. These little creatures are part of our own reproductive system; then why not we part of that of machines? . . .

We are misled by considering any complicated machine as a single thing; in truth it is a city or society, each member of which was bred truly after its kind. We see a machine as a whole, we call it by a name and individualize it; we look at our own limbs, and know that the combination forms an individual which springs from a single centre of reproductive action; we therefore assume that there can be no reproductive action which does not arise from a single centre; but this assumption is unscientific, and the bare fact that no vapour-engine was ever made entirely by another, or two others, of its own kind, is not sufficient to warrant us in saying that vapour-engines have no reproductive system. The truth is that each part of every vapour-engine is bred by its own special breeders, whose function it is to breed that part, and that only, while the combination of the parts into a whole forms another department of the mechanical reproductive system, which is at present extremely complex and difficult to see in its entirety.

Complex now, but how much simpler and more intelligibly organized may it not become in another hundred thousand years? Or in twenty thousand? For man at present believes that his interest lies in that direction; he spends an incalculable amount of labour and time and thought in making machines breed always better and better; he has already succeeded in effecting much that at one time appeared impossible, and there seem no limits to the results of accumulated improvements if they are allowed to descend with modification from generation to generation. It must always be remembered that man's body is what it is through having been moulded into its present shape by the chances and changes of many millions of years, but that his organization never advanced with anything like the rapidity with which that of the machines is advancing.[1]

---

[1] From *Erewhon, Or Over the Range*, by Samuel Butler, published in 1872. The hero of this story visits a world in which any machinery beyond the most rudimentary is strictly prohibited. He discovers that the origin of this ideological hostility to machines is *The Book of the Machines*, from which he quotes at length. This material is based on Butler's 1863 essay, "Darwin among the Machines." In Frank Herbert's *Dune* (1965), set in the far future, there has been an event in the distant past (but in our future) called "the Butlerian Jihad," during which all computers and other cybernetic devices have been destroyed and outlawed.

The Merovingian's Minions

GREGORY BASSHAM is Director of the Center for Ethics and Public Life and Chair of the Philosophy Department at King's College, Pennsylvania. A frequent contributor to the Popular Culture and Philosophy series, he is the co-editor of *The Lord of the Rings and Philosophy* (2003), the author of *Original Intent and the Constitution* (1992), co-author of *Critical Thinking: A Student's Introduction* (second edition, 2005), and co-editor of the forthcoming *The Chronicles of Narnia and Philosophy* (2005). Greg once built an APU for former National Rifle Association President Charlton Heston in his garage, but he's eighty percent sure this was before Heston was diagnosed with Alzheimer's.

NICK BOSTROM is a British Academy Research Fellow at Philosophy Faculty, Oxford University. He previously taught at Yale University. His research areas include philosophy of science, foundations of probability theory, ethics, and emerging technologies. He is one of the founders of the transhumanist movement. Many of Nick's papers can be found at his homepage: www.nickbostrom.com. He has some skill.

MARTIN DANAHAY is Professor of English at the University of Texas at Arlington. His most recent publications are *Men at Work in Victorian Culture* (Ashgate, 2005) and a scholarly analysis of *The Matrix* entitled "*The Matrix* and Business @ the Speed of Thought." Although he usually only writes about their movies, he'd actually prefer to fight the Wachowski brothers because, as Seraph says, you don't really know somebody until you've fought them. He's looking forward to getting to know them the way that only hand to hand combat can provide.

DAVID DETMER is Professor of Philosophy at Purdue University Calumet. He is the author of *Challenging Postmodernism: Philosophy and the Politics of Truth* (Humanity Books, 2003) and *Freedom as a Value: A Critique of the Ethical Theory of Jean-Paul Sartre* (Open Court, 1988), as well as essays on a variety of philosophical topics. He appeared in the crowd scene at Club Hel, his usual weekend haunt.

JORGE J.E. GRACIA is State University of New York Distinguished Professor and holds the Samuel P. Capen Chair in Philosophy. He has published over thirty-five books. He is author of *Hispanic/Latino Identity* (Oxford: Blackwell, 2000) and co-editor of *Hispanics/Latinos in the United States: Ethnicity, Race, and Rights* (New York: Routledge, 2000). Among his more than 200 articles are: "Ethnic Labels and Philosophy," "Hispanic/Latino Identity: Homogeneity and Stereotypes," "Hispanic/Latino Culture in the US: Foreigners in Our Own Land," and "Language Priority in the Education of Children." He is currently working on two articles, "The Oreo Phenomenon" and "Can Ethnic and Racial Groups Be Individuated?," and a book, *Surviving Race, Ethnicty, and Nationality*. Gracia is a very confused man; he can't tell whether he is in the Matrix of race or out of it.

THEODORE GRACYK lives in Minnesota, where he teaches philosophy. He is the author of two books on the philosophy of music, *Rhythm and Noise: An Aesthetics of Rock* and *I Wanna Be Me: Rock Music and the Politics of Identity*. Ted is currently writing a book on musical taste and is under contract to adapt *The Matrix* as a Broadway musical.

IDRIS SAMAWI HAMID is Assistant Professor of Philosophy at Colorado State University. He is the Editor-in-Chief of the *International Journal of Shīʿī Studies*, and works primarily in the fields of Islamic metaphysics and mystical phenomenology. He spends much of his spare time programming in TeX, creating the master Matrix for scholarly and critical Arabic typesetting. His first attempt was quite naturally perfect; it was a work of art. Flawless, sublime. A triumph equaled only by its monumental failure.

WILLIAM IRWIN is Associate Professor of Philosophy at King's College, Pennsylvania. He is the author of *Intentionalist Interpretation: A Philosophical Explanation and Defense* and has published articles on aesthetics in leading journals. He has edited *Seinfeld and Philosophy*, *The Simpsons and Philosophy*, and *The Matrix and Philosophy*. Bill enjoys cursing in French—Que tu es emmerdant. Le putain de ta mère. Va te faire foutre—and wiping his ass with silk.

WILLIAM JAWORSKI is not really an Assistant Professor of Philosophy at Fordham University; he just plays one in the movies. He's nevertheless published articles in the philosophy of mind, and has research interests in ethics, metaphysics, and the philosophy of science. He's occasionally been found at mid-semester rummaging through his office muttering something about a "little blue pill" he misplaced.

JAMES LAWLER teaches philosophy at SUNY Buffalo. He is the author of *The Existentialist Marxism of Jean-Paul Sartre; IQ, Heritability, and Racism;* and *Matter and Spirit: The Battle of Metaphysics in Modern Western Philosophy Before Kant* (forthcoming). He is the editor of *The Dialectic of the U.S. Constitution: Selected Writings of Mitchell Franklin* and a contributor to *Market Socialism: The Debate Among Socialists.* Jim's only regret—he still misses this place that had these really good noodles.

ANNA LÄNNSTRÖM is Assistant Professor of Philosophy at Stonehill College. Her recent and forthcoming publications include: "Am I My Brother's Keeper? An Aristotelian Take on Responsibility for Others" in *Responsibility: Boston University Studies in Philosophy and Religion,* Volume 26, forthcoming; "Forgiving Judas: Extenuating Circumstances in the Ultimate Betrayal" in Jorge Gracia, ed., *Mel Gibson's Passion and Philosophy* (2004); and as editor, *Promise and Peril: The Paradox of Religion as Resource and Threat. Boston University Studies in Philosophy and Religion,* Volume 24 (2003), and *The Stranger's Religion: Fascination and Fear. Boston University Studies in Philosophy and Religion,* Volume 25 (2004). Once she fully realizes that there is no spoon, the rest will be easy.

LOU MARINOFF is Associate Professor of Philosophy at The City College of New York (CCNY), and founding President of the American Philosophical Practitioners Association (www.app.edu). He is author of the international bestsellers *Plato Not Prozac* (New York: HarperCollins, 1999) and *Therapy for the Sane* (New York: Bloomsbury, 2003), and Editor-in-Chief of the APPA's journal, *Philosophical Practice* (published by Taylor and Francis). Lou is also on the Faculty of the World Economic Forum, the Aspen Institute, and the Omega Institute. A pioneer of the philosophical practice movement, Lou renders services to individuals, groups, and organizations world-wide (www.loumarinoff.com). He first became familiar with little red and blue pills as a hippie during the 1960s.

HENRY NARDONE is Professor of Philosophy at King's College where he has taught for the last thirty-seven years. He has also occasionally taught at Webster University, Thailand, to escape the winter winds of Pennsylvania. Henry is a co-author of *Critical Thinking: A Student's Introduction* (McGraw-Hill, 2002). He dislikes films with gratuitous violence but he enjoys swatting pesky flies.

THEODORE SCHICK JR. is Professor of Philosophy at Muhlenberg College and co-author (with Lewis Vaughn) of *How to Think about Weird Things* (McGraw-Hill, fourth edition, 2004) and *Doing Philosophy* (McGraw-Hill, second edition, 2002). His most recent book is *Readings in the Philosophy of Science: From Positivism to Postmodernism* (McGraw-Hill, 1999). Ted looks a little like the Trainman when he wakes up in the morning, and he's much less patient.

BEN WITHERINGTON III is Professor of New Testament at Asbury Theological Seminary and St. Andrews University, Scotland. He is the author of the *New York Times* best seller, *The Brother of Jesus* (with Hershel Shanks, Harper), the *Gospel Code* (InterVarsity Press, 2004), and two Biblical Studies books of the year *The Jesus Quest* and *The Paul Quest* (InterVarsity Press). Ben is currently stuck somewhere between this world and the machine world.

MARK A. WRATHALL is Associate Professor of Philosophy at Brigham Young University. He is the author of numerous articles and the editor of numerous collections on topics in phenomenology and existential philosophy, including *Religion After Metaphysics* (Cambridge University Press, 2003) and *The Blackwell Companion to Heidegger* (Blackwell, 2004). Beneath his poised appearance, the truth is he is completely out of control

SLAVOJ ŽIŽEK is a philosopher and psychoanalyst and Senior Researcher at the Department of Philosophy, University of Ljubljana, Slovenia. His recent publications include *The Puppet and The Dwarf* (MIT Press, 2003), *Organs Without Bodies* (Routledge, 2003), and *Iraq: The Borrowed Kettle* (Verso, 2004). When confronted with the choice between a juicy steak within the Matrix and the miserable reality outside the Matrix, he always chooses the steak.

The Keymaker's Index